Job Hunting
for the
Utterly Confused

Jason R. Rich

DISCARDED
TORONTO PUBLIC LIBRARY

P9-BZW-203

McGraw-Hill

New York   San Francisco   Washington, D.C.   Auckland   Bogotá
Caracas   Lisbon   London   Madrid   Mexico City   Milan
Montreal   New Delhi   San Juan   Singapore
Sydney   Tokyo   Toronto

THE SCARBOROUGH PUBLIC LIBRARY BOARD

Library of Congress Cataloging-in-Publication Data

Rich, Jason.
    Job hunting for the utterly confused / Jason Rich.
       p. cm.
    Includes index.
    ISBN 0-07-052665-6 (alk. paper)
    1. Job hunting.   I. Title.
HF5382.7.R54   1998
650.14—dc21
                                         97-44036
                                            CIP

McGraw-Hill

A Division of The **McGraw·Hill** *Companies*

Copyright © 1998 by the McGraw-Hill Companies, Inc. All rights reserved.
Printed in the United States of America. Except as permitted under the United
States Copyright Act of 1976, no part of this publication may be reproduced
or distributed in any form or by any means, or stored in a data base or retrieval
system, without the prior written permission of the publisher.

1 2 3 4 5 6 7 8 9 0   DOC / DOC   9 0 3 2 1 0 9 8

ISBN 0-07-052665-6

The sponsoring editor of this book was Betsy Brown, the editing supervisor was
Curt Berkowitz, and the production supervisor was Pamela Pelton. It was set in
Times Ten by North Market Street Graphics.

Printed and bound by R. R. Donnelley & Sons Company.

McGraw-Hill books are available at special quantity discounts to use as
premiums and sales promotions, or for use in corporate training programs.
For more information, please write to the Director of Special Sales, McGraw-
Hill, 11 West 19th Street, New York, NY 10011. Or contact your local bookstore.

This book is printed on recycled, acid-free paper containing a
minimum of 50% recycled de-inked fiber.

Contents

Preface

Dedication is the key to success. Whatever you're involved with, dedication and commitment become so important. You have to put in the necessary time and work hard to accomplish anything, whether you're playing professional sports or working in business. Obviously, you're lucky if you have talent, but the people who actually make it are the people who sacrifice the most, who are the most dedicated, and who work the hardest.

Wayne Gretzky, NY Rangers

When you were a child, people probably used to ask you, "What do you want to be when you grow up?" At the time, you might have picked a popular career, like being a firefighter, a superhero, or a circus clown. Well, you're all grown up now, and it's time for you to choose the career path you want to follow. You can choose to pursue a traditional career, or you can be a bit creative and discover ways to earn a living doing something you really love. Whatever career path you ultimately decide to follow, you first have to land a job.

Unfortunately, what you are about to embark on is a totally frustrating, time-consuming, and confusing process that's known as the job search. Your goal is to set yourself apart from everyone else, and find and then land the job that you'll be happy and prosper in. At all costs, you want to avoid landing a dead-end job, or accepting a job that's been misrepresented. You want to find a group of people you'll enjoy working with, have a boss you get along with, choose a job that will challenge you, and find a job that will allow you to learn and expand your personal and professional skill set. Finally, you want a job that you'll truly enjoy. After all, if you examine what sets highly successful people apart from others, it's their dedication and their passion for their work. It's not the paycheck that motivates successful people!

As you kick off your own job search process, you'll have to carefully define your interests and skills, and then decide what type of jobs or career opportunities you want to pursue. It will be necessary to develop a one-page resume and a cover letter that captures the attention of potential employers and allows you to showcase your skills, education, and work experience in the best possible light, and in the most concise way possible.

You'll have to find the best job opportunities to apply for, research the companies offering those jobs, spend time preparing for your interviews, and make a good impression during your actual interviews. It will be necessary to make many follow-up phone calls, network, negotiate a compensation package, and actively engage yourself in every aspect of this whole process. At the same time you're applying for jobs, you will most likely have to deal with rejection from employers that don't hire you. To be successful, however, it's necessary to keep a positive and success-oriented attitude. This book will provide you with strategies to help you stay motivated and keep you from becoming depressed or too stressed out as you apply for jobs.

What Will You Learn from Reading This Book?

At the bookstore, there are job and career books written for "idiots" and others targeted to "dummies." You are neither an idiot nor a dummy, right? There are books that claim they'll help you write the ultimate "knock-'em-dead" resume, and others that will help you write cover letters or perform well in an interview. Do you really need a whole book to help you write a one-page resume? Do you have time to read a different book in order to prepare for each step of the job search process? Probably not. Very few books on careers and jobs are designed to walk you through each step of the job search process, and provide tips and strategies that will help you to help yourself land a job that you really want. We all have something unique about ourselves that makes us particularly suitable for certain types of jobs. Knowing how to define and market your skills using your resume, cover letter, and interview(s), and every other opportunity you have to impress a potential employer, will mean the difference between landing a job and getting passed over.

The primary goal of *Job Hunting for the Utterly Confused* is to walk you through the entire job search process, taking one step at a time. This book is designed to take the confusion and stress out of your job search. By breaking down the process into a bunch of extremely manageable tasks, you'll soon discover that you can land a job with minimal frustration and stress (hard work and a time commitment on your part will still be required).

No matter what type of job you hope to land, the very best way to go about landing it is to take a highly organized and deadline-oriented approach, which is what this book will teach you how to do. Each chapter of *Job Hunting for the Utterly Confused* will focus on one aspect of the job search process, and provide valuable insight and strategies that will greatly assist you in maximizing all of your potential for landing the job you want.

The Internet is one of the most powerful job search tools you have at your disposal. Even if you don't own a personal computer, you can obtain access to a computer and the Internet at a college or university, or a public library, or by using a friend's or family member's computer. *Job Hunting for the Utterly Confused* will show you how to surf the Internet to find exciting job opportunities, obtain career advice, perform company research quickly and easily, and even apply for jobs on-line. A personal computer is also the ideal resume creation tool. Using special software, you can create professional-quality resumes that can be quickly customized for each job you apply for. Sure, you can create a resume using almost any word processing program, but making the word-processed resume look perfect will take you a lot of time. Without the resume creation software, you'll have to manually adjust margins, tabs, font sizes, and type styles until you get your word-processed resume to fit onto one page and look professional. Later in this book, you'll discover all the different ways a personal computer can be used to help you find and ultimately land a job.

Finally, as this book takes you step-by-step through the job search process, you'll learn how to avoid the most common mistakes made by most applicants. If some of the information in this book seems like common sense, then you're already one step ahead of the competition. Believe it or not, one of the most common reasons why people aren't seriously considered for a position they apply for is because their resume contains spelling mistakes or serious errors. Many applicants don't proofread their resume and cover letter before sending them out. Most human resources personnel and other people in charge of hiring new employees admit that resumes containing errors simply get tossed in the garbage (a.k.a. "filed"), even if the applicant might otherwise be qualified for the job.

Market Yourself Like a Company Markets a Product

When a company launches a new product, it develops a precise marketing and advertising campaign to help ensure its success. The goal of the company launching a new product is to set it apart from the competition and convince consumers to try it. This is often done by applying the four "P's" of marketing: product, placement, price, and promotion.

There are many similarities between finding and landing a job and launching a new product. With a bit of modification, the four P's of marketing can also apply to finding a new job. When you're looking for a job, you (as a person with unique skills, experiences, and education) are the new product. The way you actually sell your experience and skill set using your resume, etc., is your product placement. How are you better than the competition? What skills make you qualified for the job you're applying for? Your resume should answer these questions. The price of the product in this case is the salary and overall compensation package that you're willing to work for. Finally, instead of using ads, brochures, and demonstrations to sell your product, you'll be using the marketing tools of every job applicant—your resume, cover letter, interpersonal skills, communication skills, and overall presentation during your interviews.

It's your responsibility to develop the best possible way to advertise and market yourself, set yourself apart from the many other people applying for the same jobs that you are, and convince potential employers that they should give you a try by hiring you. Knowing that each time you approach a potential new employer, you only have a few seconds to make the best possible initial impression, it is vital that you focus your efforts and provide the consumer (in this case, the potential employer) with what he or she is looking for.

Just as a company must plan the marketing of a product by defining its features and benefits, its position compared with its competition, and its target market, you'll have to follow many of the same procedures to market yourself to potential employers.

Starting now, you have to start believing one thing—you will soon land an awesome job! It might not be the first job you apply for, and it will most likely take a lot of time and effort on your part to find the best job opportunity, but if you put in the effort and focus your energies, the results will be positive.

Who Will Benefit from This Book?

Soon-to-be and recent graduates who are entering the work force for the first time will benefit greatly from the information offered in *Job Hunting for the Utterly Confused.* Anyone looking for a new job, with a new employer, will also find this book to be a useful resource. In addition, this book offers advice and strategies that will benefit people hoping to land a promotion (or a transfer) from their current employer. Finally, if you're reentering the work force after an extended absence, or if you're changing careers (or industries), or if you're hoping to land a summer internship or part-time job, this book will help you discover the best opportunities and get a great job.

The Workplace Is Constantly Changing

Years ago, when people landed a job at a major corporation, they planned on spending the rest of their career working for that employer. People expected job security and looked forward to the day they'd receive their gold watch from their employer for a lifetime of dedication to the company. Those "gold watch" retirement days are virtually gone.

As we quickly approach the new millennium, "downsizing," corporate mergers, and the need for companies to operate with the smallest staffs possible have become all too common in the workplace. The result is that people are forced, for a multitude of reasons, to move from job to job during their career. These days, it's extremely common for people to work at three, four, or more jobs, at different companies, before they retire. Thus, instead of working to become excellent at filling one specific position at a company, it's becoming increasingly more necessary for people to focus on constantly expanding their skill set and to keep up with changing technology and ongoing changes in their industry.

Jobs will come and go, but the things that can never be taken away from you are your knowledge, education, motivation, and skill set. So while you're applying for jobs and answering questions from potential employers about what you can offer them, you should be thinking to yourself, "How will this job help me expand my knowledge, experience, and skill set?" and "If I were to accept this job, how will it lead to future advancement or help me achieve my long-term career goals?"

As you decide what types of job opportunities you'll be pursuing, try to focus on growth industries and choose a career path that has a bright future. Look for positions that offer training, and if necessary, be willing to take the initiative to enhance your personal skill set. For example, in the next millennium, it's been predicted that two out of three jobs will require people to operate some type of computer. If you're not already computer-literate and able to surf the Internet, consider taking an adult education class or an introductory computer class taught at a local computer store. For almost any job you apply for, being able to list on your resume that you're computer-literate and that you know how to operate popular computer programs is a plus.

The Job Search Process Begins Now

As you turn the page, your job search effort is about to begin. It's an excellent idea to read this book in its entirety so that you develop a good understanding of what you can expect from the job search process and what will be expected of you. Once you've read this book, you can refer to it as you participate in each step of the overall process. Whether you're looking for your first job or hoping to make a job switch, it's an excellent idea to find someone who can offer you support throughout the process. Obviously, you'll receive the best support from a trained career counselor, but someone who has recently been through this job search experience, or who understands the process, will also be able to offer you valuable support and motivation.

Use your support person to proofread your resume and cover letters, help you decide what to wear to interviews, assist you in preparing for interviews by asking you sample interview questions, and help you deal with the rejection that's part of the process. No matter whom you choose to offer you support, make sure he or she will be totally open and honest with you. The better this person knows you, the more help this person will be when it comes time to pinpointing your unique skills and deciding on the best ways to market yourself to potential employers.

The first step in this whole job search process is to decide what you want and determine what type of work you're qualified to do. Define your long-term career goals. You'll be spending a huge amount of time on the job, so if you want to be a happy and ultimately successful person, it's important to make the right decisions and be totally honest with yourself as you evaluate the many job opportunities and career paths that are available to you. If you're willing to work hard, you deserve to be both happy and successful, so whatever you do, don't settle for a job that you know you won't enjoy and prosper in. Since you're going to be spending the time and effort to land a new job, use this book to help you ensure your future short-term and long-term success.

Stay in Touch

If you find this book to be helpful, or if you discover a strategy for finding and landing a job that you think will benefit others, please share your ideas and comments. Send an e-mail message to Jason R. Rich at **jr7777@aol.com,** or you can visit one of these Web pages: **http://www.jasonrich.com** or **http://www.firstjob.com.**

Good luck!

Acknowledgments

First and foremost, I'd like to thank two people in my life who are extremely important to me, Mark Giordani and Ellen Bromfield, who have unselfishly helped me to grow, both personally and professionally over the many years I've known them. These two people, and their respective families, continue to be a never-ending source of love and support for which I am grateful.

I'd also like to thank Betsy Brown and Griffin Hansbury at McGraw-Hill for inviting me to work on this book project. My ongoing gratitude also goes out to Jeff Herman, my literary agent, who helps to keep me busy writing. Thanks also to Curt Berkowitz and Kurt Nelson at McGraw-Hill for helping to bring this book to publication.

Finally, I'd like to acknowledge the hard work and dedication that my sister Melissa has toward her own education and career, and thank her for sharing some of her experiences as I wrote the various sections of this book. Of course, my parents, Victor and Lois, along with my grandmother, also continue to offer me the love and support that makes life worth living.

—Jason R. Rich

About the Author

Jason R. Rich is a weekly columnist for *The Boston Herald's* Sunday career section and has written feature articles for *National Business Employment Weekly* and *The Wall Street Journal's Managing Your Career.* He's also the author of *First Job, Great Job* and has written over 20 other books, including a number of bestselling computer and video game strategy guides. Visit his Web site at http:www.jasonrich.com.

PART I

Let's Get Organized

CHAPTER 1

Defining Your Skills and Interests: Who Are You Anyway?

Do I Need to Read This Chapter?

➡️ How do I define myself?

➡️ What are my most marketable strengths?

➡️ What are my interests?

➡️ What are my weaknesses?

When you look in the mirror, what do you see? Who are you? What do you think about yourself? What do other people think about you? Before you can set off on a quest to find a job and start marketing yourself to potential employers, you have to do some serious soul searching and honestly answer some questions about yourself. You must know exactly who you are and what your strengths and weaknesses are before you can start marketing yourself to others.

This chapter will pose to you some personal questions. As you answer these questions, be brutally honest with yourself. You don't ever have to share most of your answers with anyone else, but answering each of these questions as honestly as possible will help you to define in your mind who you are and what type of job opportunities you're best suited for. As you work your way through this chapter, have a pen and pad handy so that you can write out your answers. Be prepared to spend some time thinking about your answers and what impact they have on your life now, and could have on your future.

Everyone in the world is different. People have unique looks, different personalities, things they do extremely well, and personal weaknesses. By carefully examining your own strengths and weaknesses, you can more easily set yourself apart from the competition and narrow down your job search effort so that you focus only on opportunities that you know you'll be happy with. By carefully analyzing yourself now, you will be in a better position to market yourself to potential employers as your job search gets under way. The number one rule among marketers is to know your product. Since you're the product that you'll be marketing to potential employers in the not-so-distant future, your number one task before actually starting to search for jobs is to get to know yourself. Do you prefer a desk job in an office that involves minimal interaction with other people, or are you a people-person who would prosper working in a retail environment or in a sales position?

No matter who you are, there are careers or professions that you are suited for and can be highly successful in, based on your personality, your education, your unique set of interests, and your personal skills. The people who are the happiest and most successful in terms of their careers are people who manage to find jobs that combine their interests and skills. Finding a job that you're very good at isn't good enough. Ideally, your job should also allow you to exploit most, if not all, of your personal strengths. Your work should also involve performing tasks that you enjoy. (Sure, every job will have things about it that you don't like, but the trick is to make sure that the positives outweigh the negatives by a significant margin.) As you start your job search, be looking for a job you'll love, and don't settle for anything less.

By defining your strengths and knowing what your weaknesses are (and acknowledging them to yourself), you'll be in a much better position when it comes time to market your capabilities and to downplay your weaknesses to employers. Even the smartest, most ambitious people, who are well rounded and appear to be the perfect candidates for just about any job they apply for, have weaknesses. These people, however, have learned to capitalize on and exploit their strengths, while being able to work around or compensate for their weaknesses. When analyzing a job offer, it's also important to know your likes and dislikes and what you really want out of your work experience.

One of the biggest mistakes you can make when applying for a job is lying to yourself or to a potential employer about your interests, your personality, and your capabilities. Remember, there are no right or wrong answers to any of the questions you're about to answer. Being dishonest with yourself now can lead you to a dead-end job that you'll hate.

As you review each of these questions, you might not immediately see their relevance to helping you find and land a job. That's okay for now. Just answer each of the questions as completely as possible. Later, in Chapter 9, you'll revisit these questions and the answers you provide to them. When you start actually receiving job offers and have to choose which job to accept, the answers you provide to these questions will help you to carefully analyze your possibilities and point you toward the best job opportunity for you.

Get Started

Here are some questions you should ask yourself to help you to truly define your skills, goals, accomplishments, likes, and dislikes. Throughout several chapters of this book and during various stages of the job search process, for example, when you're creating your resume, writing cover letters, and analyzing job offers, you'll be referring to the answers you provide to these questions. Again, try to answer them as completely as possible now, but feel free to add to your answers later.

The best time to work on answering these questions is when you're alone and relaxed and you have at least one or two hours to think about your responses as you write them out. Simply thinking about how you would answer these questions isn't good enough.

1. What is your personal life like now?

_____

_____

_____

_____

2. What would you most like to change about your life?

_____

_____

_____

_____

3. What are the five things that you can start doing today to help you make the necessary changes in your life actually happen?

1. _____
2. _____
3. _____
4. _____
5. _____

4. How would you define your present lifestyle?

_____

_____

_____

5. What type of lifestyle would you like for yourself 5 or 10 years down the road?

_____

_____

_____

6. What five things could you be doing, starting today, to help you make these lifestyle changes take place?

1. _____
2. _____
3. _____
4. _____
5. _____

7. How would you describe your current financial status?

_____

_____

_____

8. Assuming you'd like to improve your financial status, what five things do you think you have to do to bring about improvements over the next 1 to 5 years?

Continued

1. _____
2. _____
3. _____
4. _____
5. _____

9. What would you say are the five very best things about your life? What is the reason for each item on your list?

   1. _____
   2. _____
   3. _____
   4. _____
   5. _____

10. What are the five worst things about your life overall that you'd like to fix or improve upon?

    1. _____
    2. _____
    3. _____
    4. _____
    5. _____

11. What are the five qualities about yourself that you are most proud of? (*Sample answers:* I have an outgoing personality. I make friends easily. I'm a positive, upbeat person. I am compassionate toward others.)

    1. _____
    2. _____
    3. _____
    4. _____
    5. _____

12. What are the five qualities about yourself that you know people don't like, or you think need improvement? (*Sample answers:* People hate that I smoke in their presence. I gossip too much about other people. I am a bit overweight and can't stick to my diet.)

    1. _____
    2. _____
    3. _____
    4. _____
    5. _____

13. What can you do, starting today, to change the negative qualities that you listed in Question 12 into positive ones?

    1. _____
    2. _____
    3. _____
    4. _____
    5. _____

14. What are some of the things you know you could be doing to improve the aspects of your life that you're not happy with?

    _____

    _____

15. Are you comfortable with your educational background and personal skill set? What three skills could you improve upon to make you more qualified for the type of job you hope to land? (*Sample answers:* I could learn how to operate a spreadsheet program on a computer. I could learn how to send and receive e-mail. I could take a speed reading course to boost my overall reading speed and comprehension rate. I could perfect my time management skills to give myself more free time and ultimately become a more organized person.)

Continued

1. _____

2. _____

3. _____

16. If you were to pursue an advanced degree or continue your education, what subject(s) or degree(s) would you pursue and why?

   _____

   _____

   _____

17. What course of action can you take, starting immediately, to help you improve your skill set? (*Sample answers:* Take evening classes, self-help courses, on-the-job training, etc.)

   _____

   _____

   _____

   _____

18. If you could spend more of your free time doing something (pursuing an interest, activity, or hobby), what is it you'd like to be doing?

   _____

   _____

   _____

19. What are your long-term career, personal, and family goals?

   Career Goals:

   _____

   _____

   Personal Goals:

   _____

   _____

Family Goals:

_____

_____

20. List five accomplishments from any aspect of your life that you are the most proud of. (*Sample answers:* I increased sales in my previous job by 30 percent in a 6-month period and won the salesperson-of-the-year award. I donated my time to help organize a charity fund-raiser, and we raised $20,000.)

   1. _____
   2. _____
   3. _____
   4. _____
   5. _____

21. What marketable skills and/or special abilities do you have? (If you're having trouble listing skills, think about what skills were required to accomplish everything you listed in Question 20, and what skills you possess that helped you succeed in school, in your recreational activities, and in previous jobs.) (*Sample answers:* Public speaking, writing, computer-literate, manager/supervisor, well-organized, telemarketing, deadline-oriented, athletic, problem solver, energetic, negotiating, analyzing, selling, creating, and/or bilingual.)

_____   _____   _____

_____   _____   _____

_____   _____   _____

_____   _____   _____

_____   _____   _____

Continued

22. What were your strongest subjects in school? Which subjects were your favorites? Why?

_____

_____

_____

23. What are your interests (hobbies), and what type of work-related activities do you enjoy? (*Sample answers:* playing tennis, surfing the Internet, writing short stories or poetry, Rollerblading, skiing, travel, organizing meetings or parties, cooking, reading.)

_____	_____	_____
_____	_____	_____
_____	_____	_____
_____	_____	_____
_____	_____	_____

24. What would you say are your biggest weaknesses? (*Sample answers:* Always running late, overextended, poor dresser, poor writing skills, too shy around strangers, not a good communicator, can't break the smoking habit.)

_____	_____	_____
_____	_____	_____
_____	_____	_____
_____	_____	_____
_____	_____	_____

25. Describe what would be the ideal atmosphere for you to work in? (Do you like working with people or working alone? Do you perform better in a structured job or one that allows you to take initiative and make decisions? Do you enjoy traveling on business or spending time driving in your car to and from meetings? In what work environment are you the most productive? Do you want a smoke-free work envi-

ronment? Is working in an office building with windows that open important to you? Do you prefer a corporate atmosphere or a more laid-back work environment?)

_____

_____

_____

_____

26. What were the five things you hated about your last job? (*Sample answers:* I didn't get along with the people I worked with. The work was boring and unchallenging. The office environment was too political. My boss was a tyrant.)

    1. _____

    2. _____

    3. _____

    4. _____

    5. _____

27. What work-related tasks are you really good at? (*Sample answers:* Typing, filing, telephone sales, in-person sales, building . . . , manufacturing . . . , creating . . . , organizing . . . , managing . . . , customer service and dealing with clients and customers, designing . . . , buying . . . , purchasing, bookkeeping, marketing, public relations, writing . . .)

    1. _____

    2. _____

    3. _____

    4. _____

    5. _____

Continued

28. What are the five qualities that you hope to find in your new job? (*Sample answer:* I'd like to work with people I could also become friendly with outside the workplace.)

1. _____

2. _____

3. _____

4. _____

5. _____

29. What kind of coworkers would you like to have?

_____

_____

_____

30. What type of people do you prefer to work with? (*Sample answer:* Young people, men, women, teenagers, or people from a specific economic, ethnic, or social background.)

_____

_____

_____

31. Are there people with certain personality traits that you have trouble working with? If so, what personality traits do you despise in your coworkers?

_____

_____

_____

32. Do you know anyone who works in the industry you're interested in? List people that might be able to provide you with information, help make an introduction for you, or provide you with career guidance.

_____

_____

33. If you could have any job you wanted, what would you do for a living? What would your responsibilities be?

_____

_____

_____

_____

34. Out of all the jobs you've had in your life (including summer jobs as a teenager and internships), which were the most rewarding and enjoyable? Why?

_____

_____

_____

_____

35. In terms of work-related benefits, what is most important to you? (Flexible work schedule, vacation time, health insurance, retirement plan, overtime, child care, etc.) List the top three benefits you want your next employer to offer.

1. _____

2. _____

3. _____

36. When working on the job, how do you like to be rewarded? (A pat on the back, promotion, pay raise, additional vacation time, more coffee breaks, a plaque, etc.)

_____

_____

_____

_____

_____

Continued

37. Check out a newspaper's help-wanted section and then write a help-wanted ad for what you would consider to be the ideal job for yourself. (Be specific.)

_____

_____

_____

38. Living or dead, who is your mentor or idol? What person do you try to model yourself after from a professional standpoint? What is it about that person you admire?

_____

_____

_____

39. Years after you pass away, how would you like to be remembered?

_____

_____

_____

40. How do you define personal and professional success? What would it take for you to consider yourself personally and professionally successful?

My definition of personal success is:

_____

_____

_____

My definition of professional success is:

_____

_____

_____

You might be feeling a bit emotionally drained, and your hand is probably tired from all the writing. Before you start analyzing your answers and putting all this information into the context of finding yourself a job, take a break and do something fun for a few hours. When you feel refreshed, move on to the next chapter, which explores how to manage your time effectively during the job search process.

✔ By carefully defining your strengths, knowing your weaknesses, and examining your interests and goals, you will be much more successful when marketing yourself to a prospective employer.

CHAPTER 2

Effective Time Management for Job Seekers

Do I Need to Read This Chapter?

➡ Why are time management and organizational skills important?

➡ How can I use the A-B-C–1-2-3 method in my job search?

➡ How can I use a personal planner as a time management tool?

➡ What is scheduling/contact management software?

➡ What is a PDA, and how can one of these devices help to keep me organized and on time?

Finding and landing a new job is probably going to feel like a full-time job unto itself, and if you're currently employed, you'll have to juggle your current workload with your job search efforts. Doing this effectively is going to take careful scheduling and plenty of planning, especially if you want to keep your job search activities a secret from your current employer until you've actually landed a job and you're prepared to give notice and tender your resignation from your current job.

Even if you're currently unemployed and looking for a new job, participating in a successful job search effort will also take plenty of planning and will put your time management skills to the test. Chances are, you're going to wish you had a few extra hours in the day in order to accomplish everything you need to do.

Successful time management means a lot more than wearing a wristwatch and showing up for interview appointments on time. This chapter of *Job Hunting for the Utterly Confused* will help you to develop useful time management skills that will make your job search efforts more organized and less stressful. At the same time, this chapter will teach you ways of managing your time once you're actually hired and working at your new job. You can't add extra hours to your day, but you can make the hours you're awake more productive. Yes, you will find time to accomplish what needs to get done, but you may have to make sacrifices along the way. Determining in advance what sacrifices you might have to make, and being prepared to make them if it becomes necessary, will help you to alleviate the stress of an overburdened schedule.

Why Time Management and Organizational Skills Are Important

There are only 24 hours in a day—that's 168 hours, or 10,080 minutes, in a week. How you spend every minute is important, because once time has past, it can't be relived or recaptured. Assuming you take time to sleep every night, and you work at your job for at least 8 hours per day, that doesn't leave a whole lot of time to spend with your family or pursue personal interests or hobbies. On top of personal and work obligations which already eat up huge amounts of time, you must now find the time to find yourself a job. Start by making your job search efforts a top priority in your life. (Of course, if you have children and family responsibilities, those come first.) Understand that for the next few weeks while you're a job seeker, the more time and effort you spend finding and then trying to land the ideal job for you, the happier and more fulfilled you'll be in the weeks, months, and years ahead.

By carefully planning and managing your time, setting priorities, and making an effort to meet self-imposed deadlines, you will be able to accomplish everything you need and want to get done in a typical day and still get a good night's sleep. Staying organized will keep you in a better frame of mind and will greatly reduce the stress commonly experienced by job seekers.

Without proper planning and scheduling, trying to remember your appointments, personal and business obligations, and the tasks you need to get done is very difficult. Since it is extremely unprofessional to show up for appointments late, or blow them off altogether because you forgot about them, it's critical that you develop your own method for keeping track of your time. In addition, you must learn to successfully juggle all the different aspects of your life that demand large chunks of time, and discover how to set priorities so that you don't get bogged down trying to accomplish unimportant tasks. Part of being an organized and successful time manager requires choosing the most important tasks to do, and then determining the best and most time-efficient way to do them.

To successfully manage your time, you'll need to use some type of time management or scheduling tool, such as a personal planner, scheduling software on your computer, and/or a handheld personal digital assistant (PDA). Whatever organizational tool you choose to incorporate into your life, don't expect miraculous changes overnight. Becoming an organized person, who carefully manages his or her time, takes practice and persistence. So once you decide to incorporate some type of scheduling and organizational tool into your life, stick with it. Once your overall life becomes more organized and you become keenly aware of how you're spending your time, you will find it easier to focus on your short- and long-term goals and ultimately achieve them.

It is as easy to become overorganized or too conscious of time as it is to be totally unorganized and have no concept of time ticking away. Your goal is to find a happy medium, so that you can save time and use what time you allocate to specific tasks to the utmost advantage. How you ultimately spend your time will be based on long-term habits, the demands others place upon you (including your boss, your family, and your friends), your need to accomplish work-related tasks, your need to relax and have free time, and sudden or unexpected events that demand your immediate attention.

Knowing that you only have 24 hours in a day, you must make decisions about how you want to spend your time. This means taking into account everything you hope to accomplish in the long term, middle term, and short term, prioritizing these tasks, and blocking out time to accomplish them, starting with the most important ones that will generate the biggest benefits and rewards.

Setting Priorities Is as Easy as A-B-C and 1-2-3

Becoming organized means performing three tasks on a daily basis—*focus, plan,* and *act.* First, *focus* on what needs to get done on any given day. Take between 5 and 15 minutes in the morning and make a detailed to-do list to start planning out your day. *Planning* begins with prioritizing your tasks and to-do list items and then determining how and when you're going to accomplish them. Also, determine if larger tasks need to be divided into smaller, more manageable ones. Set aside specific times in the day to accomplish each task, after you have chosen what's important. Finally, once you know what needs to be done and you've allocated time in the day to do it, it's time to *act*—turn your goals and objectives into reality.

To help you determine what tasks in your life require immediate attention, one of the easiest things you can do is make a list of everything you need to accomplish in a day, a week, or a month. Include all your personal obligations, your work-related obligations, your job search tasks, and your to-do items, no matter how minor they may seem. Everything you do in a day takes up time, and it's your responsibility to determine how you spend your time. Once you have completed your list, place an A, B, or C next to each item.

- Items categorized as an A should be absolutely critical and require your immediate attention to complete. A items should produce the most valuable result, reward, or benefit once they're completed.
- Items marked with a B should be important, but not tasks that require immediate attention in order to meet a deadline. B items should produce an important result.
- C items are things that should get done eventually, or optional tasks, that lack importance. Thus, these tasks produce a worthwhile result, but nothing that's critical to your long-term success.

To help you further decide what tasks should get done in what order, also give each A, B, or C item a 1, 2, or 3 priority, based on when the task should get completed.

- Tasks marked with a 1 should be completed as soon as possible.
- Tasks with a 2 should get done soon, but can be pushed back if absolutely necessary.
- Categorizing a task as a 3 means it can wait. As time goes by, a C-3 task might grow in importance and eventually become an A-1 task.

When you're first starting your job search efforts, and you haven't yet pinpointed what types of companies you want to work for, you haven't yet created your resume, and you've read absolutely no help-wanted ads, a C-3 item on your to-do list might be to buy a new suit to wear to your interviews. Right now, buying a new interview suit is a C-3 item because it's very low on the scale of importance of things you need to do right now to start finding a job. Later, after you start sending out resumes and cover letters, and you start hearing back from potential employers that want you to come in for an interview, that C-3 item becomes much more important and timely. Thus, a day or two before your first job interview, buying a new suit might be reclassified on your to-do list as an A-1 or A-2 priority.

Don't Forget

Using this A-B-C–1-2-3 method of prioritizing tasks, your A-1 tasks should be only those things that absolutely must be completed immediately, and your C-3 tasks should be those unimportant tasks that don't require your attention in the near future.

The best time to create your prioritized list is first thing in the morning, before you actually start your day. An alternative time is in the evening, right before you go to bed. Plan on spending between 5 and 15 minutes per day to compile and prioritize your list. Whatever time you actually spend planning will ultimately save you countless hours of wasted time throughout the day, because you will no longer spend your time working on unimportant tasks. If you plan your time efficiently, about 80 percent of your time should be spent doing the items in the top 20 percent of your list (in other words, the A tasks), which are the most important and will result in the biggest benefits and rewards.

Don't Forget

1. As you plan out your day, always allow room for flexibility. Leave at least 1 hour per day (during normal business hours, if possible) to deal with any unexpected situations that arise.

2. Be sure to distinguish between "urgent" and "important" items, and make time for completing both. An urgent item is an emergency that must be dealt with immediately. An important item is something that needs to be accomplished before you can move on to something else.

Quick Tips

Later in this book, "success expert" Barry Farber shares some of his advice about setting goals and becoming a more organized person. He takes the concept of creating a detailed to-do list and daily schedule a step farther. After setting daily goals for yourself, Farber suggests taking each goal, and on a separate sheet of paper, rewriting it as a question. For example, if your goal for the day is to create your resume, at the top of a blank sheet of paper you'd write, "What do I have to do today in order to create my resume?" Under this heading, Farber suggests creating a list of everything you'll need to do, no matter how insignificant, in order to accomplish your overall goal. Once this list is complete, choose one of the items on your list that you can begin working on immediately, and get started. As you complete each item on the list, place a checkmark next to it and move on to the next item. This approach will help you to divide larger, almost overwhelming tasks into smaller tasks that are easily manageable. By following this strategy, you'll be able to accomplish even your most challenging goals.

Using a Personal Planner as a Time Management Tool

If you visit any office supply store, chances are you'll see a whole department that offers all sorts of personal planners, including Day-Timers, Franklin Planners, Day-Runners, Filofax, and a number of others. Day planners, also known as appointment books or schedulers, come in all shapes and sizes. Some planners are designed to fit comfortably in your pocket or purse (and are ideal for people on the go), while others have desktop designs that give you plenty of space to plan out your life. (Desktop designs are better suited for people who spend most of their time working behind a desk or in an office.)

The first thing you should do when you purchase a planner is to gather up all your scrap papers and sticky notes that contain things for you to do, phone numbers, addresses, appointments, and other important pieces of information. Immediately copy all these random notes into the appropriate places in your planner. Next, throw away those scrap papers and stop creating new ones. From this point on, all your notes, appointments, to-do items, reminders, ideas, etc., should be added directly into the appropriate space in your planner.

Reasons for using a planner include:

- It helps you take charge of your busy schedule, because you can better plan for what's coming up next in your life.
- You can enjoy a less stressful way of life because all the details regarding your appointments, meetings, to-do lists, etc., are neatly organized in one place. You can easily reference to-do items and appointments and then mark off completed items. Being able to mark off completed items throughout a day will keep you motivated to accomplish more and will allow you to see the progress you're making.
- A planner will help you develop focus in your life and maintain that focus throughout each day.

- You can begin working smarter, not harder. You'll focus your valuable time and effort doing only the tasks that are important and require your attention.

- All your important information is written down in one place, so when you need to refer to it, it will be right where it should be. This will keep you from spending time trying to remember what tasks you have to accomplish or where you wrote down someone's phone number.

- By successfully managing time, you'll discover that you will have more time to spend with family and friends, to work on hobbies, and to just kick back and relax.

Day-Timers, Inc., is one of the world's leading publishers of personal planners. The company distributes its products through office supply stores and through its mail-order catalog, which can be ordered by calling (800) 225-5005 or visiting the company's Web site at http://www.daytimer.com. Within the Day-Timers catalog, you'll find over 1400 products that you can use to organize your life without using a computer.

In addition to being able to select a planner size that meets your needs, Day-Timers offers many different planner formats to choose from, allowing you to totally customize your planner to meet your personal and professional needs. A typical Day-Timer personal planner will cost anywhere from $20 to $100 (or more), depending on how fancy you want your planner to be. Obviously, the look of your planner isn't as important as its functionality. You're going to pay more for fancy designer and/or leather planner covers that provide a nicer look, but no additional functionality.

Depending on how flexible your daily schedule is, choose a planner format that best meets your personal needs. Popular formats from Day-Timers include:

- *2-Pages-Per-Day.* This format gives you two pages to schedule each day (Figure 2.1). You can write in appointments, commitments, and deadlines in the "Appointments and Scheduled Events" portion of each day's planner pages, which divides the 8:00 a.m. to 9:00 p.m. workday into half-hour increments. You can also create a "To Be Done Today" action list for each day, and keep track of all your other notes, tasks, and to-do items in the "Diary and Work Record" area. Some of the 2-Pages-Per-Day formats also offer space to write-in phone calls and expenses. If you're juggling a full-time or part-time job along with a job search, you'll probably want to take advantage of the added space the 2-Pages-Per-Day format offers.

- *1-Page-Per-Day.* This format also allows you to plan out your 8:00 a.m. to 9:00 p.m. workday by blocking out half-hour time increments. There's also space for a "To Be Done" action list for each day (Figure 2.2).

- *Weekly Format.* This Day-Timer format allows you to view a week at a time, but provides less space to write in appointments and to-do lists for each day (Figure 2.3).

Each Day-Timer also offers extra pages for planning future activities with a monthly calendar view, plus can hold a pad of paper and pen. Additional options you can add to most Day-Timer planners include a personal address and telephone book, along with extra pages for keeping telephone call logs; for keeping track of expenses, long-term projects, and meeting agendas; and for writing down any other kind of notes.

Any type of personal planner is designed to keep all your scheduling information in one place, saving you from having to keep track of dozens of notes that you've written on scrap paper.

Don't Forget

When writing your appointments into a planner, always use a pencil so that you can neatly and easily modify your schedule as needed. Neatly print all your entries so that they can be read easily.

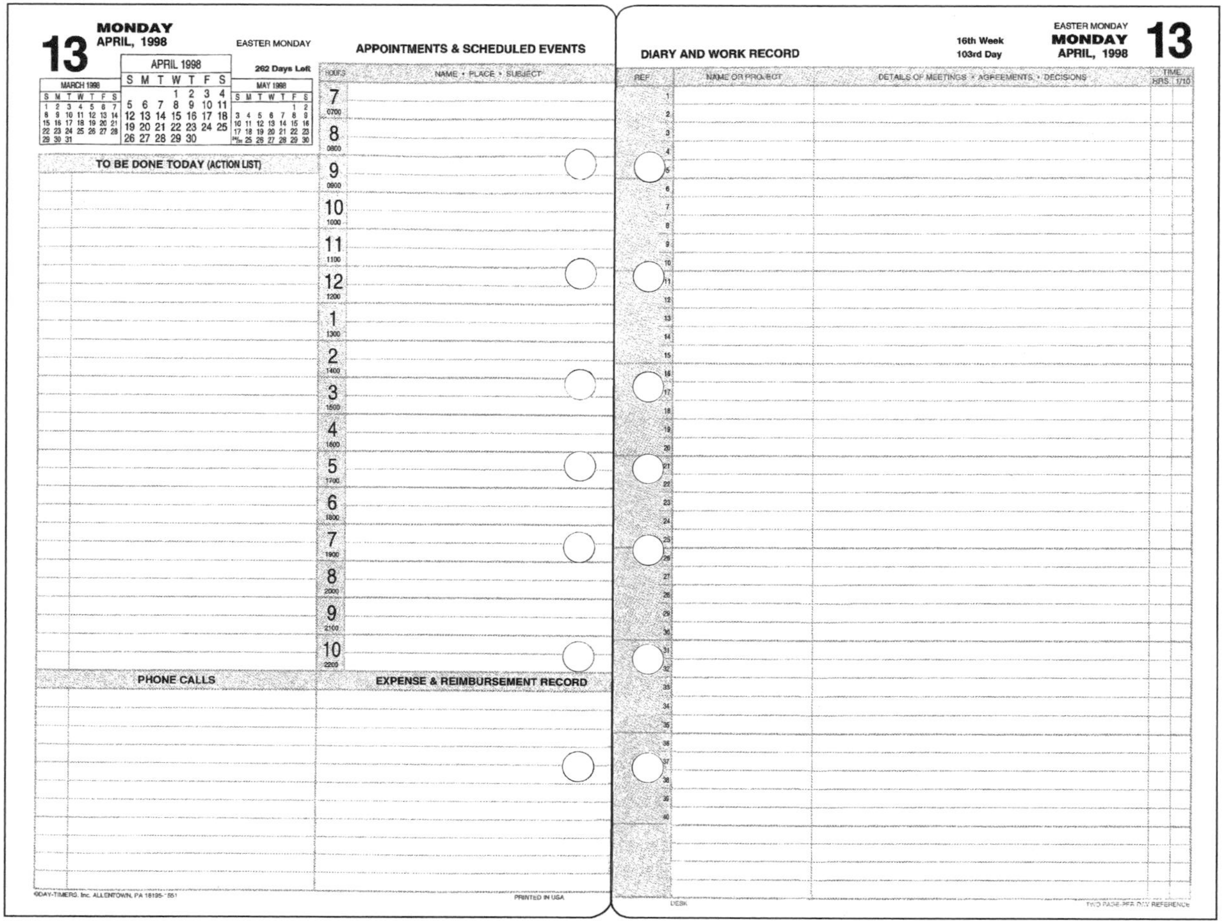

Figure 2.1 Here's what a page from a Day-Timers 2-Pages-Per-Day planner looks like. As you can see, there's plenty of room for writing your appointments, notes, and to-do lists.

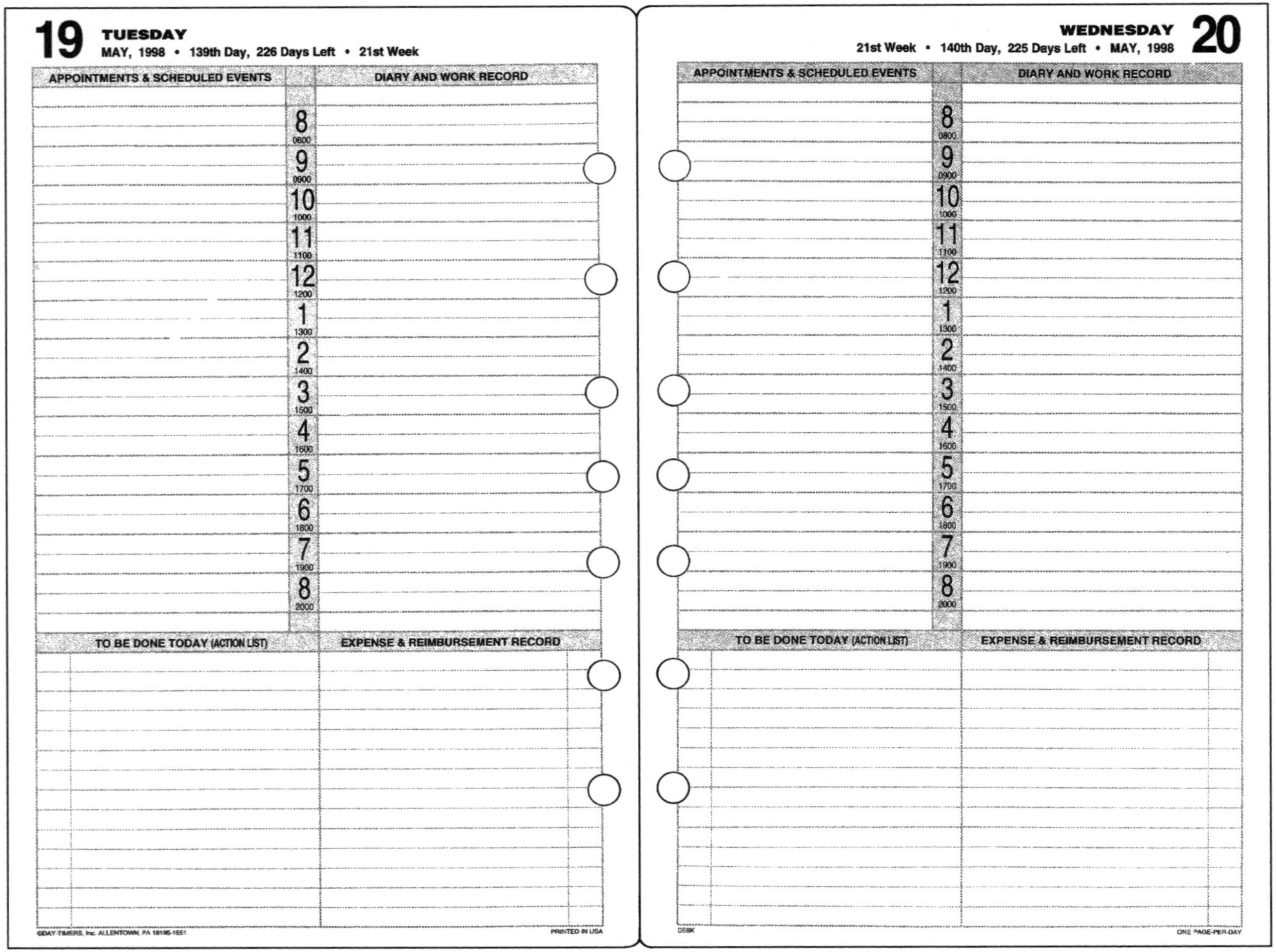

Figure 2.2 This is what a page from a Day-Timers 1-Page-Per-Day planner looks like.

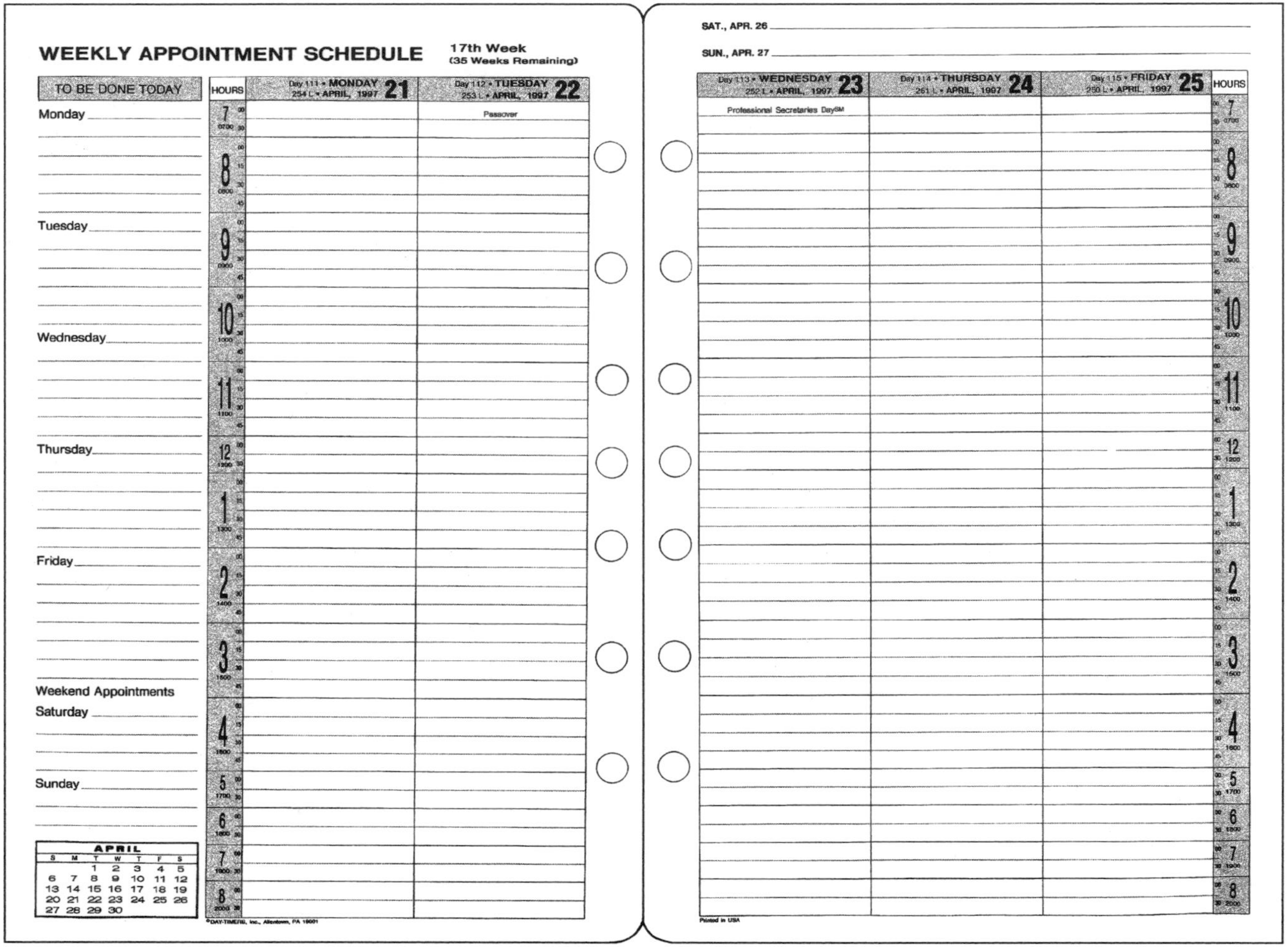

WEEKLY APPOINTMENT SCHEDULE

17th Week
(35 Weeks Remaining)

TO BE DONE TODAY	HOURS

Monday

Tuesday

Wednesday

Thursday

Friday

Weekend Appointments
Saturday

Sunday

APRIL

SAT., APR. 26

SUN., APR. 27

HOURS

Figure 2.3 This weekly format of a Day-Timer planner provides yet another way you can format and keep track of important information.

Danger!

As you write down appointments, be sure to block out extra time needed for preparation and travel. For example, if you just scheduled a job interview with The ABC Company on Tuesday at 2:00 p.m., you should first turn to Tuesday's page in your planner and block out the necessary amount of time for the interview. (For this example, we'll assume the job interview will last about 2 hours.) If you need at least 30 minutes travel time to get to the interview location, you should block out time starting at 1:30 p.m. Since you know this interview is coming up, you also need time to perform company research and prepare for the interview. You'll probably want to do this at least one day early, so on Monday's page in your planner, set aside the time you'll need to perform research and to prepare for the interview. Consider your interview preparation time to be an appointment, so that once you allocate the time for it, you will spend that time doing the necessary preparation.

MONDAY, JULY #, 199#

9:00 a.m.   Go to library and research The ABC Company. (2 hours)

9:30 a.m.

10:00 a.m.

10:30 a.m.

11:00 a.m.

12:00 p.m.   Meet Ellen to practice answering job interview questions over lunch at Bob's Restaurant. (90 minutes)

12:30 p.m.

1:00 p.m.

1:30 p.m.

TUESDAY, JULY #, 199#

12:00 p.m.	Pick up interview suit from the dry cleaner.
12:30 p.m.	Review company research notes, prepare questions to ask interviewer, and prepare for interview. (1 hour)
1:00 p.m.	
1:30 p.m.	Travel by car to The ABC Company job interview.
2:00 p.m.	Job interview with Mark Giordani at The ABC Company (applying for bookkeeping position)—123 Main Street, 3rd Floor. (2 hours)
2:30 p.m.	
3:00 p.m.	
3:30 p.m.	
4:00 p.m.	Travel home after interview.
4:30 p.m.	Write and mail out thank-you note to Mark @ The ABC Company.
5:00 p.m.	

To-Do Lists versus Appointments

Whenever you need a predetermined block of time in the day to accomplish a specific task or objective, consider it an appointment and enter it into your planner accordingly. For example, you need to spend 2 hours at the library performing research on a company you will be interviewing with the following day. In your planner, block out 2 hours of time, say, between 5:00 and 7:00 p.m., after your regular workday is over. By writing this into your planner as an appointment, you won't schedule dinner with a friend or make other plans that will detract from your research time.

The process of looking for a job has to become a top priority in your life. Thus, if you should be doing research, looking through help-wanted ads, creating cover letters, writing thank-you notes, or preparing questions to ask a potential employer, you can't spend whatever free time you have hanging out with friends, going to parties, or performing less important but time-consuming activities. With careful planning, you might be able to fit in your friends or other social commitments between work-related responsibilities and finding a job, but what you spend your time doing will ultimately be based on the priorities you set for yourself.

Quick Tips

If you have a hair salon appointment at 10:00 a.m., a job interview at 2:00 p.m., and a dinner meeting starting at 6:30 p.m., these are all specific appointments that should be added into your planner as soon as the appointments are made. In fact, when booking appointments, you should always have your planner in front of you.

To-do items are tasks or errands that you need to accomplish during the day, but that don't require a substantial amount of time or a specified time. For example, picking up your interview outfit from the dry cleaner, dropping off your resume at a print shop, or dropping your thank-you notes in a mailbox are all items that can be added to a day's to-do list. These items can be done in between scheduled appointments or whenever you have a few minutes to spare. A typical to-do item for a job seeker to do each day is to check the ads in the newspaper's help-wanted section and check the various Internet job databases (such as The Monster Board—www.monster.com) for new job listings that might be of interest.

Don't Forget

As you complete each item in your daily to-do list, place a checkmark next to it and move on to the next item.

Short Cuts

To keep from becoming overwhelmed, you might consider creating two or three different to-do lists each day, but keep all the lists in your planner. One list could include all your job-related tasks (if you're currently employed), while the second list can include the tasks you need to accomplish related to finding and landing a new job. Finally, you can create a third list containing personal or family-oriented tasks. Your to-do list(s) should be written directly into your planner on the appropriate page for each day. Items that you don't complete on a specific day should be copied over to the next day's page. Uncompleted items from the previous day should get priority treatment the following day.

It's always a good idea to divide larger projects into smaller ones. For example, if you are writing your resume, this is probably going to take many hours, so break up this task by completing one section of your resume at a time. If you have 1 week to complete your resume, allocate 1 or 2 hours per day to spend on this project. During the day, if you happen to think of something important that relates to your resume, jot it down in your planner and refer to it when you're focusing your time on your resume creation activities. Don't drop whatever it is you're doing and start working on your resume. Being able to focus on whatever task you're working on is an important time management strategy.

Using Scheduling/Contact Management Software to Better Organize Your Life

The great thing about scheduling/contact management software is that it contains many different modules to help organize your life. An electronic scheduler looks very much like a personal planner, but it appears on your computer screen. It can be used to keep track of all your appointments and time commitments. This type of software also acts as a database of your contact addresses and phone numbers. Once you enter each of your contacts into the contact management portion of the software, you can access the data directly, or easily incorporate the data into your word processing documents to generate personalized letters, memos, or faxes. Combine these two powerful applications with an electronic to-do list manager and the ability to keep track of all telephone calls, written communication, and e-mail, along with your notes regarding a contact, and you have all the tools you need to be totally organized. Having your contact information at your fingertips will also help to make you a highly successful networker.

With over 1 million users worldwide, one of the most popular scheduling/contact management software packages on the market is Symantec's ACT! 3.0 (or higher) for Windows 95 (Figure 2.4). Versions of this program are also available for Windows 3.1, Macin-

Figure 2.4 Look for the ACT! contact management and scheduling software wherever computer software is sold. You can download a demo version of this software when you visit Symantec's Web site at http://www.symantec.com.

tosh computers, and many handheld personal digital assistants. ACT! assists people in managing their business relationships more effectively, and helps to increase organization and productivity. A less expensive, scaled-down version of ACT! 3.0, called 1st Act!, is also available from Symantec wherever computer software is sold.

ACT! is an incredibly powerful program, and yet it's easy to use. This program is particularly useful for job seekers, because it allows you to keep track of all information pertaining to each job you apply for, and to keep well-organized and detailed notes about each potential employer. At the same time, you can keep track of all your appointments and to-do lists using a single program.

Just as Day-Timers and all the other companies that market personal planners offer their organizational tools in a variety of popular formats, ACT! allows you to display daily, weekly, and monthly calendars in many different formats, so you can easily schedule, and electronically be reminded of, calls, meetings, to-dos, interviews, and appointments.

One feature that any scheduling/contact manager software package offers, which no traditional printed planner can, is an electronic search option. If you have dozens or hundreds of contact names, addresses, and phone numbers (of potential employers or network contacts) entered into your database, and you need to find someone's information fast, you can perform a search based on almost any criteria—such as a first or last name, company name, city, state, phone number, job type, interview date, and other information.

You can then enter notes in that contact's database record, or import the contact's name and address into your word processor so that you can quickly send out a personalized letter, fax, or e-mail message. Another benefit to using this type of software, as opposed to a traditional paper-based planner, is that any information can easily be edited, updated, added, or deleted, and the only limit to the amount of information you can store is based upon the size of your computer's hard disk. Using your printer, you can print out a daily, weekly, or monthly itinerary, or print contact information and carry this printed information with you.

If your personal contact database contains hundreds of individuals, that's a lot of business cards or address book entries to keep track of manually. When you use a software program to manage your contacts, whether you have 10 or 10,000 contacts, keeping them alphabetized (or sorted any way you choose) is all done on your computer. You don't have to worry about losing individual business cards, and when you need to locate a contact, you don't have to remember if you filed that contact by first name, last name, or company name, because the software will locate your contact in seconds using any search criteria. Furthermore, using this type of software eliminates the need to maintain a traditional planner (for keeping track of appointments), a notepad (for keeping track of to-do lists), and an address book or Rolodex (for organizing your contacts).

If you have access to a personal computer, using ACT! (or a similar program) can greatly increase your productivity during your job search efforts. The timesaving and organizational benefits will continue once you actually land a job.

When you're looking for a job, one of the ways ACT! can come in handy is when you're first contacting many different companies and sending out your resume. Each company you contact can be added to an ACT! contact database you create specifically to keep track of potential employers. In addition to the company name, address, phone number, and other related information, you can also include in the ACT! record detailed notes for each potential employer about what job you applied for, when you sent your resume and cover letter, who your main contact is at the company, etc. You can also set an alarm to remind you to follow up your resume and cover letter with a phone call in a few days. When you call up the company, you can add detailed notes about any topics discussed and use the scheduling portion of the software when scheduling interview appointments.

Later, you can enter your company research notes directly into your ACT! database, so all the information you have about each potential employer will be located in one place. Just before you leave for your interview, you can print out the ACT! record for that company, and have a neat, well-organized printout that contains all the information you compiled about the company. After the interview, you can have ACT! remind you to make any necessary follow-up calls, and you can quickly whip out a personalized thank-you note.

In addition to being powerful, programs like ACT! are also highly customizable, so you can activate only the features you need, and you can custom-design each contact screen to display only pertinent information (Figures 2.5 and 2.6).

ACT! is available wherever software is sold. If you have access to the Internet, you can visit Symantec's Web site (http://www.syman-

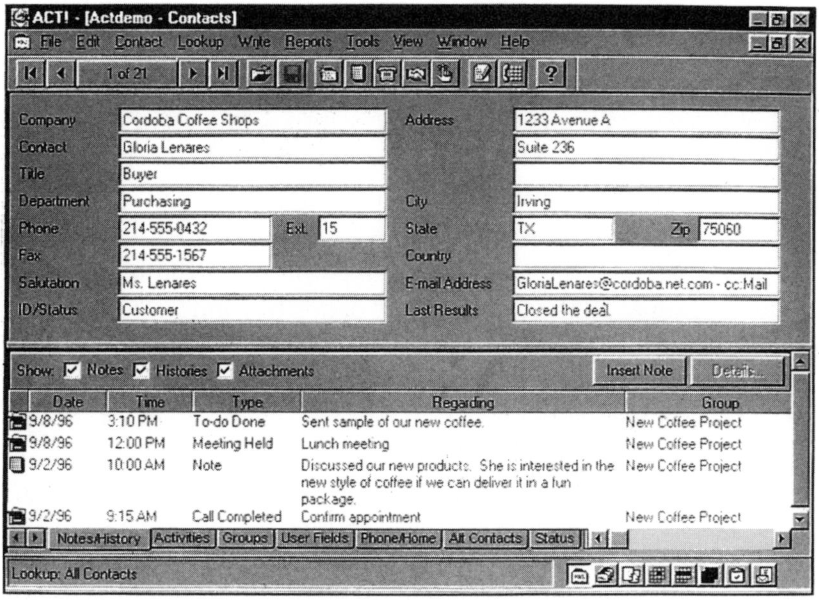

Figure 2.5 Here's a screen shot from the Windows 95 version of the ACT! software.

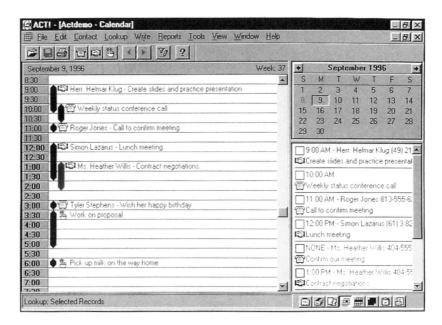

Figure 2.6   As you can see, ACT! helps you organize all your important information.

tec.com) and download a free-trial version of the software. The trial version of ACT! is the actual program and is fully functional, but you'll be limited to creating a database containing no more than 25 contacts, which is actually enough to get your job search started. Of course, when you get hooked on using the program and your personal contact database expands beyond 25 contacts, you'll need to make an investment and purchase the complete version of the software. Whether you choose to use ACT! or a similar program, you will benefit in the short and long term, because this type of software transforms your desktop or laptop computer into a powerful organizational tool that can help you maintain control over your life.

In addition to ACT! there are many other scheduling/contact management programs available for Windows- and Macintosh-based personal computers. Microsoft Corporation offers Microsoft

Schedule+ and Microsoft Outlook, which are sold separately or come bundled with Microsoft Office 95 and Microsoft Office 97 (respectively). For more information about these Microsoft products, visit your local software dealer, or check out Microsoft's Web site at http://www.microsoft.com.

Day-Timer Organizer 2.0 is a Windows- and Mac-based computer program from Day-Timers, Inc., which is basically a traditional Day-Timer planner, but in electronic form. This software is primarily a scheduling program and electronic address/telephone book that can be purchased wherever Day-Timer planners are sold, or by calling (800) 225-5005. A free demo version of Day-Timer Organizer 2.0 is available at Day-Timers' Web site at http://www.daytimer.com.

Lotus Development Corporation, the creator of the Lotus 1-2-3 spreadsheet program, offers a powerful scheduling and contact manager program, called Lotus Organizer 97 GS. You can use this latest version of Lotus Organizer to schedule appointments, create prioritized to-do lists, plan major events, store and organize addresses, track phone calls, make notes, create calendars, sort information, mark important dates, link to your favorite Web sites, and a lot more.

Like ACT! and similar programs, Lotus Organizer integrates an on-screen calendar, to-do list, planner, address book, call manager, notepad, anniversary reminder, and scheduler. Lotus Organizer has the look and feel of a paper datebook, and you can fully customize the calendar/scheduler on-screen display so that it caters to your personal needs. When you need to take your contact and schedule information with you, this program allows you to print your information in over two dozen layouts, ranging from monthly calendars to trifolds. Your information can even be formatted to fit into a traditional datebook. The latest version of Lotus Organizer is available wherever software is sold. For more information, call Lotus Development Corporation at (800) 343-5414, or visit the company's Web site at http://www.lotus.com.

Using a Personal Digital Assistant to Keep You Organized and On Time

A personal digital assistant (PDA) is a portable (often handheld) computer with built-in software specifically designed to help keep you organized, no matter where you are. The best things about a PDA are that, unlike a desktop PC or even a laptop computer, they're battery-powered and 100 percent portable. In fact, these small devices will easily fit in a briefcase, purse, or large pocket. Even the least expensive PDAs, which cost around $50, offer an electronic appointment book/scheduler, text editing capabilities, and a calculator, along with an address and phone directory.

The more powerful PDAs, often called HPCs (handheld PCs), offer the power of a desktop computer. PDAs are available from stores that sell consumer electronics and computers, and are manufactured by a wide range of companies, including Casio, US Robotics, Sharp Electronics, Hewlett Packard, Psion, NEC, Compaq, Philips Electronics, and Apple Computer, Inc. Each of these manufacturers offers several models of PDAs and/or HPCs, which have different features and capabilities. The latest generation of HPCs uses an operating system called Microsoft Windows CE, which is a scaled-down, yet powerful version of Microsoft Windows 95. The PDAs that use Windows CE come with built-in versions of Microsoft Word, Excel, Explorer, and other Microsoft Office software titles, so you can actually surf the Internet, write text documents, or create spreadsheets, and then transfer your information easily between your HPC and desktop computer.

When you use scheduling/contact management software on your desktop computer, the biggest limitation is that you can't easily take the information with you, unless you create printouts or use a PDA. Some of the most popular PDAs available are compatible with popular scheduling/contact management software programs that work on the PC, so you can automatically keep your PC and PDA data synchronized, often with the touch of a single button. Some PDAs and HPCs actually have versions of ACT! and/or Schedule+ available for them, so you can keep your important information up-to-date in both your desktop PC (or laptop) and your PDA.

Casio's popular Cassiopeia line of personal digital assistants offers Windows CE compatibility and can easily be used for maintaining your contacts and appointments, in addition to handling many other applications. The pocket-size Cassiopeia weighs less than a pound and features a 480×240 dot LCD display with a backlight, a pen-touch-sensitive screen, a small typewriter-style keyboard, and a standard PC card expansion slot (allowing you to add a modem or another type of PCMCIA-based expansion device). Casio's Cassiopeia HPCs offer the same user interface used by Windows 95 for desktop computers, and a wide range of additional third-party software titles that can be purchased to increase the power and capability of these handheld units. The Cassiopeia operates for up to 20 hours using two AA batteries, and is available in several different system configurations. By adding an optional modem, you can easily use the Cassiopeia to access the Internet's World Wide Web, send and receive e-mail, and/or to send and receive faxes from virtually anywhere (Figure 2.7).

What sets a typical PDA apart from an HPC is the unit's computing power and price. Casio's Cassiopeia HPCs start at around $500. If, however, you don't need a full-powered handheld computer, and you're looking for a device that can simply manage your schedule and contacts, Casio manufactures much less expensive PDAs. Because of the HPC's ability to easily synchronize data with a desktop PC running Windows 95 (or later) and most popular scheduler/contact manager programs, users who have access to a desktop PC will get the most benefit from an HPC running Windows CE.

For additional information about Casio's line of Cassiopeia HPCs, visit any office superstore or computer store, or check out the company's Web site at http://www.casio.com. To find out about HPCs manufactured by Casio, Philips Electronics, NEC, and other

Figure 2.7 The Casio Cassiopeia PDA offers the power of a desktop computer, but fits in the palm of your hand.

companies, you can visit Microsoft's Windows CE Web site at http://www.microsoft.com/windowsce.

Don't Forget

To learn more about the PDAs and HPCs now available, visit your local consumer electronics store, office supply superstore, or computer store. You can also visit these Web sites:

Casio: http://www.casio.com

Microsoft: http://www.microsoft.com/windowsce

US Robotics: http://www.usr.com/palm

Hewlett Packard: http://www.hp.com/handheld

Apple Computer: http://www.apple.com

Sharp Electronics: http://www.sharp-usa.com

Psion: http://www.psion.com

NEC: http://www.nec.com

Philips Electronics: http://www.philips.com

HPC.Net: http://www.windowsce.com

Now that you know how to become a more organized person, you're ready to take the next step in finding a job, which is creating a resume. In the next chapter, you'll learn how important a resume is when it comes to finding and landing a job, and you'll discover how to create a resume that captures the attention of the reader.

It's a Wrap

✔ Careful planning and time management, which involves setting priorities and meeting self-imposed deadlines, will allow you to finish what you want to get done in a typical day.

✔ Staying organized greatly reduces stress.

✔ The A-B-C–1-2-3 method only takes 5 to 15 minutes each day and will greatly simplify the act of prioritizing.

✔ You should now be able to begin using a personal planner, scheduling software, or a PDA to further organize your schedule.

PART II

Preparing
the Resume
Package

CHAPTER 3

Preparing a Resume
That Makes an Impact

Do I Need to Read This Chapter?

➡ How do I prepare a resume?

➡ What is the most appropriate information for my resume?

For many job applicants, one of the most challenging tasks as you embark on your job search is creating a resume. After all, it will most likely be the information on one single-sided sheet of 8.5 × 11 inch paper that will determine whether or not an employer has any interest in inviting you to come in for an interview. On one sheet of paper, you have to concisely summarize, using examples, all the reasons why a potential employer should hire you. As a potential employer reads (or skims) your resume, that employer has a few questions in mind that he or she wants instant answers to. Your goal with your resume is to answer the employer's questions quickly. As someone reads your resume, the answers to the following questions should be obvious:

- What are your skills and qualifications?
- What work experience do you have that directly relates to the job you're applying for?
- Are you worth the salary that you're asking for, or that the job pays?
- What can you offer to the company?
- How will hiring you benefit the company in the short term and long term?
- Can you help to solve the problems or challenges that the company is currently facing?
- What sets you apart from all the other people applying for the same job that you are?

Not only must you be prepared to answer these questions in an interview situation, but you must offer answers in your resume in order for it to make an impact. Your resume has to be powerful, positive, attention getting, yet truthful. It should shout out to the employer, "Hire me!" not "File me!"

When a company markets an expensive product, such as a computer, a car, or some type of machine or appliance, one of the first steps for getting a customer interested in that product is to provide a brochure that lists the product's unique benefits and features. The brochure is designed to get the customer excited about the product. When it comes to landing a job, your resume is the brochure that you will use to market yourself. Your resume must get the potential employer interested enough in you so that you'll get invited in for an interview. From that point, your chances of landing the job rely on your ability to sell yourself in person, but more on that later.

Upon looking at sample resumes, you probably think that you can sit down and crank one out in a few minutes. Well, you probably can. The problem is, the resume you whip together will most likely be useless. Choosing what information about yourself to include in your resume, how that information will be presented, and then how you should customize your resume specifically for the job you're applying for takes a lot of thought.

Creating a resume with impact, that will actually help you market yourself, is going to take time and a lot of thought, and probably require you to write and rewrite multiple drafts before you have a completed document that's suitable to be sent off to potential employers.

What Information Gets Included in a Resume?

Every resume, no matter what format you decide to use to convey the information, is broken down into sections. Using a pad of paper (and a pen), write down, in plain English, the pieces of information about yourself that you think belong in each section. Later, you'll condense this information, organize it, and rewrite it using action words to add impact.

While not every resume includes each of these sections, the most common sections of a resume are:

- Heading
- Job objective
- Education
- Accreditation and licenses
- Skills
- Work and employment experience
- Professional affiliations
- Military service
- References
- Personal information

Heading

At the top of the resume, list your full name, address, phone number(s), fax number, and e-mail address. If you are still in school, include your permanent address as well as your school address. Never list the phone number of your present employer (your current work number), especially if you're applying for new jobs without your current employer knowing about it.

Danger!

When you list a phone number on your resume, always make sure that the phone will be answered, 24 hours per day, when someone calls. To assure a potential employer can reach you on the first attempt, connect an answering machine to the line, hire a telephone answering service, or subscribe to the "call-answering" service offered by your local phone company. If a potential employer can't reach you easily, you might wind up getting passed over for a job.

You can use any of these sample heading formats in your resume:

John R. Doe
123 Main Street
Anywhere, NY 10###
(212) 555-1234
(212) 555-4321 (fax)
Jdoe@internet-provider.com

John R. Doe, 123 Main Street, Anywhere, NY 10###
(212) 555-1234   Jdoe@internet-provider.com

John R. Doe
123 Main Street
Anywhere, NY 10###
(212) 555-1234
Jdoe@internet-provider.com

John R. Doe
123 Main Street
Anywhere, NY 10###
(212) 555-1234
Jdoe@internet-provider.com

Note: This information can be centered, right-justified, or left-justified, as long as it appears on the top of the page. Your full name is always the first piece of information on your resume.

If you want to list two addresses on your resume, you could use this format:

John R. Doe

Permanent Address   School Address

123 Main Street   P.O. Box 1234
Anywhere, NY 10###   Universityville, CA 90###
(212) 555-1234   (203) 555-1234
Jdoe@internet-provider.com

Job Objective

This can be one of the trickiest pieces of information to convey, because the wording you use is critical. In just one sentence, you must clearly state what job position you are hoping to fill. To land a job, the objective that you list should closely (if not perfectly) match the job you're applying for. This piece of information should be customized for each resume you send out. Writing something generic at the top of your resume, such as "Seeking a challenging and rewarding opportunity," is worthless. Try to find out the exact job title or description the company you're sending your resume to uses to describe the position that you're applying for. Often, you can get this information directly from a help-wanted ad.

On your actual resume, the heading you use for this section could be "Job Objective," "Objective," "Job Target," or "Goal."

Examples:

Suppose the help-wanted ad you're replying to reads, "Project Manager. 5–10 yrs. exp., mechanical construction. . . ." For your resume's objective, you could write:

> Objective: To obtain a full-time position as a Mechanical Construction Project Manager.

Suppose the help-wanted ad you're replying to reads, "Secretary for small office. Must have bookkeeping experience. . . ." For your resume's objective, you could write:

> Objective: Seeking a full-time position as a secretary in a small office environment, which requires me to use my extensive bookkeeping, typing, filing, and telephone skills.

Education

In addition to listing traditional education, including high school and/or college information and the degree(s), certificate(s), or award(s) you've earned, you should also list any apprentice training, on-the-job training, and accredited workshops or training courses you've completed. Each item of information should contain the name of the educational institution, the date of completion, the degree(s) or certificate(s) awarded, and the city and state where the institution is located. You should also include any courses or extracurricular programs that would be of direct interest to the potential employer. On your actual resume, the heading you use for this section could be "Education," "Schools," or "Academic Record."

Danger!

Don't list your grades, class rank, or overall average unless this information is extremely impressive and will help to set you apart from other applicants. Obviously, graduating first in your class with a solid 4.0 (straight-A average) is definitely worth mentioning.

Don't Forget

When listing your educational background on a resume, the first piece of information should be the highest degree you've earned or are in the process of earning.

Accreditation and Licenses

If you have earned any type of accreditation or license that directly applies to the job you're applying for, you'll want to include this information in your resume. You'll also want to mention if you are close to obtaining a specific accreditation or license and the projected date for acquiring it.

Skills

What special skills do you have that the potential employer would be interested in? Refer to the answers you provided to the questions in Chapter 1. In addition to simply listing your skills, be prepared to provide examples of how you have successfully used these skills. Certain skills, such as being bilingual or computer-literate (with knowledge of specific software applications), are well worth listing in your resume. Employers are most interested in your skills and capabilities. The work and employment experience you list in your resume should be used to support the skills you have and to prove that you know how to competently use the listed skills to get your work done.

The following is a list of just a few of the many possible skill-related words you could list in your resume (assuming they're skills you actually have):

Analyzing	Deadline-oriented	Record keeping
Arbitrating	Decision making	Researching
Coaching	Entertaining	Scheduling
Communicating	Innovating	Selling
Conceptualizing	Investigating	Supervising
Consulting	Meeting deadlines	Teaching
Controlling	Motivating	Telemarketing
Coordinating	Negotiating	Visualizing
Counseling	Organizing	Web page design
Creating	Performing	Writing
Cultivating	Planning	
Data entry	Public speaking	

Work/Employment Experience

On your pad, begin by listing all internships, after-school jobs, summer jobs, part-time jobs, full-time jobs, and volunteer or charitable work you've done. Be prepared to include specific dates of employment, job titles, responsibilities, and accomplishments for each position. How you convey this information in your resume will be critical. It will have to be written concisely, using actions words. For now, however, just write down anything and everything you think is relevant. On your actual resume, the heading you use for this section could be "Employment," "Job History," "Work Experience," "Professional Experience," "Employers," "Employment History," or "Experience."

Danger!

1. On your actual resume, refrain from including any references to salary. If you're completing a job application and there's a question about your salary requirements, instead of answering with a specific or general dollar amount, write "negotiable."

2. Never include the reasons why you stopped working for an employer, switched jobs, or are currently looking for a new job. If necessary, this information can be brought up later, during an interview.

Professional Affiliations

Are you a member of a professional group or association that directly relates to the job you're applying for? If so, list it here.

Don't Forget

If you are involved with multiple professional organizations, you might not want to list all of them, since the potential employer might be concerned that these obligations will interfere with your regular work schedule.

Military Service

Just as you list all your work and employment experience, your time in the military is also important and can help you market yourself to potential employers. Any specialized training you received while serving in the military should be listed in the "Education" section of your resume. In the "Military Service" section, stick to when you served, your rank, and the branch in which you served. You also want to mention any special talents you developed or decorations you earned while serving.

Don't Forget

Most employers who have served in the military themselves give preferential treatment to applicants who have also served. After all, the military is known for teaching skills like self-discipline and leadership, which all employers look for.

References

Don't waste valuable space on your resume listing personal or professional references. You can, however, include a line at the bottom of your resume that states, "References available upon request." If you have letters of recommendation, or have a list of people (who are not related to you) that you know will give you excellent recommendations, you can provide this information during a job interview or include this information on a job application.

Personal Information

The law states that job applicants do not have to disclose their age, sex, sexual orientation, race, marital status, family size, or handicaps to potential employers, so whether or not you choose to include a "Personal Information" section in your resume is totally optional.

Don't Forget

If you happen to have some type of special skill or accomplishment that doesn't easily fit into any other section of your resume, but that you think makes you more attractive to employers, consider adding this information in the "Personal Information" section of your resume.

Assuming you have written out all the information required in a resume that was described in this section, and you have answered the questions posed in Chapter 1, you probably have several pages of hand-written notes. These notes contain the heart of your resume's content. Now, you must choose which pieces of information you believe are the most important, and which make you appear to be the most qualified for the job(s) you will be applying for.

Get Started

Go over your notes and place stars or asterisks (*) next to those pieces of information that you know for sure should be included in your resume. Next, place checkmarks next to the pieces of information that you would like to include, but that aren't critical to your resume. Finally, place an X next to the items that you know for sure don't belong on your resume (these pieces of information could still prove useful when preparing your cover letters or participating in interviews, so keep these notes handy).

Begin with the pieces of information in your notes that contain asterisks, and rewrite and then format each item so that it will neatly fit into your resume. To do this, you'll have to rewrite each item as concisely as possible, using action words to add impact and emphasis. Keep your sentences short and punchy (under 15 or 20 words each).

Using Action Words in Your Resume Is an Absolute Must!

An action word is usually a verb that you use to make your accomplishments sound even better, without stretching the truth. For example, if you're a financial analyst, you could state as one of your previous job's responsibilities, "Used Microsoft Excel." That's great, but you could rewrite this item so that it states, "Analyzed financial statements and created detailed cashflow projection models to assess financial risks using Microsoft Excel spreadsheets." Doesn't that sound a lot more impressive?

Your one-page resume has to successfully convey your personality, skills, education, accomplishments, and work experience, and at the same time, set you apart from the competition. What your resume says about you, and more importantly, how it's said, is what can make your resume a powerful job search tool.

As you create your resume, you want to say as much as possible about yourself using the fewest words possible. Your resume has to profile you as the ideal person to fill the job you're applying for and answer the question, "Why should I hire you?" Using short sentences containing carefully selected action words throughout your resume is one way of adding impact. The words you incorporate into your resume should relate to the skill words listed in the ad or job description you're responding to and also demonstrate an action.

Action words present themselves in a very bold fashion when they're listed with bullet points in a resume as opposed to within paragraphs of text. In today's job market, most employers will spend less than 1 minute looking over your resume, and if they don't immediately like what they see, you will get passed over.

After you have determined exactly what information you want to put into your resume, edit that information down into short sentences or phrases, and then add action words to provide impact to what you're attempting to convey.

With each item of information you will be listing in your resume, choose one or two action words that make that piece of information jump off the page. Choose action words that relate directly to your job objective and that help you to quantify your skills and experience in tangible terms that can be applied to the job you're applying for. Select action words that demonstrate efficiency and accomplishment, without stretching the truth. Never use words that you don't know the meaning of, just because you think they make you look smarter.

Action words, like *analyzed* or *created* help you to demonstrate efficiency and accomplishments. There are literally thousands of action words that you can use to add impact to your resume (and cover letters). As you rewrite each item from your notes into items that will appear in your resume, try to incorporate some action words from this list:

Accomplished	Authored	Conducted
Achieved	Authorized	Consolidated
Adapted	Awarded	Consulted
Addressed	Balanced	Contacted
Administered	Budgeted	Contributed
Advanced	Built	Controlled
Advised	Calculated	Coordinated
Allocated	Catalogued	Counseled
Analyzed	Chaired	Created
Appraised	Charted	Decreased
Apprised	Classified	Delegated
Approved	Coached	Demonstrated
Arbitrated	Collected	Designed
Arranged	Compiled	Developed
Assembled	Completed	Devised
Assigned	Composed	Diagnosed
Audited	Computed	Directed
Augmented	Conceptualized	Dispatched

Documented	Integrated	Reconciled
Doubled	Interpreted	Recorded
Downsized	Interviewed	Recruited
Drafted	Introduced	Rectified
Edited	Invented	Reduced
Educated	Investigated	Reeducated
Eliminated	Launched	Regulated
Enabled	Lectured	Remodeled
Encouraged	Led	Repaired
Enforced	Maintained	Researched
Engineered	Managed	Restored
Enlisted	Marketed	Restructured
Established	Mediated	Revitalized
Evaluated	Moderated	Scheduled
Examined	Monitored	Settled
Exceeded	Navigated	Shaped
Executed	Negotiated	Sold
Expanded	Networked	Solved
Expedited	Operated	Specified
Facilitated	Optimized	Stabilized
Focused	Organized	Stimulated
Forecasted	Originated	Streamlined
Formulated	Overhauled	Strengthened
Generated	Performed	Summarized
Guided	Persuaded	Supervised
Headed up	Planned	Tabulated
Illustrated	Presented	Trained
Implemented	Prioritized	Translated
Improved	Produced	Trimmed
Increased	Programmed	Tripled
Influenced	Projected	Unified
Informed	Promoted	Upgraded
Initiated	Proposed	Upsized
Inspected	Published	Wrote
Installed	Purchased	
Instigated	Quadrupled	
Instructed	Recommended	

A Quick Note about Electronic Resumes

If you are putting together a keyword resume that you know will be "read" by a computer instead of a human, instead of using action verbs, try to use nouns or adjectives that describe your skills, responsibilities, and qualifications. For example, instead of using the action word *managed,* use the word *manager* or *management.* Instead of *audited,* use *auditor.* Often the help-wanted ad or job description will use words that you should incorporate into your keyword-based electronic resume. If a master's degree, Ph.D., CPA, or some other type of degree is a job requirement (and a keyword you know the employer is looking for), be sure these credentials are listed in your resume. If the job you're applying for requires special skills or knowledge of certain brand-name machinery or equipment, list this in your resume as well. For example, an administrative assistant should, of course, have typing skills, but listing specific programs that you can operate, like Microsoft Word or WordPerfect, provides keywords that will likely be picked when your resume is scanned by a computer. Check out Chapter 7 for more information on electronic resumes.

Some of the benefits of electronic resumes are:

- You can send them via e-mail directly to an employer and save the postage and printing costs.
- Sending an electronic resume proves that you are computer-literate and know how to prepare, send, and receive e-mail.
- You can add your resume to on-line resume databases. This is a free service offered by many career-related Web sites, such as The Monster Board (http://www.monster.com).

Choosing a Resume Format

The first step in creating your resume involves determining exactly what type of job you plan on applying for. You should know specifically what industry you hope to work in, and what sort of positions you are qualified to fill and why. Landing the type of job you want and are qualified for is obviously your ultimate goal.

Now, with this goal in mind, you must break down and consider all the things that make you an attractive applicant. Earlier in this book, in Chapter 1, you answered a number of questions. Those answers will help you fill in your resume. The resume format you choose will help you to market yourself in the best possible way.

Each resume format has a different strategy for conveying an applicant's information. Thus, it is important that you choose the resume format that best fits your needs. There are three main resume formats: chronological, functional, and targeted.

As you'll discover later, when you read Chapter 11, there are career counselors and professional resume writers you can hire to help you choose a resume format and pinpoint the information you want to highlight within your resume.

Chronological Resume Format

This is the most popular resume format, because it makes it very easy for a potential employer to determine your work experience and education (Figure 3.1). This information is actually listed in a reverse chronological format, starting with your most recent job or work experience and going backward in time. Each past employer is listed, along with the dates of your employment. When listing the dates of employment, use years only (1992–1996 or 1995–Present). It is not necessary in your resume to list what months you began or finished a job (June 1992–September 1996).

The purpose of this format is to show that you have been steadily employed and have demonstrated upward or lateral mobility (that you're following an organized career path) as you've moved from job to job. If you have the work experience necessary to properly use this resume format, you'll be able to demonstrate your career

GERALD D. BUCKMAN

173 Any Street
Any Town, Any State 11111

Telephone: Any Number
FAX: Any Number

e-mail: anyone@anything.com

POSITION OBJECTIVE

Regional Sales Manager for an organization offering opportunities for increasing responsibilities and professional advancement.

BACKGROUND

Over 20 years of outside sales experience in a wide variety of industries with a proven record of accomplishment in the areas of sales, sales management, customer service, and sales forecasting.

SALES & MANAGEMENT EXPERIENCE

OWNER/MANAGER   1995 to 1996
Ajax Corporation   Any Town, Any State
Guided all activities associated with the successful operation of a commercial printing operation, including: sales, sales management, submitting bids, and customer service. Prospected for and developed new accounts through telemarketing, direct mail, print advertising, promotional giveaways and other marketing campaigns.

Accomplishments include:
- Managed over 200 accounts generating $1 million in annual sales.
- Implemented purchasing controls and quality control standards resulting in an 18% reduction in cost of goods over a 9-month period.
- Developed 41 new accounts in 18 months.
- Implemented a computerized billing system resulting in a 10-day average decrease in accounts collection cycle.

OWNER/MANAGER   1983 to 1994
Buckman & Associates   Any Town, Any State
Directed a manufacturers' representative organization representing manufacturers in the hardware home improvement industry and selling to retail accounts and distributors. Pioneered new product lines and developed new accounts for start-up companies. Constructed in-store displays to increase consumer awareness. Conducted in-store training classes for retail personnel to motivate and increase sales.

Accomplishments include:
- Developed 40 new accounts in 6 months for Widget Garage Door Openers. This generated $450,000 in sales in the first 9 months from a zero account base.
- Achieved a 24% average increase in sales over an 11-year period.

OWNER/SUPERVISOR   1990 to 1994
Davis, Incorporated   Any Town, Any State
Directed all operational activities, including: marketing, promotions, sales management, and cash flow management. Managed recruiting and training of new sales representatives. Implemented marketing promotions using direct mail, print advertising, register tape programs, coupon books, and discount referral cards.

Accomplishments include:
- Increased sales by 15% in the first 6 months.
- Stabilized seasonal cash flow by implementing membership programs.
- Increased the number of income streams by adding new product lines.

NATIONAL SALES MANAGER   1987 to 1990
Wilmar Clothing   Any Town, Any State
Managed nationwide sales for this clothing manufacturer. Directed sales forecasting as well as hiring and training of new sales representatives.

Accomplishments include:
- Increased sales by 21% during 1st year.
- Increased new accounts by 43% in 2 years by establishing a nationwide network of sales representatives.
- Established 3 new sales territories through coordination/participation in trade shows.

EDUCATION

Any University . . . Any Town, Any State
Bachelor of Science in Business

PERSONAL BACKGROUND

Willing to travel   Willing to relocate

Figure 3.1 Sue Nowacki and Steve Burt are the cofounders of 1st Impressions, a professional resume writing service that operates on the Internet (http://www.1st-imp.com). In Chapter 11, Sue and Steve offer advice for creating your resume, but for this chapter, they have prepared several sample resumes to demonstrate how to use a resume's format to best showcase yourself. Use these resumes as a guideline for formatting your resume, but be sure to write your own content. This resume follows a chronological format that organizes the applicant's employment history in a focused manner, showing his expertise as an owner/manager.

direction. This resume format easily demonstrates that your career has been focused. The job you're applying for now should be the next step upward from your most recent work experience (the first item listed in the "Employment" portion of your resume).

Each employment listing in your resume should include the name of the employer, the city and state in which the company is located, the dates you were employed, your job title, your primary responsibilities, and your achievements in that position. For your most recent jobs, you want to provide the most details and information, especially when listing primary responsibilities and achievements.

Who Should Use This Resume Format?

This resume format is well suited to applicants who are proud of their steady work and education record, and can demonstrate constant growth or lateral movement with each job listing on their resume. If your previous employment has been with highly respected, well-known companies, you should also take advantage of this resume format. Applicants who have had impressive job titles and can show upward mobility and growth will benefit from using a chronological resume, too.

Danger!

Who should avoid using this resume format? If there are gaps in your employment history, if you have jumped from job to job often, or if you have moved from industry to industry with little or no focus, this is easily noticeable by someone reading a resume that was created using this format. Employers don't like to hire quitters or people who have a history of being fired from many jobs. Thus, if your work history isn't perfect or highly impressive, even though this is the most favored resume format among human resources people, you should strongly consider a different format that better showcases your skills, capabilities, and potential, not your weaknesses.

This is usually not the best resume format for recent graduates. Even if you can list impressive summer jobs, internships, and/or part-time work, as a recent grad your resume should focus on demonstrating your skills, potential, and education.

Applicants who prefer to keep their age a secret, or at least not highlight it in a resume, should be careful about using this resume format. Any potential employer can do some simple math and determine your approximate age based upon listed graduation dates and the lengths of your employment at various jobs.

Don't Forget

If there's one gap in your employment history, you can get away with using a chronological resume, but don't make it obvious that there was a period of time you were out of work. Do not include a line in your resume saying, "Unemployed" or "Out of Work" along with the corresponding dates. For the time being, pretend it never happened and focus your resume on the positives. Those who have a few large gaps or many smaller gaps in their employment history should consider using a different resume format.

The Functional Resume Format

This type of resume organizes your past work experiences into functional categories (Figure 3.2). You'll use basically the same information as you would in a chronological resume, but how you convey the information will be different. The focus is on your past job responsibilities. When you use this resume format, your skills are highlighted while your previous employers, employment dates, and job titles are of lesser importance.

Functional resumes are best used by applicants who want the potential employer to discover what they can do (or are capable of

Frank M. Smith
(123) 456-7891

♦ 123 Any Street   ♦ Any City, Any State 43567
Fsmith@anynet.com

SUMMARY
- Intelligent, self-motivated technical professional offering an extensive background in technical support, applications' modification, implementation, administration, and database design. Interested in expanding knowledge to programs' and systems' analysis and design.

PROJECT DEVELOPMENT
- Designed, programmed, implemented, installed, and supported database applications and spreadsheet models for a variety of business and professional needs.

APPLICATION PROJECTS
- Billing program for medical facility
- Material price list & quoting application
- competitor product line tracking system
- Payroll & benefits tax reporting system
- Sales accounts tracking program
- Inventory management program

MANAGEMENT
- Directed all administrative and operational functions for wholesale / retail material distributor, including management of purchasing, merchandising, inventory, billing, personnel, and customer services.

NETWORKING & USER SUPPORT
- Designed, installed, and administered Windows95 / Windows for Workgroups network. Administered XENIX system.
- Provided systems and on site troubleshooting, trained users in programs, and specified upgrades. Modified systems to client needs.

TECHNICAL SKILLS
Platforms:
- Windows (3.1 and 95), Windows NT, OS/2, UNIX, XENIX

Languages:
- Visual Basic, X-Base database, Lotus 1-2-3 macro

Software:
- Microsoft Access, FoxPro, Lotus 1-2-3, Excel, Quattro Pro, Microsoft Word, Microsoft Publisher, Norton Utilities, Procomm Plus

EMPLOYMENT HISTORY

Manager   1994 - Present
ABC Company, Any City, Any State

Computer Support   1991 - 1994
DEF Incorporated, Any City, Any State

Database Manager / Sales   1987 - 1991
GHI Graphics, Any City, Any State

EDUCATION
Sampson Technical College, Any City, Any State
- Associates Degree, Business Information Systems

Figure 3.2   This resume follows a purely functional resume format. It focuses on the applicant's skills and accomplishments (previous job titles), and puts less emphasis on actual employment history.

doing) as opposed to when and where they've done whatever it is they've done. This type of resume should answer the question, "What specifically can the applicant do for the employer?"

If you choose to use a functional resume format, choose your five or six most marketable and applicable skills and list them. Under each skill, include between one and three specific achievements that required the successful use of that skill, and mention where you were employed when the skill was used.

Who Should Use This Resume Format?

This resume format is especially well suited to recent graduates, people with gaps in their employment history, people with good training but little on-the-job experience, and people with extensive unpaid volunteer work experience, or non-work-related experience that helped the applicant develop skills that will be useful in the workplace. This type of resume is also good for people changing careers, because it allows them to highlight their skills and down-play the fact that they have little or no actual work experience in the industry they're now applying for a job in.

Danger!

What are the potential problems with the functional resume format? Since most employers prefer to see chronological resumes, they sometimes assume that applicants who choose to use a different format are trying to hide something about their past. By reading this type of resume, it is hard for a potential employer to put together an applicant's employment history or determine the applicant's career path. To compensate for these potential drawbacks, it is critical that the information you include in your resume be extremely compelling and relevant to the reader and to the job you're applying for.

The Targeted/Combination Resume Format

When you have a very specific job at a specific company that you're sure you want, this is the resume format you should use. All the information included in this type of resume should help to answer the question, "Why are you perfect for a specific job?" Since you know the requirements and skills that are necessary for the job you're applying for, this resume format allows you to give specifics about why you're qualified to meet those job requirements based on the skills you have.

Using the targeted resume format allows you to combine elements of the chronological format and functional format. As you list your employment history (in reverse chronological order), stress the top skills that made you successful in that position. The dates of employment, however, can be tucked away at the end of each employment listing, so it takes the emphasis away from any gaps in your employment history, and forces the potential employer to concentrate on your skills and positive work experience.

Basically, when creating this type of resume, you want to start off by developing a functional resume and then add the employment information to provide proof or support for the skills and achievements you list. As you'll see from the following sample resume layouts, there are several ways you can organize your resume using this format (Figures 3.3 and 3.4).

Who Should Use This Resume Format?

This resume format is useful for job seekers who know exactly what type of job they want to apply for and can prove that they are qualified for that job using this resume format. This format can also be helpful to someone who has the skills needed to fill a specific job, but who doesn't necessarily have related work experience (some-

Eric S. Thomas	(123) 456-7891

♦ 12345 Any Street   ♦ Any City, Any State 98765
Ethomas@anynet.com

SUMMARY

➢ Professional individual offering a solid background in supervision and operations management within the transportation and manufacturing industries.

➢ Solid leadership background, able to provide direction for improved maintenance and production efficiencies, develop cohesive team structures, and turn company visions into viable, realized goals.

➢ Comprehensive understanding of Federal and State Regulations with regard to safety operations and procedures, as they apply to OSHA and ADA standards.

➢ Solid industry, technical, equipment, and computer tracking knowledge. Able to trouble shoot problems and offer effective, workable solutions. Computer proficient.

CAREER BACKGROUND

Supervisor   1992 - Present
Space Age Energy Company, Any City, Any State

✧ Provide direction for all departmental operations, including: workforce, maintenance, production, and operations management.

✧ Wrote Operator Training Program, including formal qualifications guidelines to quantify training goals and ensure essential training was achieved and documented for each participant. Led team building program by creating and coordinating team efforts, producing collaborative solutions in troubleshooting efforts requiring multiple specialized skills. Reduced operational redundancies, and increased solution speed and shift productivity by 25%.

✧ Conduct operator and employee safety training programs, assuring employee adherence to established company policies. Completed *Confined Safety Training Program*, and reside on the Confined Space Rescue Committee.

✧ Team with engineers to produce effective production solutions, including development of a new distillation process which increased productivity by 10% and improved overall efficiency.

✧ Revised inventory management and storage methods, and created a flat-file database (using MS Access) that allowed inventory search and tracking by name or part number. Inventory restructuring enabled company to recapture $120K in redundant stock, and $165K in tax and administrative savings. Reduced inventory management time by 50%.

✧ Managed and oversaw various complex installation and overhaul projects with budgets in excess of $1 million. Provided contract negotiations with contractors and vendors, and coordinated efforts of contractors, plant personnel, vendors, and outside services.

Supervisor   1987 - 1992
Stateman Shipping, Any City, Any State

✧ Directed evening operations, personnel management, and monitored compliance to DOT regulations.

✧ Managed customer relations for delivery of expedited overnight parcels and materials.

✧ Worked closely with field operators, directing efforts for location of mechanical problems and providing timely, effective solutions.

✧ Created and implemented computerized tracking and inventory management system.

EDUCATION

University of High Esteem, Any City, Any State

✧ *Bachelor of Science degree, Management*

Figure 3.3   This resume is just one style of a targeted resume.

WILLIAM COLLINS

421 Any Street
Any Town, Any State 11111
Any Phone Number

POSITION OBJECTIVE	Financial position in the investment industry with an organization offering opportunities for professional advancement.
EDUCATION	Any University Any Town . . . Any State **Bachelor of Science in Finance**, December 1996 **Minor: Economics** GPA: 3.5 in major; 3.2 cumulative Coursework in Finance includes General Finance, Debt Management, Equity and Capital Markets, and Financial Management.

HONORS AND ACTIVITIES	International Economics Honor Society
	Financial Management Association
	XYZ Fraternity
	   • **Treasurer** - Held weekly meetings with the fraternity's accountant / financial manager. Developed and managed the fraternity's operating budget. Managed accounts payable and accounts receivable.
	   • **New Member Educator**
	   • **Rush Chairman**

RELATED EXPERIENCE	**FINANCE INTERN** Spring Semester 1996
	Thomas and Associates Financial
	Any Town, Any City
	   Principal accountability for management of company's portfolio valuations. Also performed general office duties. Received training and became proficient in use of Morningstar, industry-related software.
	
	FINANCE INTERN Summer 1993
	XYZ Partners
	Any Town, Any City
	   Provided detailed stock analysis for investment company. Also performed general office duties. Worked with the Bloomberg System, investment software.

COMPUTER SKILLS	Proficient in Bloomberg Investment Software, Morningstar Software, Windows 95, and America Online.
PERSONAL BACKGROUND	References available Willing to travel and relocate Follow the activities of the stock market on a daily basis.

Figure 3.4 This sample resume focuses on the applicant's educational background. Clearly, this person has little actual work experience, and so the resume highlights the person's educational achievements, skills, and internship work.

one changing industries or going from being self-employed to applying for a job at another company).

Danger!

What are the potential problems with the targeted resume format? The only major problem with this resume format is that if the employer doesn't believe you're the right person for the specific job your resume was targeted for, you might not be considered for similar opportunities available from that employer.

Using any of these widely accepted resume formats, you can adopt many different styles to help you capture the attention of potential employers. Some resumes are designed specifically to showcase accomplishments. Others focus more on an applicant's education and potential. And some resumes are designed to focus specifically on the reasons why an applicant is suitable for a very specific position. There are also keyword resumes, used primarily when you know that your resume will be scanned into a computer database and never actually be read by humans. Based on your personal situation, choose the resume format that you believe will market you the best.

Quick Tips

Resume preparation tips and strategies:

• Keep your resume short and to the point. If your resume is more than one side of an 8.5 × 11 inch piece of paper, shorten it. One of the most common complaints employers have about resumes is that they contain too much information and information about the applicant that's not relevant to the job. Another popular complaint about resumes is that the information isn't organized well, making it difficult for the person reading the resume to quickly find pertinent information about the applicant.

Continued

- Your resume *must* be typed, but don't use any fancy fonts or type-styles. If at all possible, generate your resume using a computer (not a typewriter). Submitting a resume created on a typewriter implies that you don't know how to use a computer, and that's the wrong message to send.

- Keep your sentences short, under 20 words each. All paragraphs should be 10 lines or less (less is better).

- Whenever possible, remove words that aren't absolutely needed. All redundancy should be removed. If you clearly state something in your resume once using powerful action words, there is no need to repeat the information.

- Use action words to add impact to the items listed in your resume. Try to start each sentence with an action verb.

- Consider obtaining a list of job titles that apply to your industry, and use it as reference as you put together your resume. From this list, you might be able to find better ways of explaining your previous work experience.

- Remove any technical jargon from your resume.

- Print your resume on good-quality white paper. Your finished resume should look neat and well-balanced on the page. It should be inviting to the reader and not look cluttered. Never send a photocopy or poorly printed copy of your resume.

- Customize your resume to match the job you're applying for.

- Make sure you apply for jobs that you're qualified for. A recent graduate who is qualified for an entry-level position should not be applying for managerial or executive-level positions. If your ultimate goal is to become a top-level executive, that's great and it's something that should be brought up during an interview to show that you are motivated and have a defined career path, but don't expect to be hired for that type of position right out of school.

- No matter what, *never* lie on your resume.

- Don't include personal information (height, weight, age, race, religion, sex, marital status, sexual orientation, etc.) or hobbies in a resume, unless they relate directly to the job you're applying for or help to portray you as the perfect person for the job.

- Do not include your current salary or earning history in your resume.

- Whenever possible, try to stress teamwork in your resume. Potential employers love to see applicants who can work well with others. Also, stress any leadership positions you've had in order to demonstrate that you can take charge of a situation or a group of people.

- If the company you'll be submitting your resume to uses a computerized resume management system and will be scanning your resume into its system, use as many keywords and phrases as you can in order to describe your work experience and goals. (Try to incorporate the keywords used in the actual help-wanted ad or in the job description you're applying for.) Also, keep the format of your resume simple. Never use multiple columns.

- Reread your resume carefully, and fix spelling mistakes and typos. Now, reread it two or three more times to ensure that you've fixed all mistakes. Finally, have someone else read your resume to make sure it's absolutely perfect—before you send it out to a potential employer.

- Don't just send your resume to the human resources or personnel department of a company. Also, target an executive within the company who's in charge of the division you're hoping to work in. If you're applying for a job in the marketing department of a company, for example, send a copy of your resume to the vice president of marketing at the company. Be sure to read Chapter 6, which focuses on networking strategies and how and when to make contact with executives at companies you'd like to work for.

- Write a personalized and custom-written cover letter to accompany each resume you submit. Keep your cover letter short, but make it upbeat and attention getting. Be sure to highlight any skills and/or

Continued

experiences that are not featured in your resume. Don't repeat information. Be sure to read Chapter 4, which tells you how to write a powerful cover letter.

· Don't address your resume to a company president, CEO, or top-level executive and mark the envelope "Private" or "Personal." If you are sending an unsolicited resume to a company executive, most of the time it will either be tossed in the trash or be forwarded to human resources. If, however, you make contact with the executive first and he or she requests a resume, that's another story.

Putting Your Resume Together

Creating a really good resume is going to take a lot of thought, and mostly likely require you to write and rewrite several drafts until you have a document that you're proud of and willing to send out to potential employers. Remember, the resume is a marketing tool that should be used to highlight your positives (and not mention your negatives). If you have negative situations in your employment history that require an explanation, save it for the job interview, so that you can explain the situation in the most positive way possible.

Danger!

The most common mistake made by applicants is that they send out resumes containing spelling errors and/or grammatical errors. Even the slightest error in your resume could easily cause the person reading it to toss it. If two applicants apply for a job and both are totally qualified, but one person has a small spelling error in his or her resume, while the second applicant's resume is perfect, who do you think will get the job? The purpose of your resume is to set you apart from the competition and

offer a preview about why you're the ideal candidate for the job opening
you apply for. Thus, you want the person reading your resume to focus
on its informational content (your skills and achievements), not the fact
that you were too lazy to check your resume for spelling errors before
sending it out.

How Can You Tell If Your Resume Is Working?

Well, the biggest indication that your resume is working is that you
get invited in for interviews. If you receive a negative response from
a potential employer after submitting a resume, try to determine
why that employer believes you are not suitable for the position
you applied for. Ask questions!

Perhaps your resume doesn't stress enough work experience or
the right educational background, or perhaps it doesn't depict you
as having the right skills for the job. Listen to whatever input is
offered by potential employers and consider making modifications
to your resume (without stretching the truth). Based on comments
and feedback you receive, you might want to add more focus (or
make your resume a little less focused) when applying for similar
positions at other companies.

If you find yourself getting invited in for interviews, but not
receiving job offers, this could mean several things. The most common reason for this is that during the interview, you didn't live up to
the expectations created by your resume. Consider working on your
interviewing skills. In this situation, if you told the truth in your
resume, got invited in for an interview, but didn't receive a job offer,
your resume is working perfectly as a job search tool. However,
there's something about your overall appearance or presentation
that didn't fit what the employer was looking for.

Stumped? Maybe You Should Get Some Professional Help

A professional resume creation consultant is someone who specializes in writing resumes. Consultants charge either a flat fee or an hourly fee for their services. The benefit to using a resume consultant is that the consultant will spend time interviewing you and help you to choose what information should be included in your resume. The consultant will then help you choose a resume format, take your information, and create a professional-looking resume. If you're asked simply to fill out forms instead of participating in an in-person or telephone interview with the resume preparation expert, find someone else. Also, if the person you hire to create your resume encourages you to lie or stretch the truth in your resume, fire him or her and find someone else.

Resume consultants advertise in the telephone book and on the Internet (using any Internet search engine, type in the keyword *resume* or *resume preparation*). Before hiring a resume consultant, ask to speak with several of the consultant's previous clients and ensure that they were satisfied customers. You can also request a free consultation meeting so you can see firsthand if the person seems talented. Ideally, you want to hire a resume consultant who is familiar with the industry you want to work in.

Upon contacting a resume preparation consultant, ask about fees up-front, and find out exactly what those fees include. Will the consultant update your resume or customize it for each job you apply for? If so, how much extra will this cost? Will you be provided with a computer disk containing your resume in a format that you can edit yourself using a word processor?

Will a resume preparation expert perform magic and guarantee you a job? No! What these people will do is take the information you make available to them and format it into a resume. (A similar task can be accomplished using specialized resume creation software.)

Resume Worksheet

Based on the notes you took as you read this chapter, you should have the information necessary to fill in all the information requested in this worksheet. If certain information doesn't apply to you, skip it. Otherwise, include as much detail as you can, but keep your answers short and to the point.

HEADING INFORMATION

Your Full Name: _____

Permanent Street Address: _____

City, State, Zip: _____

Telephone Number: _____

Fax Number: (Optional) _____

Pager Number: (Optional) _____

E-mail Address: (Optional, but recommended) _____

School Address: (Optional) _____

Your Phone Number at School: (Optional) _____

OBJECTIVE

Write a one-line description of the job you're seeking. In this sentence, try to incorporate how you can use your skills to the employer's benefit.

_____

_____

EDUCATION

Most Recent College/University That You Attended: _____

_____

City, State: _____

Year Started: _____

Graduation Year: _____

Degree(s) or Award(s) Earned: _____

Your Major: _____

List Accomplishments, Extracurricular Activities, Etc.: _____

_____

College/University That You Attended: _____

City, State: _____

Year Started: _____

Graduation Year: _____

Degree(s) or Award(s) Earned: _____

Your Major: _____

List Accomplishments, Extracurricular Activities, Etc.: _____

_____

SKILLS AND ABILITIES

What is your primary marketable skill? _____

Give three examples of how you used this skill in the workplace:

1. _____

2. _____

3. _____

What is another of your marketable skills? _____

Give three examples of how you used this skill in the workplace:

1. _____

2. _____

3. _____

What is another of your marketable skills? _____

_____

Give three examples of how you used this skill in the workplace:

1. _____

2. _____

3. _____

(List all your marketable skills. On your resume, you'll want to narrow this information down to no more than five skills, and be able to support each listing with examples of how the skill was used in the workplace.)

WORK HISTORY

Most Recent Employer: _____

City, State: _____

Year You Began Work: _____

Year You Stopped Working: (Write "Present" if you're still employed.)

_____

Your Job Title: _____

Job Description: _____

What are your two or three proudest accomplishments?

1. _____

2. _____

3. _____

Employer: _____

City, State: _____

Year You Began Work:_____

Year You Stopped Working: (Write "Present" if you're still employed.)

_____

Your Job Title: _____

Job Description: _____

What are your two or three proudest accomplishments?

1. _____

2. _____

3. _____

(List all your past employers.)

MILITARY SERVICE (If applicable)

Branch of Service:_____

Years Served:_____

Rank: _____

Decorations or Awards Earned: _____

Special Skills or Training You Obtained: _____

ACCREDITATION AND LICENSES

List any accreditations and/or licenses that you have earned, especially those that relate to the job you're seeking:

_____

_____

HOBBIES AND SPECIAL INTERESTS

List any hobbies, special interests, or non-work-related skills that will help to separate you from the competition and will position you as the perfect applicant for the job you're applying for:

_____

_____

AMBITIONS

What are your long-term goals and ambitions?

_____

_____

_____

If you don't have the qualifications for a job, you won't get it, unless you lie on your resume. When the employer discovers you lied, however, you will most likely be fired on the spot, so don't lie!

To learn more about resume preparation experts and how the services they offer are different from what career counselors offer, check out Chapter 11.

Remember, even if you follow the advice and resume creation strategies to the letter, how useful your resume will actually be will be determined by the information you choose to include in your resume as well as the way you present that information. What you say, how you say it, and how it looks on the page are all elements of a resume that work together to promote you to the reader.

As you start distributing your resume to potential employers, you must also submit cover letters, and if you're lucky enough to get invited in for an interview, you'll have to follow up by sending the interviewer a thank-you note. These documents are part of your overall *resume package*.

Every element of your resume package must look consistent, must be written in the same professional tone, and should be printed on the same type of paper. Creating a look for your resume package and writing powerful cover letters and thank-you notes are the topics covered in the next chapter.

It's a Wrap

✔ You can increase your resume's impact by taking the time to craft a polished and professional design that makes great use of limited space.

✔ Action words will greatly enhance the information you've chosen to describe yourself.

✔ Choose the appropriate resume format—chronological, functional, or targeted—based on your experience and the position that you seek.

━━━━━━━━━━━━━━━━━━━━━━━━━━━━━━━━━━

CHAPTER 4

Complete Your Resume Package with a Powerful Cover Letter and Thank-You Note

━━━━━━━━━━━━━━━━━━━━━━━━━━━━━━━━━━

Do I Need to Read This Chapter?

→ How do I create an overall "look" for my resume package?

→ What is the best type of paper for printing my cover letters and resumes?

→ How do I write a cover letter that will make me stand out as an applicant?

→ How do I write thank-you notes to interviewers and people who have assisted in my job search?

Most people think that a resume is their primary marketing tool when looking for a job, and a cover letter is an unimportant additional piece of correspondence that gets attached to a resume as a matter of formality. The truth is, your cover letter is as important as your resume when it comes to marketing yourself to a potential employer. Some employers read your cover letter followed by your resume, if you manage to peak their interest. Others exclusively read cover letters *or* resumes to save time. Thus, there's a chance that your cover letter will be your only opportunity to convince a potential employer to continue on by reading your resume, and then invite you in for an interview.

If used correctly, your cover letter should nicely complement your resume from both a visual and an informational standpoint. Without duplicating too much information that's already in your resume, a cover letter is an ideal tool for introducing you to an employer and for telling the reader a few things about you that are directly relevant to the job you're applying for. Basically, your cover letter should seize attention, peak interest, provide information, briefly demonstrate your skills and accomplishments, and ask for an action to be taken. Every cover letter should highlight things about you that are of direct interest to the recipient. Using bullet points in your cover letter is an ideal way to convey much of this information.

When you send a resume and cover letter to an employer, you must develop an overall message and package to market yourself that should be consistent. Whenever possible, the envelope, stationery, print color, typestyle(s), and font(s) should all match, and each piece in your resume package should work together to promote you—the applicant. Every aspect of your overall package has the ability to make a strong positive or negative impact on whether or not you will be invited in for an interview. Your immediate goal is to write cover letters that make the best possible impression.

What Is a Resume Package?

A resume package consists of your resume, cover letter, envelope, and any additional inserts (such as a personal business card) that you send to a potential employer in hopes of landing an interview. You'll discover from this chapter that using matching papers and envelopes in your resume package is an absolute must. When your package is received by a potential employer, it will most likely arrive with dozens, perhaps hundreds, of other pieces of mail. Someone will sort that mail, and your resume package, it is hoped, will reach its intended destination—human resources or the executive within a company who is expecting to receive it.

Sending your unsolicited resume to an executive within a company is like sending a piece of junk mail. A very small percentage of unsolicited resumes that a top-level executive receives will actually be read. Most will systematically be forwarded to human resources or tossed in the garbage unread. Chapter 6 discusses how to successfully network and contact executives within a company you'd like to work for, but simply sending your resume package to an unsuspecting recipient won't work about 99 percent of the time.

Creating an Overall Look for Your Resume Package

While the content of your resume and cover letter is critical, first you must capture the attention of the reader by making your resume package look spectacular, yet highly professional. The first step in this process is to choose a type of paper that you'll print your cover letter and resume on. You must also obtain matching envelopes and thank-you note cards or stationery. Resume paper can be purchased from an office supply store, a local print shop, or a mail-order company like Paper Direct.

As a general rule, you'll want to choose a professional-looking white, off-white, or cream-colored paper. If you visit an office supply store or print shop, you'll immediately notice that there's no such thing as standard "white" resume paper. In addition to dozens of different color variations, there are also different paper weights and paper content to choose from. The cost of each sheet of premium or high-quality resume paper will range from a few cents up to $1 or more, depending on the actual paper you select.

Selecting a good-quality paper is important, but you don't want to overdo it. Paper Direct is a mail-order paper company that offers a wide range of the highest-quality paper stocks available, many of which are perfectly suited for resumes and cover letters. You can request a free catalog by calling Paper Direct at (800) A-PAPERS, or by visiting the company's Web site at http://www.paperdirect.com.

Quick Tips

Linda Ireland is Paper Direct's director of marketing, and Mark Clark is the company's associate product manager for business communication essentials. These paper experts share their advice in this section on how to choose the highest-quality cover letter and resume paper to meet your specific needs. Ireland begins by explaining the kind of paper the company carries:

The papers that Paper Direct carries cover a broad range, while what you'll probably find at an office supply superstore falls in the lower end of that range. With so many paper choices available, what you definitely want to avoid is using standard 20-pound, white ream paper that's commonly used in photocopy machines and laser printers. For a resume and cover letter, Paper Direct highly recommends choosing paper with at least 50 percent cotton content. In late-1997, we introduced a brand-new line of specialized designer resume papers that are exclusive because they contain designer image content on them. The screened images convey a highly professional attitude and can help a resume and cover letter stand out just enough to get noticed.

Paper Direct's designer resume paper is currently available in six different themed designs, several of which cater to specific fields, such as technology. Ireland continues:

We've tried to create a design element that is suitable for resumes, but that isn't so prevalent that it's distracting to the person reading the resume. A CPA applying for a job at an accounting firm or Fortune 500 company should probably stick with a resume and cover letter printed on white paper using black ink. Someone hoping to work in a less formal industry might want to add a bit of personality to their resume using one of our designer resume papers.

Aside from using generic 20-pound photocopy paper, one of the most common mistakes job seekers make is selecting a paper that's too colorful or too outrageous. Ireland goes on:

I recommend selecting one of our specially designed resume papers or choosing a very plain, but high-quality paper with at least 50 percent cotton content. Paper Direct also offers a very nice grouping of subtle, professional papers that are excellent for resumes.

Clark adds:

A lot of different characteristics make up what a paper is. Choosing a paper with a watermark is not a necessity for a resume, but watermarks are just one more feature that can improve the overall image and professional look of your cover letters and resume. We strongly recommend choosing a paper that has a high cotton content, because those papers are the highest quality for business correspondence. As a job seeker, you should be prepared to pay a bit more for a higher-quality paper to use for your cover letters and resume than you would use for normal business letters. As for the weight of the paper you ultimately select, most people choose either a 24- or 28-pound bond paper, but there are also paper stocks that are a bit heavier. One way to help your resume stand out is to use a heavier paper stock; however, you don't want to fold a resume that's printed on a heavy paper stock (over 28-pound basis weight). All of Paper Direct's designer resume paper packs feature 24-pound, 100 percent cotton paper stock.

Continued

As for the color of the paper you choose, Paper Direct suggests using the safest choice, which is bright white or ultra white. These shades of white are the most traditional when it comes to resumes and cover letters. Definitely avoid using bright-colored papers other than white. Clark advises:

> Ivory, slate blue, or gray colored papers are nice alternatives that convey a professional image and can help your resume package stand out. The use of a limited amount of colored text within a resume is another way to help your resume and/or cover letters stand out, but by adding colors, you're moving away from what's traditional, and that can be risky. For easy readability and professionalism, print your text using black ink, or another dark color, such as blue or burgundy.

One of the benefits of purchasing resume paper from companies like Paper Direct is that they offer special packages containing matching resume paper, cover-letter paper, thank-you note paper, and envelopes. Ireland notes:

> By matching all of your papers, you're making a subtle statement that you're coordinated, well thought out, and that you've developed a package to market yourself in a professional manner. I believe that even your thank-you note cards should coordinate with the paper stock you choose for your resume and cover letters.

> Paper Direct's designer resume paper comes in packages containing 50 resume sheets, 50 matching #10 envelopes, 100 coordinating sheets for cover letters, and second sheets for your resume and/or thank-you letters. These complete paper packages are priced around $40. Many different, less expensive, nondesigner, but premium cotton, papers are also available.

When choosing a resume paper, be sure that it's suitable for use with a laser printer or can be used by professional printing equipment if you choose to have a local print shop duplicate your resume. Keep in mind that not all paper stocks work well with ink-jet printers. While there are certainly high-quality ink-jet printers available, the look of your final resume and cover letters will be much better if you use a laser printer to print out your documents from your computer.

Don't Forget

Make a point of actually seeing and touching a sample of the paper you choose before spending a lot of money purchasing a package of that paper. Upon request, Paper Direct will send customers a free sample of any of its paper stocks. If you're buying your paper from an office supply store or print shop, ask for a sample. The paper you ultimately select is a matter of personal preference, and you want to choose the type of paper that you like the most.

Quick Tips

The paper selection checklist:

- Avoid using the generic, 20-pound, white bond paper that's typically used in photocopy machines and laser printers. For a resume package, you want to project a more formal image.

- Choose a paper that has between 50 and 100 percent cotton content and a basis weight between 24 and 28 pounds. You can use a heavier paper stock to help your resume stand out a bit more, but if you do use heavier paper, use large-size 9 × 12 inch envelopes so you can avoid folding your resume and cover letter.

- Papers that contain watermarks add an additional touch of formality to your resume package, but these papers cost more and won't add a huge amount of impact to your resume package's appearance.

- When selecting a paper color, bright white or ultra white are the most traditional shades of white that are used for resumes and cover let-

Continued

ters. You can, however, use ivory, slate blue, or gray paper, but nothing that's too bright or that doesn't convey the professional image you're trying to achieve.

- One way to help your resume package stand out is to stray from using traditional black ink when printing your resume and cover letters. Always use a dark-color ink, however, such as blue or burgundy. A second-color ink, such as red, can also be used to sparingly highlight key points in your documents, but this can be risky, depending on the industry you're applying to work in. Using two ink colors in a resume is not considered traditional.

- Before ordering paper for your resume and cover letters, ask for a sample to make sure that you really like the paper and that it will convey the image you want to project for yourself. Also, make sure matching envelopes are available. If matching note cards are available, you'll want to use them for your thank-you notes, so that everything looks consistent.

Once you have selected the paper you'll use for your resume package, and you have your resume written and designed, the next step is to create cover letters that complement your resume in terms of content and appearance.

Writing Cover Letters

Cover letters allow you to introduce yourself to a potential employer, peak the employer's interest in you as an applicant, and let you prove that you know how to communicate using the written word. In addition to evaluating what is said in your cover letter, the writing style, spelling, punctuation, and format will also be evaluated by the employer. Thus, in addition to choosing what you want to say in your cover letter, you must also think carefully about how you say it, and make sure that your overall presentation is professional and visually appealing.

In almost every circumstance, a cover letter should be written in a business-letter format. Each letter should be custom-written for the job you're applying for, and also personalized using the name and title of the recipient.

Cover letters are used when you're sending a resume in response to a help-wanted ad or job opening announcement, when you're following up a job lead given to you by an acquaintance, or when you're sending an unsolicited resume to a company. (An unsolicited resume is a resume that has been sent even though it has not been specifically requested by the recipient and is not in response to a help-wanted ad or job opening announcement.)

Danger!

Before sending your resume package, call up the company and ask for the recipient's full name and title. Ask the receptionist to spell the person's first and last name, so that it will be 100 percent accurate in your letter. Also, make sure you have the correct spelling of the company's name. Don't make any assumptions. If you're told the vice president of human resources is Mark Gerald, confirm the spelling of that person's name. You could discover that this *Mark* spells his name *Marc*, and that *Gerald* is spelled *Gerrald*. Accidentally spelling someone's name incorrectly is insulting to the recipient and totally unprofessional. Even the slightest spelling error could result in your resume package getting thrown out.

Cover letters are typically addressed to:

- Someone in the human resources department at the company you want to work for.
- An executive or department head at the company you want to work for.
- A professional headhunter or job placement specialist.

- A friend, former business associate, or network contact who currently works for (or is associated with) a company you want to work for. You will be asking your contact to act on your behalf and forward your resume to the appropriate person at the company, along with a personal recommendation.

As you sit down to write your cover letter, you'll need to know the following information:

- The recipient's full name
- The recipient's job title
- The company name
- The mailing address
- The phone number
- The exact position you're applying for (Unsolicited cover letters and resumes should be less targeted, so that you'll be considered for a wider variety of job openings.)
- The recipient's fax number (optional)
- The recipient's e-mail address (optional)

Since your resume succinctly summarizes your accomplishments, education, and skills, your goal with the cover letter is to introduce yourself and explain in plain English what exactly you can do for the company you're applying to. Remember, just as your resume was only one 8.5 × 11 inch page in length, your cover letter should also be one page. The shorter the better, since most people don't have time to carefully read long letters. Within your cover letter, use bullet points whenever possible to stress key points, skills, or your work history. Using bullet-point lists eliminates the need for long paragraphs of text and also makes your cover letters easier to read. After all, you want potential employers to be able to pinpoint your strengths quickly and easily when they read your cover letter.

At the top of the letter should be your address and phone number, followed by the recipient's address and the date. Next come the salutation, opening paragraph, your marketing message, support paragraph, your request for an interview, and finally some type of closure. The formatting and placement of your address, the recipient's address, and the date will be demonstrated in the sample cover letters that follow.

The Salutation

Every business letter begins with a salutation such as:

> Dear Mr./Mrs./Ms./Dr. (insert recipient's last name):
> Dear (insert recipient's first name),
> To whom this may concern:
> Dear (insert job title):
> Dear Sir or Madam:

When you're writing a personalized, formal cover letter to a specific individual, your salutation should read, "Dear Mr./Mrs./Ms./Dr. (insert recipient's last name)." The only time you should consider addressing someone by his or her first name is if the person is a relative or close friend. If you're responding to a help-wanted ad that only lists a contact person's first name, with no telephone number, then obviously you should address your cover letter to that person using the first name.

Danger!

1. Never use a generic salutation such as "Dear Sir or Madam," "Dear (insert job title)," or "To whom this may concern." As far as the employer is concerned, if you can't spend the necessary time to research the ideal person your letter should be addressed to, you shouldn't be sending it at all.

2. Some names, such as Pat, can belong to either a male or female. Make sure that you know the gender of the person you're writing to

Continued

and address him or her correctly in your salutation. If you don't know someone's gender, call the company and ask. Don't make any assumptions. Remember, even the slightest error will make you look bad, which is something no job applicant can afford.

3. If you're sure the recipient of your letter is a woman, but you don't know if she is married or not, the safest approach is to use "Dear Ms. (insert last name)" as your salutation. These days, "Miss" is virtually never used in a business letter.

The Opening Paragraph

Who are you and why are you writing this letter? What is your overall objective in writing this letter? These are the questions you should answer in the opening paragraph. Keep this part of your cover letter short and directly to the point. (No longer than two or three sentences.) For example, you could write:

I read your advertisement in the (insert date) of (insert newspaper/publication name) and believe that I have the skills and work experience necessary to successfully fill the (insert job title) position that you have available. For your consideration, please find my resume enclosed.

I am writing in response to our telephone conversation on (insert date) regarding the job opening (insert company name) has for a (insert job title). Enclosed please find my resume for your consideration.

In response to your company's ad, which I saw in the (insert date) issue of (insert newspaper/publication name), I would like to be considered for the (insert job title) opening your company has available.

Our mutual colleague, (insert name of colleague), suggested I contact you regarding the (insert job title) job opening that your company currently has available.

(Insert someone's name) suggested I contact you regarding the opening for a (insert job title) that your company has available. Enclosed please find a copy of my resume for your consideration.

Your Marketing Message

This next paragraph or two in the body of your cover letter is important, because what you write should set you apart from the competition and position you as the best applicant for the job. Your goal in this section of the letter should be to address the employer's primary needs using examples of how you can fill those needs. One way to begin this paragraph is by posing a question such as:

Are you looking for an energetic, qualified, highly talented (insert job title)?

Are you interested in . . . ?

Did you ever ask yourself . . . ?

Don't you need . . . ?

Don't you wish . . . ?

Wouldn't you like to . . . ?

Are you ready for . . . ?

Or you can use an opening statement such as:

It's no secret that . . .

You've probably noticed that . . .

Think about . . .

Believe it or not . . .

Today, more than ever . . .

If you've been waiting for the right _____ to come along, your wait is over.

Let's face it, . . .

Often, making statements with an impact works better than asking a question to which the answer is obvious. For this portion of your letter, you can save space by using bullet points. For example, you could write:

For your consideration, I am enclosing a copy of my resume, which demonstrates some of the skills I possess and used regularly in my previous jobs:

- Related accomplishment/work experience/skill
- Related accomplishment/work experience/skill
- Related accomplishment/work experience/skill
- Related accomplishment/work experience/skill

If the ad you're responding to states, for example, that "5 years' experience as a public relations account executive with major media contacts" is a job requirement, you want to address the employer's needs directly. You could write, "As you'll see from my resume, I have _____ years experience working for the ABC Public Relations Company. Some of my major clients have included (insert company names). As an account executive, I have developed extensive local and national newspaper, magazine, radio, and TV media contacts that have allowed me to generate a substantial amount of publicity for my high-profile clients." Thus, in three short sentences you have demonstrated that you meet the job opening's qualifications and that you have related work experience. In your cover letter, be sure to mention specifically what job opening you're applying for, especially if you're responding to an ad.

Don't Forget

Answer the questions you know potential employers have on their minds—Do you have the skills, education, and work experience necessary to meet the job's qualifications? Are you knowledgeable about the industry and the company? Can you communicate well on paper? Do you have what it takes to succeed at the company? What sets you apart from other applicants?

The Support Paragraph

In this paragraph of your cover letter, answer the question, "What specifically is it about the employer that appeals to you?" This is your opportunity to kiss up, compliment the employer, and demonstrate that you have done some research. Prove that you know what the company is all about.

Don't Forget

1. Within your cover letter, you want to stress your experience and accomplishments. Avoid personal topics such as your age, race, religion, health, physical or mental disabilities, hobbies, social security number, or references to your physical appearance.

2. Just as you wouldn't discuss salary in your resume and during an interview, avoid discussing previous salary or expected salary in your cover letter. Once again, you can write that your past salary has been

Continued

"competitive," without providing actual figures. If your salary history is specifically asked for, provide a range, not specific numbers.

3. Since your cover letter is a marketing tool just like your resume, you should include as many action words as possible. Refer to Chapter 3 for a list of powerful action words that you can incorporate in your cover letter to add impact. Don't select words, however, that will make you look arrogant, and never use words that you don't know the meaning of.

Request an Action to Be Taken

If you want to schedule an in-person or telephone interview, this is the portion of the cover letter that should contain your request. The person you are writing to is busy, so take it upon yourself to follow up with a telephone call and mention that you'll be doing this in your letter. Don't simply send out your resume package and then sit by the telephone waiting for a response. Within this paragraph you could write:

I will be in the (city, state) area on (insert date), and would enjoy the opportunity to meet with you in person. I'll call you next week to schedule an interview.

✓ I look forward to speaking with you further about this job opportunity. I will give you a call later this week to schedule a convenient time for an interview. In the meantime, please don't hesitate to give me a call at (###) ###-####.

✓ After you have reviewed my resume, I would appreciate an opportunity to meet with you in person to discuss job openings at your company. I'll give you a call later this week to schedule a convenient time.

The opportunity to meet with you in person would be a privilege. To this end, I will contact you later this week to schedule an appointment.

Don't Forget

Mention in your letter that you will be making a follow-up phone call, but give the employer at least 3 to 5 business days to read your cover letter and resume before making that follow-up call. Make sure that your address and telephone number(s) are listed at the top of your resume and cover letter, in case an employer wishes to contact you.

Closure

Your cover letter should conclude with a formal closure and your signature. Thank the reader for his or her interest, time, and consideration. A few ways to end the letter are Sincerely, Regards, Best regards, Yours truly, or Respectfully.

Example:

Thank you, in advance, for taking the time to review my resume. I look forward to having the opportunity to meet with you in person.

Sincerely,

(signature)
Your Typed Name

The Cover-Letter Worksheet

Before you actually start writing a draft of a cover letter, fill out this short questionnaire. The answers you provide here will help you to write a well-organized cover letter that gets across the necessary key points.

Whom are you writing to (full name)?_____

Is the recipient a male or female?_____

What is the recipient's exact job title? _____

Recipient's mailing address: _____

Recipient's phone number: _____

Recipient's fax number: _____

Recipient's e-mail address: _____

What is the exact position you want to apply for? _____

How or where did you hear about this job opportunity? (If you're responding to an ad, write down the date the ad was published and in what publication.) _____

What makes you suitable for the job? (List three skills/accomplishments.)

_____

_____

_____

Why do you want to work for the company you're applying to? (You might like the corporate culture, the company's reputation or success rate, or its products or services.) _____

_____

_____

✓ What do you hope to accomplish by writing and sending this letter along with your resume? _____

_____

_____

✓ What key points about your skills, work experience, and/or education do you want to stress in your cover letter? _____

_____

_____

Develop a short one- or two-sentence synopsis that states who you are and what type of job you're qualified for and hope to land. You'll want to incorporate this synopsis into your cover letter, but also use it when you call a company on the phone and/or at the conclusion of an interview to quickly summarize what's special about you as an applicant.

_____

_____

_____

_____

The Layout of Your Cover Letters

Traditional business correspondence can follow several basic formats, any of which are acceptable cover-letter formats. With the possible exception of the thank-you note (which you should definitely send out immediately after each of your interviews), all correspondence should be typed or created on a computer—not handwritten. See the following sample layouts for cover letters.

Sample Layout 1

Your Name
Your Address
Your Phone Number
Your Fax Number (optional)
Your E-mail Address (optional)

Date

Recipient's Full Name
Recipient's Title
Company Name
Address
City, State, Zip Code

Dear (Mr./Mrs./Ms./Dr.) (Insert recipient's last name):

All the text in your letter should be left-justified (lined up against the left margin of the page) or left/right-justified (a feature available when writing your letters using word processing software on a computer). When using a block business-letter format, do not indent the first line of each paragraph. This paragraph is left-justified.

This paragraph is left/right-justified. In between each paragraph of your letter, leave one blank space. Leave two spaces in between your final paragraph and your closing. In between your closing and your full name, there should be two or three blank spaces, giving you room for your signature.

The term Encl. at the bottom of the page is short for *enclosure,* which signifies that within the envelop is an additional document, in this case, your resume. You can use the abbreviation *Encl.* or *Enc.* or spell out the word Enclosure and place it at the bottom of your cover letter.

At the end of your letter, here's a sample of what you could write: "Thank you for taking the time out of your busy schedule to review my resume. I will give you a call next week to schedule an interview. In the meantime, I can be reached at (###) ###-####, should you have any questions."

Sincerely,

(Your Signature)
Your Full Name Typed

Encl.

Sample Layout 2

Your Name
Your Address
Your Phone Number
Your Fax Number (optional)
Your E-mail Address (optional)

Date

Recipient's Full Name
Recipient's Title
Company Name
Address
City, State, Zip Code

Dear (Mr./Mrs./Ms./Dr.) (Insert Recipient's Last Name):

Notice that the sender's address and phone number and other pertinent information are centered at the top of the page; however, this letter still follows the basic block business-letter format. All the text in your letter should be left-justified (line up against the left margin of the page) or left/right-justified (a feature available when writing your letters using word processing software on a computer). Do not indent the first line of each paragraph.

In between each paragraph of your letter, leave one blank space. Leave two spaces in between your final paragraph and your closing. In between your closing and your full name should be two or three blank spaces for your signature. The term Encl. at the bottom of the page is short for enclosure, which signifies that within the envelope is an additional document, in this case, your resume.

Sincerely,

(Your Signature)
Your Full Name Typed

Encl.

Sample Layout 3

Your Name
Your Address
Your Phone Number
Your Fax Number (optional)
Your E-mail Address (optional)

Date

Recipient's Full Name
Recipient's Title
Company Name
Address
City, State, Zip Code

Dear (Mr./Mrs./Ms./Dr.) (Insert Recipient's Last Name):

In this example, the sender's address and phone number and other pertinent information, along with the date and signature, are right-justified. This is yet another variation of the block business-letter format. All of the text in your letter should be left-justified (line up against the left margin of the page) or left/right-justified (a feature available when writing your letters using word processing software on a computer). Do not indent the first line of each paragraph.

Every cover letter should be less than one page and should be printed using an easy-to-read text font, such as Times Roman or New Century Schoolbook. As for type size, use either 10-point or 12-point type. Anything smaller would be difficult to read. A larger type size would look totally unprofessional. Never mix font sizes, because as you can see, it looks awful. Also, use single-line spacing.

Sincerely,

(Your Signature)
Your Full Name Typed

Encl.

Your Name
Your Address
Your Phone Number
Your Fax Number (optional)
Your E-mail Address (optional)

Date

Recipient's Full Name
Recipient's Title
Company Name
Address
City, State, Zip Code

Dear (Mr./Mrs./Ms./Dr.) (Insert Recipient's Last Name):

     Notice that the first line of each paragraph is indented approximately ½ inch. The remaining text in your letter should be left-justified (line up against the left margin of the page) or left/right-justified (a feature available when writing your letters using word processing software on a computer).

     The use of white space in a cover letter is also important for maintaining a professional look. Use standard left and right margins of 1.25 inches, and top and bottom margins of 1 inch. Also, don't mix fonts. Use **bold,** <u>underlining</u>, and/or *italics* very sparingly, or you'll distract the reader.

Sincerely,

(Your Signature)
Your Full Name Typed

Encl.

Sample Layout 5

Your Name
Your Address
City, State, Zip

Your Phone Number
Your Fax Number (optional)
Your E-mail Address (optional)

Date

Recipient's Full Name
Recipient's Title
Company Name
Address
City, State, Zip Code

Dear (Mr./Mrs./Ms./Dr.) (Insert Recipient's Last Name):

If you're using word processing software on your computer, you can desktop-publish personal stationery and print it on the high-quality paper that you purchase. Creating stationery will help to make your cover letter stand out visually. It is acceptable to use a decorative font and typestyle for your name, address, and phone number, and even add a decorative line, as long as the overall document maintains a professional look. Use a basic text font, such as Times Roman, for the body of your letter, as well as for the main text in your resume.

When you're ready to print out your desktop-published cover letter (on personal stationery), use the same paper for your cover letter as you use for your resume. It's also important to have matching envelopes.

Sincerely,

(Your Signature)
Your Full Name Typed

Encl.

Quick Tips

The following are some general guidelines and tips that will help you to create professional-looking cover letters that will get attention.

- Follow the style of a formal business letter when writing your cover letter.

- Use a standard text font, such as Times Roman, New Century Schoolbook, or Courier. Stick with an easy-to-read font size, between 10 and 12 points. The font and typestyles you select should be identical to the one(s) used to create your resume. Using a font size larger than 12 points looks unprofessional, and one smaller than 10 points is very difficult to read.

- Make sure your cover letter is visually appealing and utilizes plenty of white space on the page. Try to use standard 1.25-inch left and right margins and 1-inch top and bottom margins.

- If you use a computer, your cover letter should be printed on a laser printer or high-quality ink-jet printer. An alternative (although antiquated) method for creating a cover letter is to use a high-end typewriter.

- Every cover letter should be customized for the job you're applying for.

- Your cover letter should be personalized, using the recipient's full name and title.

- In the salutation, write, "Dear Mr./Mrs./Ms./Dr. (insert recipient's last name)."

- Keep your cover letter short (less than one page).

- All your sentences should be less than 15 words and have a specific point that you are trying to get across. No paragraph should be longer than three or four sentences. It is acceptable to have a one-sentence paragraph in a cover letter.

- Use bullet points whenever possible to keep your cover letter short and still get your ideas across to the reader. Each bulleted item can

Continued

be one or two sentences long, using as few words as possible in each sentence. Every bulleted item should make an important statement or convey an important piece of information about yourself.

- Your cover letter should be grammatically correct and contain no spelling errors.

- If you're responding to a help-wanted ad or publicized job opening, state in your letter specifically where you heard about the job opportunity. If you're acting upon a referral, mention in the letter the name of the person who referred you and the person's relationship to the reader. For example, "John Smith, your brother-in-law, suggested that I contact you directly regarding the job opening for a _____ that you have available." Or "John Smith, a senior analyst in your company's finance division, mentioned that (insert company name) has a job opening for (insert job title)."

- Avoid filling your cover letter with clichés or overly used phrases such as "In response to your advertisement . . ." or "My name is (insert name), and I am writing to . . . ." (Your name is displayed at the top of the page and at the conclusion of the letter. There is no need to reintroduce yourself by name in the body of the letter.) Try to be innovative and original, but not gimmicky.

- Within the first paragraph, specifically mention what position you're applying for.

- Don't lie or stretch the truth in your cover letter. Never include anything about your skills, education, or work experience that you can't support with evidence.

- Maintain a positive and upbeat tone throughout the letter. Make sure your letter flows and that the voice and tense are consistent throughout the letter.

- Don't list your references within a cover letter. At the bottom of your resume, you might want to include a line stating, "References available upon request." However, it's pretty much a given that as an applicant you have references that you can provide to the employer at the time of the interview.

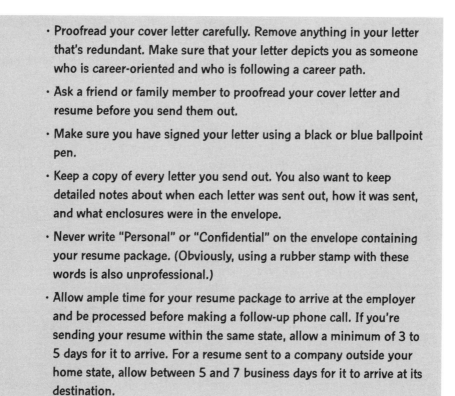

- Proofread your cover letter carefully. Remove anything in your letter that's redundant. Make sure that your letter depicts you as someone who is career-oriented and who is following a career path.

- Ask a friend or family member to proofread your cover letter and resume before you send them out.

- Make sure you have signed your letter using a black or blue ballpoint pen.

- Keep a copy of every letter you send out. You also want to keep detailed notes about when each letter was sent out, how it was sent, and what enclosures were in the envelope.

- Never write "Personal" or "Confidential" on the envelope containing your resume package. (Obviously, using a rubber stamp with these words is also unprofessional.)

- Allow ample time for your resume package to arrive at the employer and be processed before making a follow-up phone call. If you're sending your resume within the same state, allow a minimum of 3 to 5 days for it to arrive. For a resume sent to a company outside your home state, allow between 5 and 7 business days for it to arrive at its destination.

Remember to Always Say Thank You!

Within 24 hours after your job interview, you should send the interviewer a personalized thank-you note to show your appreciation to him or her for taking the time to see you. Some interviewers will actually hold out on making a job offer to see if an applicant sends a thank-you note in a timely manner.

Writing and sending a thank-you note takes just a few minutes, but the potential benefits to you as an applicant are tremendous. In a typical week, an interviewer might see 30 or even 50 different applicants. After a while, it becomes extremely difficult for the interviewer to remember who was who. Simply by sending a thank-you note, you can help to set yourself apart from the crowd of applicants, show you have an interest in the job you applied for, prove that you have strong follow-up skills, and demonstrate that you are a true professional.

Even if you know for sure that you will not be receiving a job offer after your interview, or you absolutely hated the interviewer, you should still promptly follow up with a note.

A thank-you note can be typed, using a formal business-letter format, and then printed on the same paper you used for your resume and cover letter; or you can handwrite your personalized message on a note card. The note card should match your cover letter and resume paper. However, if a match is not possible, go to any greeting card store and pick up a box of thank-you notes that convey a professional image. (Find cards that simply say "Thank You" on the outside and are blank on the inside. Avoid fancy cards containing flowers, colored papers, or anything that distracts from the professionalism of your note.) Either typing or writing a thank-you note is considered appropriate, although a handwritten note adds a more personal touch to your message.

Get Started

Keep your message short, but within the note be sure to:

- Thank the interviewer for his or her time and consideration.
- Once again state the exact position you're applying for.
- Briefly mention something specific from your interview (to jog the interviewer's memory regarding who you are).
- In one sentence, describe why you're the best applicant for the job.

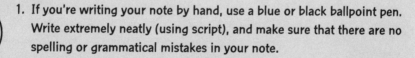

Don't Forget

1. If you're writing your note by hand, use a blue or black ballpoint pen. Write extremely neatly (using script), and make sure that there are no spelling or grammatical mistakes in your note.

2. If you had personal business cards printed that contain your name, home phone number, and address, feel free to insert a card in the envelope with your note. Again, this will help the interviewer remember exactly who you are.

Even though you now know the interviewer personally, keep your thank-you note professional by addressing the interviewer as "Mr./Mrs./Ms./Dr. (insert last name)." A typical handwritten note, sent the day after your interview, might read:

(Insert Date)

Dear Mr. Jones,

Thank you for taking the time to meet with me yesterday afternoon, and for considering me for the (insert job title) position your company has available. I really enjoyed our conversation about how (insert company) plans to outperform the competition by implementing a new marketing campaign. Using my extensive experience marketing similar products, I am certain that I would make an excellent addition to (insert company)'s marketing team. I look forward to the opportunity to make a contribution.

Sincerely,

(Signature)

Don't Forget

Interviewers aren't the only people who should receive thank-you notes. Anyone who offers you personal assistance or advice should also be shown gratitude. For example, if a friend makes an introduction for you to an employer, send the friend a short note of thanks for his or her assistance. Not only will thanking people for their support encourage them to assist you again in the future, but it might cause them to think of another way they could help you.

If you've been doing the necessary work as you read this book, by now you should have incorporated some type of time management tool into your daily life. You should also have created a resume and have made a few first attempts at drafting cover letters and thank-you notes to potential employers. These are all important job search tools that are used to help generate interest in you as an applicant. The next chapter will help to prepare you for your interviews.

✔ Your resume, cover letters, and thank-you notes should convey a highly professional image and showcase your skills, work experience, education, and unique talents that you believe make you the ideal candidate for the job you're applying for.

✔ Your resume package should have a consistent look and tone. The appearance of the resume package is greatly affected by the choice of a paper that is consistent for the resume, cover letter, and thank-you note.

✔ Properly written thank-you notes will set you apart from the other applicants.

✔ Creating a powerful resume package will result in invitations for job interviews. It will be through these in-person interviews that you can sell yourself and convince the interviewer to offer you a job.

PART III

Putting Your Best Foot Forward

CHAPTER 5

The Interview Process

Do I Need to Read This Chapter?

→ How do I prepare for interviews? What should I wear?

→ How can I make an excellent first impression?

→ What types of questions will I be asked, and what types of questions should I ask the employer?

→ What are the best ways to sell myself and set myself apart from the competition?

→ How should I explain the negative aspects of my employment history, if necessary?

→ How do I overcome nervousness?

→ How do I complete a job application?

While every aspect of the job search process is important, the interview is your primary opportunity to meet face-to-face with a potential employer and to sell yourself—your skills, accomplishments, personality, and, most importantly, what you can offer to the employer.

For many people, this is the most stressful aspect of their job search, because an interview requires applicants to meet with one or more total strangers, prove their worthiness as applicants, and satisfactorily answer all the questions posed to them. Unfortunately, it's human nature for people in this situation to become nervous, which can sometimes make it difficult to think clearly.

Scheduling Your Interviews

After sending in your resume and a cover letter to a potential employer, if all goes well, within a short amount of time your telephone will ring and you'll get invited for an interview. A wave of excitement runs through your body, and the anticipation immediately starts to build up. When that telephone rings, however, you want to maintain a clear head, so that you can act professionally and obtain some information from the person calling you.

If you're calling a potential employer back after he or she leaves a message on your telephone answering machine, find a quiet and private place where you can return the call. If you're calling from home, be sure to turn off your phone's Call Waiting by pressing *70 before dialing the phone number. If you must return a call from a pay phone, use a telephone credit card. In the middle of your important conversation, you don't want to hear recordings asking you to drop additional money into the coin slot or get disconnected for not having enough change.

During your conversation with a potential employer, always act professionally. Even if the person on the other end of the phone is abrupt or even rude, be kind and courteous, even to secretaries, assistants, or receptionists. If you're placed on hold for any reason during your conversation, assume that the person is still listening, so don't say anything stupid.

Your primary goal for this initial conversation is to schedule a convenient time and day for the interview. Ask the potential employer what looks good for him or her, and immediately open your personal planner to ensure that the date and time picked will fit into your schedule. Obviously, you want to do everything within your power to accommodate the interviewer's schedule. If you absolutely can't get away from your current job, or if you already have other interviews scheduled, you should briefly provide a reason for the scheduling conflict and immediately suggest one or two alternative times and/or days. As you choose alternative interview dates and times, don't put it off for too long. At this point, you want to make an extra effort to demonstrate your interest in the job and your willingness to do whatever it takes to reach a mutually convenient interview day and time in the near future.

As you schedule your interview, leave plenty of time in between commitments. Think about how long it will take you to get to the interview location and how you'll get there. Ideally, you don't want to schedule more than one interview per day, but this isn't always possible. If you have multiple interview commitments, make sure you leave plenty of time to travel in between appointments (allow ample time for getting stuck in traffic, getting lost, finding a place to park, running into delays with public transportation, etc.). Whenever possible, avoid scheduling an interview for the same day that you're invited in for that interview. Try to allow yourself at least one day to prepare and do your research.

Traveling Long Distance for an Interview

If going for an interview will require long-distance travel, determine beforehand if the company will be paying for your travel

Get Started

While you're on the phone scheduling your interview, during the conversation you should also determine:

1. Who exactly will be conducting the interview(s)—get the name(s) and title(s) of the interviewer(s).

2. Exactly what position you're being invited in to interview for.

3. Approximately how long the interview will take. If the employer becomes interested in hiring you, after your formal interview(s) you may be asked to meet with other people at the company. Be prepared to stay longer than the time quoted to you.

4. Confirm the company's address and, if necessary, get detailed directions on how to get there. Make sure you write down what floor and/or office number you should go to when you arrive at the company, and find out whom you should ask for.

5. Write down the name of the person you speak with, and get the person's phone number and extension.

expenses. Who will be making your travel arrangements? Will you have to pay for your travel and then get reimbursed? If so, what will the procedure be for reimbursement? If the company is making all the arrangements and prepaying for the travel, how will you obtain the airline tickets, rental car voucher, car service/taxi confirmation number, and/or hotel reservation confirmation number?

No matter who schedules your travel, the day before you're supposed to leave, call up the airline, hotel, and rental car company and confirm all the travel arrangements. Make sure you leave ample time to contact the employer in case mistakes were made in your travel arrangements. During your travels, save all your receipts.

Don't Forget

When scheduling an interview that will require you to travel between time zones or for many hours, try to do the traveling the day before the scheduled interview, and get a good night's sleep upon your arrival. You don't want to fly several hours, develop jet lag, and then have to meet a potential employer immediately. If you've ever flown from the East Coast to the West Coast (or vice versa) and then went from the airport directly into a business meeting, you know how difficult it is to think clearly and act alert. For an interview, you always want to look and feel your absolute best, and that's virtually impossible immediately after a long flight, train trip, or drive.

What to Pack When You Have to Travel

If you're traveling specifically for an interview and will be returning home after the interview, try to pack your clothing in a lightweight garment bag or in some type of suitcase that you'll be able to carry with you onto the airplane. (You don't want to deal with the possibility of the airline losing the luggage that contains your interview outfit.)

Don't Forget

Be sure to check what the weather is like in the city you'll be traveling to and pack accordingly. You can get weather reports from around the country by watching the Weather Channel, by checking a national newspaper (such as *USA Today*), or by watching a national morning TV show (*The Today Show, Good Morning America,* or *CBS This Morning*). You can also call the hotel where you'll be staying and ask for a local weather report. While reading a newspaper or watching a news program, be sure to catch up on current news events and be prepared to discuss current events during your job interview.

What to pack in your suitcase or garment bag:

- Your interview outfit (with all accessories).
- Shoes.
- A second, backup outfit.
- Toiletries (items such as toothbrush, hairbrush, shampoo, cosmetics, hair drier).
- Your travel documents.
- Copies of your resume.
- Your company and industry research.
- A briefcase and/or portfolio (containing a pad and pen).
- Your personal planner.
- A jacket and/or umbrella.
- A book to read on the plane.
- Credit cards and extra cash (always carry a few one dollar bills for tipping, plus have some cash on-hand in case of emergencies).
- A photo ID (driver's license or passport)—when you check in at the airport, for security reasons, you must present a valid photo ID.

Preparing for Each Interview: Conducting Research

Not being totally prepared for an interview is one of the most common mistakes an applicant can make. As soon as you have an interview scheduled, you must spend time preparing for it. A potential employer will be able to tell instantly if you are prepared for an interview or if you're trying to bluff your way through it. Being unprepared is as unprofessional as showing up late for the interview. It says to an employer, "Don't hire me. I don't want this job. I am just wasting your time as well as mine by showing up."

The first step in the interview preparation process is to do your research. You want up-to-date and accurate information about:

- *The Job You're Applying For.* You want to know exactly what position you're hoping to fill, what the requirements are for that position, and what skills and training are required. Often, you can obtain this information directly from the help-wanted ad you are responding to. You can also ask for a detailed verbal or written job description from the employer when you schedule your interview.

- *The Industry You'll Be Working In.* How big is the industry? Who are the main players in the industry? Where does your potential employer fit in the industry? What size market share does your potential employer currently have? What are the challenges facing the industry as a whole? Is the industry growing?

- *The Company You Will Be Interviewing With.* What is the company's history? What sets it apart from the competition? What are the company's main products or services? What are the strengths and weaknesses of the company? What are the company's revenues? Who is the company's target customer? Has the company been featured in the news recently? If so, did it receive positive or negative publicity? What challenges is the company currently facing?

- *The Person Who Will Be Interviewing You.* What is the title of the person interviewing you? What are his or her responsibilities? How long has the person been with the company? What is his or her background?

Performing Research

One of the best ways to learn about a company is to request an annual report (if it's a publicly held company) and a press kit directly from the company. There are also many other places to find additional information about public and privately owned companies.

If you have access to the Internet, be sure to visit the company's Web site, and also the Web sites of the company's main competition. You can find a company's Web site on the Internet by asking a potential employer for its Web site address, or by using an Internet search engine such as Yahoo! (http://www.yahoo.com) or Excite (http://www.excite.com) and entering the company name as the keyword to search for. You can also use the Internet, or one of the major on-line services, to search local and national newspapers and magazines for recently published articles about a company or industry.

It's easy to obtain information about virtually any company simply by calling its public relations office and/or investor relations office (if it's a public company). A public company's annual report to the stockholders tells all about its corporate philosophy, history, products and services, goals, financial status, and top-level executives. If you're applying for a government job, similar information is available from most government offices upon request. All it takes is one telephone call to obtain the information.

Press releases, company newsletters, and magazines are also useful sources of company and industry information. These materials are available directly from a company. Chapter 7 explains how to use on-line services and Web sites for performing company and industry-related research. Web sites like Businesswire, PR Newswire, and the Electronic Library are all excellent resources.

Another abundant source of company and industry information is a public library, which will have an assortment of reference directories that can provide basic information about public and private companies. In the reference section of any library, check the holdings catalog under "careers," "vocations," and your chosen job or occupation or profession.

If you're hoping to work for a mid-to-large-size company, be sure to check 3 to 6 months' worth of back issues of several popular business magazines, such as *BusinessWeek, Forbes, Inc., Fast Company,* and *Crain's Small Business.* Recent back issues of the *Wall Street Journal* and *Investor's Business Daily* are also good sources of company and industry news and information.

Ask the librarian to see a directory of publications and periodicals, and look up what industry-specific magazines, newsletters, or publications are available that relate directly to the industry you hope to work in. If you can't find these publications at your local library, obtain the publisher's telephone number from the directory and then call to order recent back issues (and the current issue) of the industry-specific newsletter or magazine.

While visiting a library, ask the librarian for these and other directories:

- *Dun & Bradstreet's Million Dollar Directory*
- *The Dun & Bradstreet Database*
- *Standard & Poor's Register of Corporations*
- *Directors and Executives*
- *Moody's Industrial Manual*
- *Thomas' Register of American Manufacturers*
- *Ward's Business Directory*
- *Business Periodicals Index*
- *Readers' Guide to Periodical Literature*
- *Wall Street Journal Index*
- *New York Times Index*
- *Occupational Outlook Handbook*
- Your local *Business-to-Business Yellow Pages*
- *The Adams Job Almanac*
- *The Almanac of American Employers*
- *Directory of Leading Private Companies*
- *Encyclopedia of Associations*
- *Directory of Occupational Titles*
- *Job Hunter's Sourcebook*
- *National Trade and Professional Associations of the United States*
- *Newsletters in Print*

- *Hoover's 500: Profiles of America's Largest Business Enterprises*
- *Hoover's Top 2,500 Employers*
- *Hoover's MasterList of Major U.S. Companies*
- InfoTrac (CD-ROM). If your library doesn't subscribe to Info-Trac, ask if it has a similar CD-ROM database of magazine and newspaper articles that can be searched by keyword or topic. InfoTrac is distributed on CD-ROM, but is similar to The Electronic Library, which is available on the Internet.

The career office at any high school, college, university, or vocational school will have information about employers that might not be available from libraries. Even if you aren't a student or alumnus, a school's career office will often give you access to its materials. (Don't expect to receive guidance from the school's career counselor, however, unless you are a student or graduate of the institution.)

State employment agencies (listed in the telephone book) are another source of information. You can also check with the chamber of commerce in your city or town. Networking is an ideal way to obtain subjective data about a company. A few days before an interview, or if you think you're interested in pursuing a job opening with a specific company, during lunch hour visit that company and strike up a conversation with a few of the employees. You can always find people outside of the building eating lunch, going to or from the parking lot, or hanging out in designated smoking areas.

Get the Facts Faxed Fast

Standard & Poor's maintains an up-to-date and accurate database of over 4600 public companies. Standard & Poor's Reports-on-Demand division will fax you a detailed financial and informational report on the company of your choice within minutes of receiving your order. To request a report from this automated service, you'll need to know the stock ticker symbol of the company you're interested in. There is a charge for each report ordered, although you can obtain one free report when you try out the service for the first time. For a free trial of this useful company research service, call (800) 642-2858. For more information, call (800) 292-0808.

Another fax-on-demand service is Company News On-Call, which is sponsored by PR Newswire. This free service allows you to obtain press releases, quarterly financial information, and company news from thousands of public and privately owned companies that subscribe to the PR Newswire service. All you need is a fax machine. Within minutes, an abundance of up-to-the-minute company news reports and press releases will arrive on your fax machine.

To use this service, from your fax machine, call (800) 753-0352, extension 662, and when prompted, enter your fax machine's telephone number. A nine- or ten-page document containing complete directions for using this service, along with a listing of company names whose press releases and news reports are offered from this service, will immediately be faxed to you. Next to each company name on the list will be a six-digit ID number.

When you're ready to start receiving information, dial (800) 758-5804 to obtain the press releases and company news reports you're interested in. Using a push-button telephone, you need to enter each company's ID number and your fax machine's telephone number. There is no charge for using this service. All you pay for is the fax paper you'll need to print out all the information you request.

Don't Forget

If you don't have access to a traditional fax machine, most personal computers can send and receive faxes when you equip the computer with a fax/modem and special fax software. If you already own a computer with a modem, check the manual that came with your modem. You may already have everything you need to transform your PC into a fax machine that will allow you to use any of these fax-on-demand services with ease.

Choosing What to Wear

Later in this chapter, you'll find a checklist that will provide you with some personal grooming advice. Before your interview, obviously you want to shower and shave and choose an outfit that fits within the corporate culture of the company you're interviewing with. It would also be advisable to remove jewelry used with body piercings (multiple earrings, tongue posts, nose rings, etc.). How you look when you show up for an interview says a lot about you, and greatly impacts the first impression the interviewer formulates.

At the bare minimum, you want to dress exactly how all the current employees at the company dress, making sure that you adhere to the company's established dress code. It's always an excellent idea, however, to show respect to the interviewer by dressing a bit more formally. There are very few industries where this advice doesn't apply. As a general rule, dress in formal business attire that's conservative.

Fashion Tips for Men

For men, in almost every case, you can't go wrong by wearing a nicely tailored and recently dry-cleaned and pressed two-piece suit to your interview. The best color choices are shades of navy blue, charcoal, or light gray. Darker colors are more conservative and businesslike. (If possible, avoid wearing solid black. Brown, tan, or beige is acceptable, although not preferable.) It doesn't matter if your suit is a solid color or pinstripe, as long as the stripes themselves are narrow.

Wear an ironed (wrinkle-free) white or light blue, long-sleeved, cotton dress shirt. Choose a silk (or silklike) tie that nicely coordinates with your suit. Complete the outfit with dark socks (black, navy blue, or gray, as long at they coordinate with your suit) and dress shoes. Freshly shined black or brown leather shoes are the most suitable. Avoid trying to make a fashion statement by wearing a brightly colored or extremely flashy tie.

Do not wear any flashy jewelry (neck chains, rings, earrings, or pins). It's an excellent idea to avoid wearing any religious jewelry or anything with a political party, club, or organization's logo. Your wristwatch should also fit nicely with your outfit. It doesn't have to be expensive, but it should look businesslike. A sports watch or a watch with a colorful design on its face should not be worn.

If you choose to go a little less formal, you can wear a nice sport jacket or blazer and dress slacks. Again, stick with businesslike colors, such as a navy blue blazer with gray dress pants.

Complete your outfit with a nice briefcase or portfolio. This will add to your overall professional image and give you something to carry copies of your resume, pad, pen, and research materials in.

Don't Forget

1. Choosing an outfit from an expensive designer isn't necessary. However, it is absolutely critical that your suit be clean and pressed (wrinkle-free) and tailored so it fits you perfectly.

2. Most men hate to iron, so be sure to bring your interview outfit to a dry cleaner to have it cleaned and pressed before each interview.

3. If you're not up on the latest men's fashions, visit a department store and ask the salesperson for assistance. You can also check out the latest issue of *GQ*, or get help from a friend with good taste in fashion. Also, before the interview, try to visit the company and see what the other male employees wear to work.

4. As a general rule, in the business world, men don't wear their hair long or in a ponytail. Being an applicant, you want your hairstyle to be businesslike, conservative, and clean-cut.

Fashion Tips for Women

As you choose your interview outfit, you want something that looks businesslike, yet is currently in style. While men are pretty much restricted to wearing traditional suits, women can be a bit more creative in their wardrobe selection, which gives them a chance to show off their personal style, as long as it fits within the company's dress code.

When choosing your outfit, avoid plunging necklines, sheer blouses, and miniskirts. Select a pair of shoes that matches your outfit. The shoes should be closed-toed pumps or flats in a neutral color. Apply minimal makeup (less is more). The "natural" look is always in style when it comes to cosmetics. If you choose to wear earrings, choose a pair that complements your outfit without attracting attention. Your nails should be nicely manicured. As for nail polish, select one solid color that complements your overall outfit, but that isn't too flashy. Avoid wearing cheap-looking jewelry or any type of flashy jewelry that will distract the interviewer.

Finally, to be safe do not wear any perfume. This can be highly distracting to an interviewer, especially if the interview is taking place in a small, confined area.

Your outfit should be clean, well-fitting, flattering, and wrinkle-free. Your clothing should also be free of static cling. There are many women's fashion magazines that provide fashion tips for working women. You can also solicit the advice of a salesperson from a major department store or fashion boutique. Be sure that you make it perfectly clear to the salesperson that you're looking for a conservative business outfit to wear to a job interview.

Make sure that your hairstyle also fits within the corporate culture of the company you're interviewing with. It's advisable to avoid applying too much hairspray or a styling gel that has a lasting odor. In most cases, you want to create an image of being a low-maintenance but well-groomed professional. It's an excellent strategy to avoid wearing any religious jewelry or anything with a political party, club, or organization's logo. If you don't want to reveal your marital status, remove your engagement and wedding rings.

Don't Forget

1. If you're planning to wear a pair of pantyhose, always take an extra pair along in your purse in case of a run.

2. Avoid wearing bright colors. If possible, it's always an excellent idea to visit the company a few days before the interview to check out what other female employees are wearing and then dress accordingly. In the business world, it is acceptable for a woman to wear a red dress or business suit.

3. Using a bit of fashion creativity and common sense, it is very easy to dress professionally without spending a fortune on designer labels. Looking clean, neat, and wrinkle-free, and wearing an outfit that fits perfectly, is much more important than looking like you spent a fortune on an outfit from a well-known designer.

Making a Perfect First Impression

In addition to arriving at the interview totally prepared, one of the most important things you can do is to arrive early, no matter what. Employers become extremely annoyed with applicants that show up for interviews even 1 minute late. Ideally, you want to arrive about 15 minutes early, check in with the receptionist, hang up your coat, and wait. Be sure that you plan out your day carefully so that you allow plenty of travel time and arrive for your interview with time to spare. Barring a personal medical emergency, there are very few acceptable excuses for being late to a job interview, and anytime you use an excuse, it will be held against you.

Prior to the interview, you want to follow the preinterview check-list at the end of this chapter and ensure that you look your absolute best. As soon as you arrive for your interview, check in with the receptionist, or find the office of the person you're supposed to meet and check in with the person's secretary or assistant. Politely introduce yourself to the receptionist and then give the name of the person you have an appointment with. Keep in mind, you're being evaluated based on every move you make, and often even the receptionists, secretaries, or assistants have input into the hiring process, so make as many friends as possible.

When you're instructed to wait in a waiting room, lobby, or seating area, take off your coat and hang it up. You don't want to be wearing or carrying your coat into the actual interview office. Make sure, how-ever, that you keep your briefcase and/or portfolio and your personal planner with you. When you are first introduced to the person who will be interviewing you, show respect by addressing him or her as "Mr./Mrs./Ms./Dr. (insert the last name)," look the person directly in the eye, smile, and shake hands. If the interviewer asks that you use his or her first name, feel free to do so from this point on.

As you get escorted into the office where the interview will be held, don't sit down before the interviewer does. Wait for him or her to be seated or invite you to sit down. When you sit down, make sure you sit up straight. Never slouch!

Don't Forget

Try to sit down at the same time or after the interviewer. If possible, avoid allowing the interviewer to look down upon you while you're sitting down and he or she is standing up.

Throughout the interview, always try to maintain as much eye contact as possible and avoid fidgeting. If you know you have ner-vous habits, such as tapping your foot, looking at your watch, touching your face, chewing your pen, twirling your hair, or banging your pen against a desk, do your best to maintain control of your actions and avoid giving in to these nervous habits.

Keep in mind, the person interviewing you does this often. As a result, the interviewer is trained to read your body language. Avoiding eye contact and touching your face often are signs of someone who is not being truthful. During the interview, never give into the urge to smoke a cigarette, even if the interviewer lights one up.

The interviewer knows that if you show several signs that you're nervous, you are probably unprepared for the interview, you have something to hide, or you feel threatened. Even if this is the case, you don't want to show it. Participating in practice (mock) interviews is one way to help yourself learn how to control your nervous habits.

Often, as the applicant, you will be offered a drink at the start of the interview. Accept whatever drink is offered, and don't make a point of ordering something unusual, such as coffee prepared a particular way. To avoid caffeine, consider asking for water. If the employer offers you a beer, or another form of alcoholic beverage, decline, but ask for something nonalcoholic.

During your interview, be prepared to make small talk, about the weather, the way a local sports team is performing, or a major news story. Whatever you do, avoid getting into an argument with the interviewer, and avoid controversial topics such as politics or religion. Try to find something that you and the interviewer have in common, such as a hobby or a mutual acquaintance, but avoid spending too much time during your interview gossiping. Establish a common bond and then focus on landing yourself a job.

Throughout the interview, even if the interviewer is taking a very casual approach, you are still being evaluated, so never let down your guard. Keep smiling, and answer all questions openly and honestly and in complete sentences. Make sure that you always think before you speak. Every question that you are asked, even if it seems to have no relevance to anything, is being asked for a reason. Some employers like to see how you react to bizarre questions, and to see if you can think on your feet. Often, what you provide as an answer to these off-the-wall questions isn't as important as how you answer them. If you don't know the answer to a specific question, never lie or make up an answer.

During the interview is when you can promote yourself as confident, intelligent, outgoing, dedicated, and enthusiastic. Asking questions during the interview is as important as answering the questions posed to you. Feel free to use your hands to express yourself.

Don't Forget

1. Some people who study body language recommend that job applicants try to mimic the interviewer's physical behaviors. If done correctly, this can be beneficial, because you can develop an unspoken bond with the other person. If done incorrectly, it becomes very obvious what you are trying to do, and you'll look foolish. As a general rule, pay attention to the interviewer's body language, and if you feel comfortable using some of the same gestures, use them, but not at the same time as the interviewer.

2. During any interview situation, make a point to come right out and ask for the job at least two or three different times (but wait until the middle or end of the interview). Be sure to explain exactly why you want the job, what you can offer to the company, and why you're the best candidate for the position. Yes, it's totally obvious that you're sitting in an interview because you want the job, but state the obvious. Say something like, "I'm really excited about everything you've been telling me about this company. I really hope you'll give me the opportunity to prove myself as a (insert job title). With my skills and experience, I know I could offer a lot to the company." Be sure to provide specific examples of your skills or accomplishments that would be beneficial to the company.

Believe it or not, it doesn't take much effort on your part to make an excellent first impression. Make sure you're looking your absolute best, show respect to everyone you meet, and act enthusiastic, confident, and energetic. Maintain eye contact, sit up straight, and answer all questions posed to you in complete and coherent sentences. Be open and honest with the interviewer, and most importantly, be yourself. No matter what happens, always act in a professional manner.

Anticipating the Questions You'll Be Asked

One excellent way to help yourself prepare for an interview is to talk with friends who are also currently looking for a job, and discuss your interview experiences in detail. Make sure that the people you talk to aren't applying for the same position(s) that you are, or the information you get from them might not be 100 percent accurate. Talking with a career counselor at your college or university's career guidance office is also a smart move (plus it's totally free).

Part of your preinterview preparation should be determining the types of questions the interviewer will ask you, and spending time developing well-thought-out, complete, and intelligent answers to these questions. Ask a friend or relative to participate in a mock interview with you. Have him or her pretend to be the employer and ask you questions. Thinking about answers in your head or even writing out answers on paper to help you prepare will be helpful. But what will benefit you the most is actually practicing answering interview questions out loud and having your friend or relative honestly evaluate your responses. If you're working with a professional career counselor, ask the counselor to help you to prepare for an interview by participating in a mock interview.

Most of the questions you'll be asked will be pretty obvious. However, be prepared for an interviewer to ask you a few questions that are unexpected or unusual. By doing this, the interviewer wants to see how you react and how well you think on your feet. Also, be prepared to turn negative questions into positive ones. If asked, "What is your biggest weakness as an employee?" don't talk about all the reasons why the interviewer shouldn't hire you. Instead, mention a job-related strength, like you work too hard or you worry too much about details. You can also talk about how your husband/wife/boyfriend/girlfriend always complains that you stay too late at the office trying to get your work done.

As you answer all the interviewer's questions:

- Use complete sentences and proper English.
- Always be upbeat and keep smiling.
- Provide complete and straightforward answers. Don't be evasive, especially if you're asked about negative aspects of your employment history.
- Never imply that a questions is stupid or irrelevant.
- Never lie or stretch the truth.
- Be prepared to answer the same questions multiple times. Sometimes an employer will ask the same question two or three different ways. Make sure your answers are consistent, and never reply, "You already asked me that."
- Never apologize for mistakes or negative information regarding your past.
- No matter how smart and well educated you are, never talk down to an interviewer or make an interviewer feel inferior or less intelligent than you are.

How you answer questions about yourself can impact how enthusiastic the interviewer will become about hiring you. As you answer questions, try to incorporate positive words into your answers. Check out this list of words and think about how you can incorporate some of them into how you describe yourself, your skills, and your previous work experience:

Able	Effective	Personable
Accomplished	Efficient	Polished
Accurate	Energetic	Polite
Adaptable	Experienced	Productive
Aggressive	Fast	Professional
Alert	Flexible	Proficient
Ambitious	Friendly	Qualified
Analytical	Goal-oriented	Reliable
Articulate	Happy	Resourceful
Artistic	Hardworking	Responsible
Astute	Highly trained	Self-reliant
Bilingual	Honest	Sincere
Bright	Honorable	Skilled
Capable	Imaginative	Stable
Clever	Innovative	Successful
Competent	Intelligent	Talented
Computer savvy	Licensed	Trustworthy
Confident	Managerial	Upbeat
Congenial	Moral	Valuable
Consistent	Motivated	Well educated
Creative	Multitalented	Well organized
Dedicated	Nonsmoking	Well rounded
Dependable	Organized	Well traveled
Detail-oriented	Outgoing	Willing
Driven	People-oriented	Worthy
Dynamic	Perceptive	

With each answer that you provide, you should somehow be selling yourself, your capabilities, your experiences, your personality, and your potential to the employer. Don't rely on your resume, cover letter, and references to do your selling for you. During the interview process, you have an opportunity to sell yourself in person, and that should be your primary goal.

Always try to focus on and bring attention to your accomplishments, skills, and abilities. One of the most common ways an interviewer kicks off an interview after the initial introductions is to turn to the applicant and say, "So, tell me about yourself." This is your first chance to highlight some of the reasons why you're qualified for the job you're applying for. Use specific examples of your past accomplishments, or talk about how you used specific skills in previous work experiences. As you do this, you can demonstrate that you're a team player and that you work well with other people by saying things like, "When I was working for (company name), we did. . . ." The keyword in this sentence is *we*. You could say, "When I was working for (company name), I did . . . ," but that doesn't show that you're a team-oriented worker. Most people applying for a job bring up the fact that they're team-oriented and that they enjoy working with people. Your goal is to bring this up subtly, without coming right out and saying it.

Don't waste time talking about your personal life, your family, hobbies, favorite foods, or the place you visited on your last vacation. Use your replies to an interviewer's questions to explain what you can do for the employer if you were to be hired for the job. From your research, you should have a good idea about the type of skills that are required for the job, so talk about how you possess the necessary skills and how you'll apply them to the job when you get it.

Questions Applicants Should Be Prepared to Answer

Before each interview, think about how you will answer the following questions. Also, make a list of job-specific questions that you'll probably be asked, and plan specifically how you'll answer them.

In italics next to many of the following questions is advice on the best way(s) to respond. Depending on what type of job you're applying for, not all of these questions will be applicable, but to be prepared for your interview, think carefully about potential answers for each of these questions anyway.

- What can you tell me about yourself? *[Stress your skills and accomplishments. Avoid talking about your family, hobbies, or what you like to eat for dinner.]*

- How would you describe your personality? *[Try to promote yourself as a positive, people-oriented, motivated, goal-oriented, and organized person.]*

- How would your previous employers and coworkers describe you? *[Be sure to answer this questions honestly. When the interviewer checks your references, this can be verified.]*

- Why have you chosen to pursue your current career path? *[Try to give specific reasons or examples why you have chosen to pursue your career.]*

- What skills do you possess that help you to excel in your chosen career path? *[Here's a chance for you to talk about your personal skill set. Think about the skills you listed in your resume and how you answered the questions posed in Chapter 1 of this book. Be sure to give examples of how you have used your skills in the past.]*

- What are two of the biggest obstacles you have overcome to achieve your success thus far? How did you overcome those obstacles? *[Be sure to provide specific examples of what you have done to overcome your obstacles or challenges.]*

- In your personal or professional life, what has been your greatest failure? What did you learn from that experience? *[Be open and honest. Everyone has had some type of failure. Focus on what you learned from the experience and how it helped you to grow as a person.]*

- Why did you leave your previous job? *[Try to put a positive spin on your answer, especially if your were fired for negative reasons. Company downsizing, a company going out of business, or some other reason that was out of your control is a perfectly acceptable answer. Another good answer is that the employer was insisting that you relocate, and you didn't want to.]*

- What would you consider to be your biggest accomplishments at your last job? *[Refer to the questions you already answered in Chapter 1.]*

- In a typical week, how much overtime did you put in at your last job? *[This response can be easily verified when the interviewer contacts your previous employer, so be honest.]*

- Have you ever been fired from a job? If so, why? *[If you have been fired, acknowledge you did something wrong, explain the situation, and talk about how you learned from the experience. Being fired is different from being let go due to a company downsizing, relocating, or going out of business.]*

- Do you enjoy working with other people? Can you give me an example of how you worked within a group to accomplish a goal while at your last job? *[Most employers want to be sure that you can work well with your coworkers. Be sure to provide examples of how you worked well within a group.]*

- How well do you deal with stress? Can you give me an example of how you successfully managed a particularly stressful situation while in your previous job? *[If you took medication to help you deal with your stress, or if you have had a nervous breakdown, be careful how you reveal this information. Try to put a positive spin on your past, and talk about how you have learned to better deal with stress in your life.]*

- What motivates you to excel in your work? [*Answering that money is your primary motivator is* not *the right answer. Talk about why your work is rewarding to you.*]

- Who are your mentors? Whom do you look up to?

- What do you want to get out of your next job? *[Try to turn this question around and talk about what you can offer to the company. You don't want to come off as someone who is concerned only with his or her own well-being and future. You can, however, talk about how you are excited to learn and gain new experiences, etc.]*

- Could you please describe what would be your ideal work environment? *[Try to match your description with what you already know about the company you're interviewing with. This is why research is important.]*

- In college, I see you were a (insert subject) major. Why did you choose (insert subject) as your major?

- How have the classes you completed as part of your major helped you to prepare for your career? *[Try to provide specifics.]*

- Why did you choose the college or university you attended? *[If you attended the same school as the interviewer, or what would be considered a rival school, think carefully about how you answer this question. You don't want to accidentally offend the interviewer.]*

- Looking back, is there anything you would change about your educational history? [*Be careful answering this question. You do* not *want to imply that you made poor decisions when choosing your courses, or that you don't consider yourself well enough educated. You want to stress that you have a well-rounded education, but you also took the required number of courses that relate directly to your major.*]

- Do you plan to eventually attend graduate school? If so, when? *[If you plan on attending grad school, you might not want to mention this now. An employer might not want to hire and train you, knowing that in a year or two you may leave the company to pursue an advanced degree. You can reply by saying you have no immediate plans to attend grad school. If you know that the company will support your pursuing a higher education in the future, you could reply that it's something you'd be interested in down the road.]*

- Would you attend grad school full-time or at night after work? *[Before answering this questions, it's helpful to know if the employer supports employees who want to pursue a higher education. Will the company pay for the education or allow you to work part-time while you're in school? Again, this is often something you can determine when researching a company before an interview.]*

- What extracurricular activities did you participate in while in school? In what ways did these activities help you to prepare for your career? *[Stress any leadership roles you had. Were you an officer of an on-campus organization or club?]*

- While you were in school, what was your most challenging subject? *[Be honest, but be careful how you respond. If you're applying for a job in the finance department, you don't want to acknowledge that math and accounting were your worst subjects. Likewise, if you're applying for a marketing or public relations job, or a job that will require a lot of writing, don't say that you didn't do well in your English, composition, or writing classes.]*

- What was your best subject in school? *[Go ahead and boast. Obviously, if your best subject somehow relates to your career, you'll look that much more qualified for the job you're applying for.]*

- Tell me about your summer jobs or internships while you were in school? *[By asking this question, the employer is trying to determine if you were career-oriented while in school. Did you take just any summer job, goof off during vacations, or pursue jobs that would give you valuable experience in whatever career you're currently pursuing?]*

- What are your long-term goals? *[As you answer this question, talk about how you have been following a career path thus far with all your previous jobs, and where you think this career path will take you in the future.]*

- How do you plan to reach your goals? *[Refer to your answers from Chapter 1.]*

- Where do you see yourself five years down the road? Ten years? *[Employers are not supposed to ask you direct personal questions. By asking this type of question, an employer could be trying to get you to volunteer personal information about yourself, so be careful how you answer. For example, if you're a newly married woman, even if you plan on having a bunch of kids, you might not want to bring this up during your interview. Some employers may think that with the new kids will come maternity leave and then the responsibilities of motherhood that could interfere with your work responsibilities. Is this sexist? Yes! But as long as employers don't come straight out and ask these questions, they can use any personal information you voluntarily provide against you.]*

- How do you define success? *[Don't reply by making a reference to earning a lot of money. Talk more about managing more responsibility and achieving more.]*

- What would it take for you to consider yourself successful on the job? *[Refer to your answers from Chapter 1.]*

- What are the skills you have that will help you the most if you were to receive this job (the one you're applying for now)? *[Make sure your answer is consistent with the skills you highlight in your resume and cover letter. Elaborate on this information as you answer this type of question.]*

- How did you hear about this job opening?

- What skills do you think this job requires? *[By doing your research beforehand, you'll know exactly what the employer is looking for. Feed this information back and stress that you have the necessary skills and experience.]*

- What is it about this job that caught your attention?

- Why do you think you're the most qualified person to fill this job? *[Talk about the positive things that set you apart from the competition. What's unique about you, your skill set, and your past experience?]*

- What work-related experience do you have that relates directly to this job?

- Why do you want to work for this company? *[Talk about what excites you about the company, based on the information you learn while doing research.]*

- Have you simultaneously applied for jobs at other companies? Which companies? *[Answer this question honestly, but stress that the other jobs you applied for were as backup, just in case this job, which is definitely your first choice, doesn't come through.*

Demonstrating that you have a backup plan shows that you think situations through and you're prepared for whatever happens.]

- If you were to receive this job, how long do you anticipate staying with this company? *[If you plan on leaving for any reason after a short period of time, don't mention this to the employer. Stress that the job you're applying for is the one you really want, and you plan on staying with it indefinitely.]*

- What interests you the most about this industry?

- What have you heard about this company that was of interest to you? *[Try to refer to any positive publicity or media attention that the company has recently received. This shows you've done your research.]*

- Can you describe some of the ways you could contribute to this company? *[You already should know the job requirements, and you've already talked about how you've applied your skills to past jobs. Now talk about how you can use your skills and experience to excel in the job you're applying for.]*

- How many employers have you worked for in the past years? What was it about your previous jobs that caused you to leave them? *[Answer honestly. Your answer can easily be verified.]*

- How did your supervisor or superior from your last job react when you gave notice that you were leaving the company? *[Answer honestly. Your answer can easily be verified.]*

- What will your previous employer miss the most about you? *[Once again, you have an opportunity to stress the various ways you'll be able to help the company you're applying to work for by talking about your past work experience.]*

- What did you like the most about your previous job? *[Avoid talking about your salary or the benefits package. Never say something like, "I enjoyed the fact that we could take long lunches or leave early from work whenever we wanted."]*

- What type of work did you enjoy the most at your previous job? What type of work did you like the least? *[Stress that you enjoy work that is challenging and that allows you to constantly grow as a person. Use specific examples. As for what type of work you like the least, choose an activity that isn't required for the job you're applying for.]*

- What did you like the least about your previous job? *[Don't talk about any conflicts you had with past bosses or coworkers.]*

- Outside of work, what do you do for fun? *[Now is the time to talk about your hobbies, etc.]*

- What else can you tell me about yourself that isn't listed in your resume? *[This is yet another opportunity for you to sell yourself to the employer. Take advantage of the opportunity while you can.]*

Illegal Interview Questions

There are some interview questions that an employer is not legally allowed to ask you. The following is a sampling of those questions. If you find yourself being asked one or more of these questions during an interview, you can avoid answering them by coming up with a witty response. For example, if you are asked if you are married, you can respond by saying, "Sometimes I think I'm married to my job. I'm always working so hard."

Your alternative is to state that you choose not to respond to the question. If the interviewer continues to ask you highly personal and illegal questions, you should strongly consider politely walking out of the interview and contacting that person's superior. It goes without saying that if an interviewer makes any kind of sexual advance during the interview, you should walk out and report that individual.

The National Association of Colleges and Employers established these guidelines for what questions an employer can and cannot legally ask:

Topic—National Origin/Citizenship

Illegal Questions: Are you a U.S. citizen? Where were you or your parents born? What is your "native tongue"? What is your religion? What temple, church, or house of worship do you belong to?

Legal Questions: Are you authorized to work in the United States? What languages do you read, speak, or write fluently? (This question can only be asked if this ability is relevant to the performance of the job.)

Topic—Your Age

Illegal Questions: How old are you? When did you graduate from college? What is your birth date?

Legal Question: Are you over the age of 18?

Topic—Marital/Family Status

Illegal Questions: What is you marital status? Whom do you live with? Do you plan to have a family? If so, when? How many kids do you have? What are your child-care arrangements?

Legal Questions: Would you be willing to relocate if necessary? Would you be willing and able to travel as needed by the job? (This question can only be asked as long as *all* applicants for the job are asked it.) Would you be able and willing to work over-time as necessary? (This question can only be asked as long as *all* applicants for the job are asked it.)

Topic—Affiliations

Illegal Question: To what clubs or social organizations do you belong?

Legal Question: What professional groups, trade groups, or other organizations do you belong to that you consider relevant to your ability to perform this job?

Topic—Personal

Illegal Questions: How tall are you? How much do you weigh?

Legal Questions: Are you able to lift a 50-pound weight and carry it 100 yards, as that is part of the job? (Questions about height and weight are not acceptable unless minimum standards are essential to the safe performance of the job.)

Topic—Disabilities

Illegal Questions: Do you have any disabilities? Please complete the following medical history. Have you had any recent or past illnesses or operations? If yes, list dates. What was the date of your last physical exam? How's your family's health? When did you lose your eyesight? How?

Legal Questions: Are you able to perform the essential functions of this job with or without reasonable accommodations? (This question is okay if the interviewer has already thoroughly described the job.) As part of the hiring process, after a job offer is made, you will be required to undergo a medical exam. Do you agree to this? (Exam results must be kept strictly confidential, except medical and safety personnel may be informed if emergency medical treatment is required, and supervisors may be informed about necessary job accommodations, based on the exam results.) Can you demonstrate how you would perform the following job-related function?

Topic—Arrest Record

Illegal Question: Have you ever been arrested?

Legal Question: Have you ever been convicted of (insert specific crime)? (The crime should be reasonably related to the performance of the job in question.)

Topic—Military

Illegal Question: If you've been in the military, were you honorably discharged?

Legal Questions: In what branch of the armed forces did you serve? What type of training or education did you receive in the military?

Don't Forget

While interviewers can't legally ask you certain personal questions, they can and will ask you open-ended questions in hopes that you'll volunteer personal information about yourself.

What You Should Ask the Employer

The answers you provide to the questions posed to you are important; however, interviewers will also pay careful attention to the questions you ask. By asking the right questions, you can demonstrate a strong knowledge of the company and the industry, and at the same time, show you're interested in the job you're applying for. Simply asking generic questions will demonstrate both a lack of preparation and your ignorance.

Prior to any interview, part of your preparation should be to think of at least five intelligent and relevant questions that you can ask the employer.

In asking questions during the interview, you want to find out as much about the job you're applying for as possible. Knowing what the job is all about and what will be expected of you will help you evaluate a job offer if one is extended.

Here are some questions that will help you learn more about the job you're applying for and the company as a whole. If an interviewer tries to evade your questions or refuses to provide answers, you should seriously reconsider your interest in working for the company.

Questions You Can Ask Potential Employers during an Interview

- Could you please provide me with a detailed job description for the position I am applying for?

- How would you describe the corporate culture (or the work environment)?

- How does the position I'm applying for fit into the overall structure of the organization?

- Who would be my immediate superior(s)?

- Are there plans to expand or make major changes to the division I'll be working in?

- Does the job I'm applying for require travel? If so, how much? Does the company pay all travel costs, including mileage reimbursement if I use my own car?

- Who will my coworkers be?

- How big is the division I'll be working in? What are the overall goals for the division?

- What other divisions can I expect to interact with as part of my everyday responsibilities?

- What are the overall responsibilities for someone in the position I'm applying for?

- What is a typical workday or workweek like? What type of work will I be doing on a daily basis?

- Are my hours flexible, or am I expected to work specific hours (9:00 a.m. to 5:00 p.m.)?

- In the first 6 months of employment, what would you expect someone working in my position to accomplish?

- How much decision-making authority and autonomy are given to new employees?

- How are employees evaluated? How often?

- Does the company hire from within for higher-level positions?

- If I were interested in moving up within the organization, what opportunities would be open to me?

- What type of on-the-job training is available?

- Does your organization encourage its employees to pursue additional education and training?

- What are the qualities that make a good employee in this organization?
- Why is the position I'm applying for open?
- How would you describe your organization's management style?
- While I'm here visiting the company, would it be possible for me to meet my potential coworkers and/or supervisors?
- I really would like this job. I think I could do excellent work and excel. Would you consider hiring me for a 30-day trial period so I could prove myself?

Don't Forget

If the job you're applying for requires employees to wear uniforms, ask if they're provided by the employer and who is responsible for cleaning the uniforms. If you have to pay for your own uniforms, how much do they cost? How many uniforms will you need to purchase? How much should you expect to spend cleaning and maintaining your uniforms?

Topics and Questions to Avoid Asking

During your initial interview, avoid asking questions about salary, benefits, paid sick days, and vacation time. Wait for the employer to bring up these topics, or wait until you receive a job offer. If you're asked about the salary you're looking for, never provide a figure. Instead, ask what someone already working for the company in a similar capacity gets paid, or say that your salary is negotiable. Try to push the employer to make you an offer, and negotiate from there. Chapter 8 delves into salary negotiation strategies and offers plenty of advice on this topic.

The questions you ask should demonstrate your interest in learning more about the company and about how you can help the company succeed. Thus, you want to avoid questions that relate to what the company can do for you (i.e., how much you'll be paid).

Also, avoid asking the interviewer personal questions or questions relating to his or her own career.

Participate in a Conversation

A job interview should be a friendly and open conversation. Your goal is to learn as much about the job opportunity as possible, while the interviewer learns everything he or she can about you and why you're suitable for the job. The best interviews take on a conversational style, in which both the interviewer and interviewee spend an equal amount of time talking. As the applicant, it's up to you to avoid getting trapped in an interrogation-style interview.

The best way to avoid being interrogated is to answer the questions asked, but also pose plenty of your own questions. Use complete sentences and provide lots of specific examples. As you describe your work experience, pretend you're telling a story. Never just nod your head or answer a questions with a yes or no answer.

One excellent way to keep a conversation going is to find things you have in common with the interviewer. As you do this, however, avoid the pitfall of gossiping about specific individuals who are mutual acquaintances. Remember, this is still an interview, and even if you develop an instant bond with the interviewer, you both still have specific objectives you're trying to accomplish.

The easiest types of interviews for the applicant are the ones where the interviewer simply reads from a predefined list of questions and sticks to an agenda. If this is the case, try to maintain a conversational style as you answer the questions posed, and then ask your own questions. You never want to make the interviewer feel threatened or defensive.

Some interviewers will take on a sales-pitch approach to their interview style. They'll start off by babbling for a while about how wonderful their company is and what the job opening is all about.

You'll then be asked if you have any questions. As you ask questions, try to reveal some information about yourself by talking about your skills and experiences. If an interviewer adopts this type of interview style, you'll have to take an extra initiative to sell yourself.

Confrontational interviews are often the most difficult to handle, because it's difficult to predict what to expect next. When interviewers adopt this type of interview format, they may ask you questions designed to make you nervous and put you on the spot. If you find yourself in this situation, it's critical that you simply relax and have some fun with it. As you answer questions that are designed to put you on the spot, respond by saying, "In my opinion . . . (complete the answer)" or "I believe . . . (complete the answer)." If you simply state your answers as fact, you might come off as arrogant. No matter how bizarre the question, answer it to the best of your abilities, don't try to hide anything, and maintain eye contact with the interviewer. There is absolutely no reason to feel threatened by an interviewer. An interviewer can't smack you, bite you, yell at you, or inflict any type of pain if you answer a question incorrectly. Many questions the interviewer will be asking are purely subjective, so there are no right or wrong answers. A question might begin, "What would you do if . . ." or "If you were the president or CEO of the company, and (insert a negative event) happened, how would you handle it?"

Always listen carefully to the questions posed to you. By asking a certain question, does the interviewer have a hidden agenda? Is the interviewer looking for information that's none of his or her business? Are you being asked some type of trick question? It's perfectly okay to take a moment after a question is asked to formulate an appropriate response in your head before opening your mouth. Having a moment of total silence during the interview can work to your advantage, because it shows that you think before you speak and you don't jump to conclusions.

Never start answering a question before an interviewer finishes asking it. If you don't fully understand a question, ask for it to be clarified before you give your answer. Likewise, if you are nervous and "zone out" while a question is being asked, ask the interviewer to clarify the question, rather than repeat it.

If you find yourself starting to babble, end your response quickly by making a point. You never want to start talking for 2 or 3 minutes, pause, and then ask the interviewer, "What was your question again?"

As you answer each question, the interviewer will be studying your body language, evaluating your voice inflections, and listening to your answers. Never be fake or adopt a totally phony attitude. If the interviewer doesn't think you're genuinely excited about the job, you won't get it.

Dealing with Interruptions

Sometimes you'll be interviewed by a human resources person, but for some jobs, it will be an executive within the company who conducts the interview. If you are brought into an executive's office for an interview, go in knowing that the executive is extremely busy, and that you'll probably be interrupted multiple times by incoming phone calls and other unexpected events. If the interviewer does get distracted several times during your interview, it will be hard for him or her to focus on what you're saying. Make an extra effort to be patient and understanding, but sell yourself a bit harder. If 30 minutes was allocated for your interview and 12 minutes of that time the interviewer was on the phone, you have to make the time you have the interviewer's full attention work to your maximum advantage.

When the interviewer's telephone rings and it looks like he or she will have to spend several minutes on the phone, offer to excuse yourself and wait outside the office to give the interviewer privacy. If you're told to sit still and wait, pick up your resume or information about the company that has been provided to you and start reading it. Don't eavesdrop on the conversation. If necessary, stare at some artwork or photographs on the wall, but remain relaxed.

As noted earlier, if you're being interviewed by an executive at the company, you can also expect interruptions from the executive's coworkers, who will knock at the door requesting a moment of time with the person interviewing you. Yes, this can be distracting and break up any momentum you have going in terms of the actual interview. However, chances are, you'll be introduced to the people that show up at the door, and any of them could be a top-level executive with the company. Be polite to everyone. When you are introduced, make a point to stand up and shake hands. If the interviewer doesn't bring it up when you're introduced to the person at the door, mention what job you're applying for and how excited you are about the possibility of working for the company.

Not All Interviews Take Place in an Office Setting

Some employers prefer to conduct interviews outside the office, over lunch or dinner at a restaurant. This can be a good thing, because the overall tone of the interview will be a bit more relaxed, and you know you'll have the interviewer's full attention during the meal.

In addition to following all the other interviewing tips provided in this chapter, if your interview is taking place at a restaurant, here are some additional suggestions that will help the interview go smoothly:

- Compliment the interviewer on the choice of restaurants.
- Before ordering, ask the interviewer what dishes he or she recommends.
- Order a light meal, because you want to spend as much time as possible answering and asking questions, not stuffing your face with food.

- As you order, make sure you stay away from foods containing garlic, onions, or anything else that will cause bad breath or gas. No matter what, it's an excellent idea to excuse yourself at the end of the meal, visit the rest room, and use some breath freshener, or eat a mint when you're done eating.

- When placing your food order, choose something directly off the menu. Don't make your request complicated. If you spend 5 minutes ordering your food to be prepared in a special way, that could send the wrong message to the interviewer.

- Never order an alcoholic beverage, even if the interviewer does. Stick with water, juice, or decaffeinated coffee.

- Throughout the meal, as you're being interviewed, never talk with your mouth full. If the interviewer catches you when you're chewing, indicate that you need a moment to swallow, take a sip of water, and then answer the question.

- At the conclusion of the meal, as the check is being paid, thank the interviewer for the meal and mention that you had a really nice time. Later, when you're parting company outside the restaurant, thank the interviewer for taking the time to interview you; and as a closing thought, bring up how much you'd like the job and, in a nutshell, what you could offer to the company.

Sell Yourself and Set Yourself Apart

From the moment you walk in the door of a potential employer, you want to do whatever you can to set yourself apart in a positive way. Keep in mind, all the applicants that are trying for the job are going to be dressed in their best-looking interview outfit, are going to have a resume that makes them seem like the perfect person for the job, and are going to appear upbeat and excited about the job opportunity. In addition, everyone will have basically the same core qualifications.

What this means is that you must use your personality and intelligence to set yourself apart. Don't try to stand out by wearing an outrageous outfit or printing your resume on brightly colored paper. These tactics will only make you look unprofessional and foolish.

The employer is looking for someone who is qualified for the job, but also who will work well with everyone else. The employer wants someone who will fit easily into the corporate culture, yet be able to think independently, make decisions, and act responsibly and professionally.

One easy way you can set yourself apart is to have photo business cards created for yourself that feature your headshot, home address, phone number, fax number, and e-mail address. This business card can be handed to an interviewer at either the very beginning or very end of an interview, and can be attached to or filed with a resume. Since your picture is on the card, you will be more easily remembered and will stand out better in the interviewer's mind when he or she goes back and reviews everyone's resume. (Never include a photograph as part of your actual resume or cover letter, unless you're working in show biz or the modeling industry.)

You can order photo business cards from any print shop, such as CopyMax, Sir Speedy, Copy Cop, or Minute Man Press, or from a large office supply store. Photo business cards cost more than traditional business cards, but the positive impact you'll make with employers is worth the investment.

Be sure that the photograph you provide to be printed on the cards shows you from the shoulders up and is flattering. Don't use your driver's license photo or a passport photo. Also, don't use any fancy typestyles or fonts. You want the photo business card to look professional and fit nicely with your resume and cover letter.

Following are two sample photo business card styles that you can have printed on white business card paper stock, using black ink (except for the color photo).

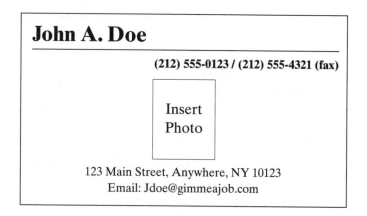

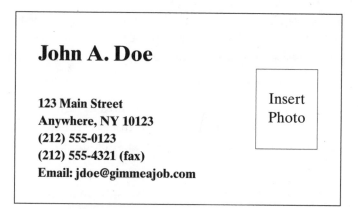

Explaining Negative Aspects of Your Employment History

Let's face it, not everyone has a perfect employment history. Whether you have been fired from a job, you have gaps (times of unemployment) in your employment history, or you've jumped from job to job, these are negatives that the interviewer is probably going to notice and ask you about.

Choosing the right resume format will help to make these negatives less obvious, but when the interviewer inquires about something negative involving your employment history, you should be

Don't Forget

Another way you can differentiate yourself from other applicants is by referring to your interviewer by name multiple times during the interview. People like to hear their own names. For example, when you're first introduced to the interviewer, you could respond, "It's a pleasure to meet you. Thank you for taking the time to see me." A better reply, however, is, "It's nice to meet you, Mr./Mrs./Ms./Dr. (insert last name). . . ." Be sure to refer to the interviewer by name several times during the interview and again at the conclusion of the interview. At the conclusion of the interview, say something like, "Thanks again for meeting with me, Mr./Mrs./Ms./Dr. (insert last name). . . ." Always address the interviewer as "Mr./Mrs./Ms./Dr. (insert last name)" unless you are specifically invited to interact with the interviewer on a first-name basis.

ready to provide an intelligent and believable response that will put a positive spin on the negative situation. Never lie about negative information or try to hide it. But at the same time, wait for the employer to bring it up.

As you explain whatever negative information the interviewer brings up, try to act as unemotional as possible. Show no resentment or bitterness toward past employers, and try to focus on what you learned from the negative situation. Answer these negative questions to the best of your ability and move on as quickly as possible to more positive subjects.

To explain gaps of several months in your employment history, if you don't have a good reason for these gaps, stating that you were job hunting is a valid reason, especially if you were laid off from your previous job due to the company downsizing, relocating, or going out of business.

If you've jumped from job to job many times, it is probably a good idea to only list the most positive work experiences on your resume and avoid using a chronological resume format.

Overcome Nervousness—How to Avoid Letting the Stress Get to You

Almost all people get nervous when they enter into a new or unknown situation. The trick, however, is to not allow your nervousness to take control of your actions. Before the interview, think about what happens to you when you become nervous or stressful.

- You sweat.
- Your hands shake.
- Your hands become cold or clammy.
- You touch your face often.
- You tap your foot.
- You tap your pen against a table.
- You rock back and forth in your chair.
- You get nauseous.
- You forget things.
- You have trouble concentrating.
- You become hyperactive.
- You bite your fingernails.
- You start saying "umm" between every sentence.

Whatever your nervous habits are, if you're aware of them you can control them with practice. When you go into an interview situation, you want to be well rested and totally prepared. If you know deep in your heart that you are prepared for the interview and you have the skills and knowledge necessary to land the job, you'll go in with more confidence, and your nervousness will fade away within minutes.

Part of your interview preparation should be to quietly sit alone in a room, close your eyes, and, in your mind, visualize the entire interview. Think about how good you're going to look, how you're going to act, what answers you're going to provide, and what questions you're going to ask. Professional athletes and many successful people use visualization techniques as a way to prepare themselves and deal with stressful situations. If you have visualized every detail of what will be your highly successful interview before it happens, when you're actually participating in the real-life interview, it will feel almost like deja vu.

Just before an interview, while you're sitting in a waiting room (or when visiting a rest room), close your eyes for a few seconds, clear your mind, and take five to ten deep breaths. Slowly inhale through your nose and exhale through your mouth. Think about your visualization and get into an interview mind-set. Think to yourself, "I have the right skills. I've done my research. I know I am totally qualified for this job. I am ready to wow 'em during this interview!"

If you are extremely nervous at the start of an interview, feel free to mention this to the employer. Just admitting that you are nervous will often help to alleviate your nervousness. Whatever you do, however, don't apologize for being nervous. Say, "You know, I'm very excited about this job opportunity, but I am a bit nervous, so please bear with me."

Throughout the interview, keep in mind your list of nervous habits, and constantly check yourself to see if you are giving into any of them. Obviously, you can't control sweating (leave that for your deodorant and antiperspirant). If you find yourself giving into any of your other nervous habits, make a conscious effort to stop.

For example, if you're rocking in your seat, place both feet on the floor and sit up straight. If you're tapping your pen on the table, put the pen in your pocket. If your hands are shaking, place them calmly on your lap. For those of you who tend to get nauseous when you're nervous, don't eat a heavy meal before the interview. Instead, stick with something light that won't upset your stomach.

In some situations, you'll be interviewed by multiple people at the same time. Don't feel like you're being ganged up on. If you have any public speaking experience, pretend you're making a speech. Instead of being intimidated, imagine that the people interviewing you are in their underwear. Very few people look intimidating wearing nothing but their underwear.

Think of the interview process as a game with no losers. The grand prize is a job offer. The prize for the runner-up is valuable experience in an interview situation. Go into the interview knowing you have absolutely nothing to lose and nothing to be worried about. You are not expected to know every answer to every question asked.

Danger!

Avoid drinking any beverages containing caffeine (soda, tea, or coffee) for several hours prior to the interview, and make sure you use the rest room before your interview.

Concluding the Interview

As your interview draws to a close, if the employer does not offer you a job right on the spot or mention when you will hear about a decision, ask when you may call to find out. Before leaving the interview, you should know exactly what the next step will be.

- Should you sit tight and wait for an offer?
- Is it necessary to contact the interviewer again?
- Do you have to provide additional information?
- Does the employer need to conduct additional interviews before making a decision?
- Do you have to schedule another interview for yourself? (If so, schedule that interview on the spot.)
- Approximately when does the employer plan to make the final decision?

If, at the end of an interview, you don't know the answers to these questions, it will be necessary for you to ask additional questions before you leave. Before finishing the interview, look the interviewer in the eye, smile, thank the interviewer for his or her time, and reaffirm your interest in the job. It wouldn't hurt to once again come straight out and ask to be hired. You should do this even if you think that the interview went very badly and that you have no shot of landing the job.

Completing a Job Application

Before most interviews, you'll be asked to complete a job application. A job application is simply a sheet of paper with questions on it. You are not going to be graded, and there are no right or wrong answers. There are, however, options. You can choose how you want to answer each question, and if you're uncomfortable supplying a certain piece of information, you can choose to leave it blank. (Instead of actually leaving a blank space, however, write "See me" or "Not applicable" in the space provided. Don't just skip questions.) Your goal when completing a job application should be to answer the questions as completely and honestly as possible in the space provided.

Keep in mind, if you're filling out the application by hand, that someone has to be able to read what you write, so print your responses as neatly as possible. Think about your answers before you start writing, and try to avoid crossing out mistakes. Using a typewriter to complete the application will help you keep the application neat and makes it easier to read.

As an applicant, you have a legal right to privacy. During an interview, or on a job application, most

Quick Tips

Request two copies of the application. Complete the first copy, but if you have a lot of cross-outs or mistakes, recopy your answers neatly onto the second application before submitting it. If you can only obtain one copy of the application, make one or two photocopies and fill out the photocopied version first as practice.

employers cannot ask you highly personal questions regarding your height, weight, age, religion, political affiliation, sex, marital status, race, or handicaps. (There are exceptions to this rule. For example, you could be asked one or more of these personal questions if your response will somehow impact your ability to do a job. For example, you may have trouble applying for a job working for the Democratic National Committee if you are a registered Republican.)

Many of the questions you will be asked to complete in an application can be answered by referring to your resume, so make sure that all the information you provide to the employer is consistent. The application is also used by employers to measure your writing skills and ability to communicate using the written word, so pay careful attention to spelling and punctuation and make sure you write complete sentences. Always print your answers using a pen, not a pencil.

Since you probably didn't include references in your resume, be prepared to include the names, addresses, phone numbers, and affiliations of your references as you complete your job application. The best references are past or current bosses, coworkers, or respected business professionals who know you. Refrain from listing relatives as references, because they are usually not considered credible. Make sure that you notify the people you list as a reference beforehand, so that they are prepared for a call from your potential employer. Never list someone as a reference without his or her permission, and make sure you ask the reference what telephone number you should provide the interviewer with. Some people don't like their home telephone number or direct office line to be given out.

As you list previous employers and schools, colleges, or universities you attended, keep in mind that the interviewer will most likely make contact with whoever is listed on your application to verify your information. Make sure that any names, addresses, and telephone numbers you provide are accurate. Some employers will also ask for your social security and/or driver's license number so that they can obtain a copy of your credit report. Thus, if you know your credit report contains negative information, such as a past bankruptcy, it might be a good idea to bring this up during the interview so that you can explain the situation.

Just as you did in your resume, avoid answering any questions that relate directly to how much money you've earned in the past. If a question asks about your previous salary, do not write in an amount. Instead, write "competitive."

Either on the job application or during the interview, you will probably be asked if you know anyone who currently works for the company. If, in fact, you have a friend or relative who works for the company, only mention that person's name if you know the person has a reputation as being a good employee. If your friend or relative is a troublemaker or poor worker, you don't want to be associated with him or her at this point.

The final portion of the actual job application is almost always some type of "agreement" that states that all the information you provided is 100 percent accurate and that any misrepresentation is grounds for immediate dismissal. You will be asked to sign and date the application.

If you receive a job offer, you may be asked to undergo a medical exam and/or a drug test. This is acceptable, but only after you have been given a firm job offer. Prior to your interview (or during the interview), in most cases the employer cannot legally ask about your health.

Don't Forget

Many job applications ask for your social security number and/or driver's license number. This is common for an application, but should not be included in a resume.

Application for Employment

Personal Information

Date: _____

Name: _____   Social Security Number: _____

Present Address: _____

City: _____   State: _____   Zip: _____

Phone Number: (_____)_____

Permanent Address: _____

City: _____   State: _____   Zip: _____

Phone Number: (_____)_____

Referred By: _____

Employment Desired

Position: _____   Date You Can Start: _____

Are You Currently Employed: ____ Yes ____ No   Salary Desired: $_____
If yes, can we contact your current employer? ____ Yes ____ No

Have you ever applied for a job at this company before? ____ Yes ____ No
If yes, where? _____ When? _____

Education

	Name of Institution	Year(s) Attended	Did You Graduate?	Subject(s) Studied
Grammar School				
High School				
College				
Graduate Education				
Other Training				

Special Training/Skills: _____

_____

_____

U.S. Military or Naval Service: _____ Rank: _____

(Continued on other side)

Former Employers

Date (Month/Year)	Name & Address of Employer	Salary	Position	Reason for Leaving
From				
To				
From				
To				
From				
To				

References

Provide the names of three persons, not related to you, whom you have known for a minimum of one year.

Name	Address	Phone Number	Business	Years Known
1.				
2.				
3.				

Authorization

"I certify that the facts in this application are true and complete to the best of my knowledge and understand that, if employed, falsified statements on this application shall be grounds for dismissal.

I authorize investigation of all statements contained herein and the references and employers listed above to give you any and all information concerning my previous employment and any pertinent information they may have, personal or otherwise, and release the company from all liability for any damage that may result from utilization of such information.

I also understand and agree that no representative of this company has any authority to enter into any agreement for employment for any specified period of time, or make any agreement contrary to the foregoing, unless it is in writing and signed by an authorized company representative."

Date: _____ Signature: _____

Get Started

For safety's sake, all pilots use a checklist to ensure that they inspect every aspect of an airplane before takeoff. Sure, pilots have gone through this process many times, and they know it by heart, but using an actual checklist ensures that they don't forget anything.

On the day of each of your interviews, review this list carefully and make sure you've done everything within your power to properly prepare. Knowing you're prepared for an interview will give you an added level of confidence.

_____ Get a good night's sleep before the interview. You want to look and feel rested and be totally awake and alert for your interview.

_____ Take a shower, shampoo your hair, clean your fingernails, and shave before an interview. You want to look and feel clean. After all, your appearance is the first thing a potential employer is going to notice when you arrive for an interview.

_____ Brush your teeth and use a mouthwash or breath freshener (preferably one that doesn't have a medicinal smell). Try to avoid eating between the time you brush your teeth and your interview appointment.

_____ Apply deodorant and antiperspirant. If you're nervous, if it's hot in the room, or if the employer poses difficult questions, you're probably going to sweat. To maintain a calm and cool appearance, make sure you use a good deodorant and antiperspirant.

_____ Put on your best interview outfit. Make sure, however, that it's clean, pressed, and wrinkle-free.

_____ Shine your shoes.

_____ Avoid wearing any type of perfume or cologne. Most interviews take place in an office or confined space. If your perfume or cologne is too strong (or even noticeable), it will distract the person interviewing

Continued

you. In addition, many people are allergic to perfume or cologne, and you don't want the interviewer getting a negative allergic reaction during your interview.

_____ Don't wear any flashy jewelry. For most jobs, you want to look professional, so if you're female, limit yourself to wearing only one earring in each ear. Guys—removing all earrings is probably a good idea. Also, remove tongue posts, nose rings, and any other form of highly expressive jewelry. A job interview is not the time to be showing off your individuality or making a fashion statement. Avoid wearing religious jewelry or anything with the logo of a political party, organization, or club.

_____ As for wearing makeup, less is more. Don't overdo it. If you visit any upscale department store, a salesperson in the cosmetics department will be happy to offer you free advice or even a free makeover. Most beauty salons also have makeup artists or cosmetics specialists on staff who can help you define your professional appearance when it comes to applying cosmetics. The "natural" look is always the best.

_____ Make copies of your resume and bring them along.

_____ Make copies of any letters of recommendation and your list of referrals that you want to present to the interviewer.

_____ Within your briefcase or portfolio, be sure to include a pad of paper and a working pen.

_____ Make sure you bring along your personal planner.

_____ Within your planner, or on your pad of paper, write down the name, address, telephone number, and directions to the location of the interview, and be sure to include the name of the person you have an appointment with.

_____ Plan your travel route to the interview location in advance, and make sure you leave plenty of time so that you arrive at least 15 minutes early. Whatever you do, don't be even 1 minute late.

_____ Bring along any research notes that you have gathered. If you arrive for the interview a few minutes early and you have to sit in a waiting room, it's the perfect time to review your notes.

_____ Leave your cigarettes and matches home. You don't want to smoke just before or during the interview, even if the interviewer is smoking and invites you to join him or her.

_____ Don't drink any beverages containing caffeine (cola, tea, or coffee) prior to an interview. The caffeine will act as a stimulant and could make you more nervous.

_____ Use the rest room before your interview. In addition to doing "your business," you can comb your hair, check your makeup, make sure your tie is straight, and give your overall appearance one last check.

_____ Spit out your chewing gum before entering the location of the interview.

_____ The morning of your interview, read a local newspaper or watch the local news to learn about the current news stories. Chances are, some current event will come up during the interview, and you want to appear knowledgeable about what's happening in the world around you.

_____ Just before the interview, take a few moments to visualize yourself in the interview, acting totally calm as you answer in complete sentences the questions posed to you, and generally making an excellent impression. Take a few deep breaths and try to relax. If you have done your work preparing for the interview, you already know what types of questions you'll be asked, how you plan on answering those questions, and what questions you want to ask the interviewer.

_____ Remember, the moment you arrive at the interview location and step through the front door, you should be in interview mode. Act professionally, and be polite to everyone.

_____ The final step in this preinterview checklist is to go into the interview and wow 'em!

On a Final Note

Your "performance" during an interview will be evaluated by the employer based on your appearance, personality, composure, suitability for the job, conversation, preparation, knowledge, personal skill set, work experience, and attitude. Knowing this in advance, you can properly prepare for your interview and make the best impact.

Immediately after the interview, send the interviewer a thank-you note and take any follow-up actions that you talked about during the interview.

Don't Forget

After your interview, while everything is still fresh in your mind, take out your pad and pen and write notes to yourself as you evaluate your overall interview performance and experience. Ask yourself:

- What could I have done better?
- What mistakes did I make that can be avoided in the future?
- What did I learn from the interview?
- What didn't I learn from the interview that I still need to know?
- What follow-up actions need to be taken?
- Did I do everything possible to sell myself and my skills to the interviewer?
- Could I have answered specific questions in a better way?
- Did I deal with my nervous habits appropriately?

How you present yourself before, during, and immediately after any job interview will play a major part in whether or not you ultimately receive a job offer. In addition to looking for highly qualified applicants who will be an asset to the company, employers look for applicants that they believe they'll work well with and that will fit nicely within the company from a personality standpoint.

Now you have the basic tools and knowledge necessary for landing jobs. However, finding available positions is a challenge since almost 80 percent of all job openings never get advertised in the help-wanted section of the newspaper or on the Internet. As you'll soon discover, networking plays a critical role in the job search process, so that's the topic covered in the next chapter.

✔ The best way to make an excellent first impression is to come prepared and to look great.

✔ Research the company and the industry in which you would like to work. This will help you to anticipate the types of questions you'll be asked. It will also be a great source of questions for you to ask the interviewer.

✔ Be prepared to fill out an employment application.

CHAPTER 6

Mastering the Art of Networking

Do I Need to Read This Chapter?

→ What is "networking," and how can I benefit from "network contacts"?

→ How should I manage my network contacts? How do I make new ones?

→ How, when, and where can I expand my network contact database?

→ How can networking be a powerful tool for discovering job opportunities?

→ How can I use a referral from a network contact to get my foot in the door at a company?

→ What are the best ways to request assistance from a network contact without being a pest or taking advantage of the contact?

Yes, networking is an art, but it's also a skill that anyone can learn and take full advantage of. Sometimes it's not what you know, it's who you know when it comes to discovering exciting job opportunities. Up to 80 percent of all job openings at companies of all sizes are never actually advertised in the help-wanted section of the newspaper or on the Internet. Instead, employers fill their openings by hiring friends, acquaintances, and even relatives of their current employees. These people come recommended by people the employer respects and relies upon—current employees.

Discovering unadvertised job opportunities requires knowing the right people and having your resume in their hands at the right time. Believe it or not, word of mouth is a highly useful tool for job seekers. On a piece of paper, write down the names of between 10 and 25 friends, relatives, and acquaintances that you could call up right now in order to ask them if they know of any job openings that might be suitable for you. Even if you call up each person on your list and none of them is able to help you directly, you're virtually guaranteed that someone on your list will know someone else who can help you find and land the job you're looking for. Each of the 25 people you know most likely also know 25 people. So, by asking 25 friends and family members if they know of any job openings, you could potentially tap the knowledge of over 625 people. This is what networking is all about!

Even if a job is advertised and dozens of applicants apply, often knowing the right people, either directly or through relatives, friends, acquaintances, or business associates, is enough to get your resume package moved to the top of the employer's pile. After all, if you were an employer, would you prefer to hire a total stranger who has no connections with anyone at your company or someone who comes highly recommended by one of your reliable employees or relatives? Having someone provide an introduction for you at a company will help you to get your foot in the door. This will also give you much more credibility than someone walking in off the street applying for a job.

Quick Tips

It's not necessary for your network contact to be a top-level executive at a company in order for him or her to give you a recommendation or provide an introduction for you. Even if your contact is a low-level employee, as long as that employee has a good record with the company, his or her recommendation or introduction will carry a lot of weight. According to Howard Lincoln, chairman of Nintendo of America, Inc., "If I receive a resume cold, without a personal referral, it almost automatically gets forwarded to human resources without getting any personal attention from me. If the resume comes with a personal referral or is delivered to me by someone I know, or someone who works at Nintendo, then it has a much better chance of getting my personal attention."

For job seekers, the term *networking* is loosely defined, because it involves making contact or reinitiating contact with everyone you know, and even people you don't yet know, in order to ultimately land a job. You might not be able to pick up the phone and call the CEO, president, or a top-level executive at the company you really want to work for in order to get yourself an interview; however, someone you know might be able to make that call on your behalf.

Networking isn't a skill used only by those in search of employment. In fact, networking is an increasingly more important part of doing business, no matter what type of work you're involved in. So, if you haven't yet mastered the art of networking, now is an excellent time to acquire these vital skills.

As you'll soon see, networking is easy, and it can be both fun and rewarding. Chances are, in your life, you've probably already tapped your networking skills, whether you realized it or not. Humans are highly social creatures, and those who truly enjoy interacting with others will find networking to be an exciting and beneficial experience. It's never too early or too late to begin developing and exploiting your networking skills.

This chapter of *Job Hunting for the Utterly Confused* explores what networking is all about, and offers ideas on how to incorporate networking skills into your job search in order to uncover job opportunities and to better position yourself when applying for jobs. As you read this chapter, think about everyone you know, the people you're related to, people you have met in the past, and any well-respected and influential people you have access to either directly or indirectly. Also, think about the people whom you would really like to get to know, who might be able to assist you in landing the job you want.

Who Are Some of Your Network Contacts?

Off the top of your head, write down the names and phone numbers of 10 people you know who might be able to assist you in finding and landing a job.

1. Relative's Name: _____

   Phone Number: (____)_____

2. Relative's Name: _____

   Phone Number: (____)_____

3. Relative's Name: _____

   Phone Number: (____)_____

4. Friend's Name: _____

   Phone Number: (____)_____

5. Friend's Name: _____

   Phone Number: (____)_____

6. Friend's Name: _____

   Phone Number: (____)_____

7. Coworker's Name: _____

   Phone Number: (____)_____

8. Coworker's Name: _____

   Phone Number: (____)_____

9. Former Professor's Name: _____

   Phone Number: (____)_____

10. Former Boss's Name: _____

    Phone Number: (____)_____

What Networking Is All About

According to the Tenth Edition of *Merriam Webster's Collegiate Dictionary,* a *network* is "an interconnected or interrelated chain, group, or system" and *networking* refers to "the exchange of information or services among individuals, groups, or institutions."

Just as the thousands, perhaps millions, of computers that are connected and exchange information make up the network known as the Internet, the people whom you know or who are related to you make up your personal network. Your personal network most likely consists of dozens, perhaps hundreds, of personal and professional relationships. Each person in your network can be considered a "network contact," and when you put all your contacts together into your personal phone directory, you have created a database of network contacts. Networking is all about constantly building, maintaining, and utilizing your contacts, in this case, in order to find and land yourself a job. You'll be surprised how willing most people will be to lend you a hand or offer you advice.

By tapping your network contacts, you can:

- Obtain career advice and guidance
- Talk with others working in the industry that interests you
- Get referrals regarding other people to speak with about possible job opportunities

- Obtain information about specific companies
- Discover unadvertised job openings
- Obtain a valuable recommendation for a job
- Receive help getting your foot in the door at a company

What Are Network Contacts? How Can You Benefit from Having Them?

A network contact is anyone you know or have met that you can call upon to get a question answered or to ask for a professional favor. Thus, a network contact can be virtually anyone—a friend, a relative, a former coworker, a past boss, a former professor, a fellow health club member, a religious leader, your hairdresser, or a past classmate.

Get Started

As you begin your job search process and you're looking for job openings to apply for, go through your personal network contact database and start calling the people you know. Start by dialing the telephone.

1. Get your network contact on the phone.

2. Ask for the person's assistance. Tell the person you need a favor, and you're hoping that he or she will help you out.

3. Explain to your network contact that you're looking for a job, and describe the exact type of job you're hoping to land. Be as specific as possible when describing the type of work you're looking for.

4. Ask your network contact if he or she knows of any job openings off-hand. If your contact does, ask for the name and phone number of the person you should call regarding that job opening. Try to gather some basic information about the person you'll be calling, and determine how your network contact knows this person. Ask specifically if

it's okay for you to use your network contact's name when making the call to the person you are being referred to. Ask if your network contact would consider giving you a recommendation, or on your behalf, if he or she would actually call the person you should speak with.

5. Ask your network contact, if possible, to refer you to one or two other people whom you could call for additional assistance, or who work in your field of interest.

6. Before ending the conversation, thank your network contact for helping.

7. After getting in touch with the person your network contact referred you to, call back your network contact and tell how you made out.

8. Once someone offers assistance, send the person a thank-you note; or if you wind up landing a job as a direct result of the person's help, consider buying the person dinner or sending the person flowers to show your gratitude.

Since some people are busy, and very difficult to get on the phone, you could always send your network contact a short letter, e-mail message, or fax asking for help. After sending your written or e-mailed request for help, if you don't obtain a response, make a follow-up telephone call.

Here's a sample letter that you could send to a network contact who you think can assist you in your job search. *The scenario:* You would very much like to schedule an interview with the ABC Company, and apply for a job in the marketing department. A guy, named Jack, whom you met a few months ago at a cocktail party that was held in honor of your mutual friend Bill's 35th birthday, works for the ABC Company's finance department. You remember Jack telling you how wonderful it is to work for the ABC Company, and you kept his business card in your personal contact database, so you decide to drop him a note to see if he can assist you.

Sample Letter

John Doe
321 Second Avenue
Anywhere, NY 10002
(212) 555-5555

June 13, 1998

Mr. Jack Simon
The ABC Company
123 Main Street
Anywhere, NY 10001

Dear Jack,

Several months ago, we met at our mutual friend Bill Smith's 35th birthday celebration, and I remember you mentioning that you work for the ABC Company. I am currently seeking a new employment opportunity, and would very much like to apply for a position in ABC's marketing department.

On my behalf, would you please forward the enclosed copies of my resumes to the vice president of marketing and to the human resources department at the ABC Company? As you'll see from my resume, I have spent the past six years working in the marketing department of Widget Company, Inc., and believe I could contribute a lot to ABC's marketing efforts. After hearing your high praises for the company, I think it would be a wonderful place to work.

Anything you could do to help me obtain an appointment for an interview would be greatly appreciated. Should you have any questions, please call me at (212) 555-5555.

Thank you, in advance, for your assistance.

Sincerely,

(Signature)
John Doe

Don't Forget

1. When you correspond with a network contact who isn't a close friend or relative, be sure that you immediately refresh the person's memory about how this person knows you and when and where you met. You'll have much better results when you ask people you know or have met in person to speak with their superiors or coworkers on your behalf. Few people are willing to go out of their way to help friends of friends whom they have never met. If a friend of yours tells you that he or she has a friend who can probably help you, make a point to meet that friend in person before asking for assistance.

2. As you ask your network contacts to do you a favor, spell out specifically what you want them to do. For example, ask them to "please forward my resume to . . . ," "please introduce me to . . . ," or "please help me schedule an interview with. . . ." Don't simply send them your resume, tell them you want a job, and rely on them to figure out how they can best help you. Asking someone to forward a resume to a coworker with a recommendation takes only minutes of someone's time, and most people are extremely willing to help out someone they know.

3. Be sure to briefly explain to your network contacts exactly what type of job you're looking for and provide them with a short summary of your most impressive work experience and/or skills. You want your contacts to know something about you, so they can speak highly of you to their superiors or coworkers.

How to Manage Your Network Contacts

The first rule of networking is to always trade business cards with the people you meet. While you're in between jobs, it's an excellent idea to have business cards printed with your home address, telephone number, and e-mail address displayed on them.

Every time you meet new people who you think should be added to your personal network contact database, you'll want to obtain basic contact information about them, and keep your files up to date. Here's a summary of the information you'll probably want to keep for each of your network contacts:

Full name
Title
Company
Work address
Work phone number
Work fax number
E-mail address
Pager/beeper number
Assistant's/secretary's name

If you develop a friendship with a contact, or if the contact is a relative, you'll also want the contact's:

Home address
Home phone number
Home fax number
Spouse's name
Child's (children's) name(s)
Birthday

Over the course of a month, a year, and your entire career, you're going to compile a vast database of network contacts. Obviously, you're not going to keep in touch with everyone you meet. However, you should never toss away business cards or contact information. Part of being a good networker is establishing a method of organizing your contacts in a way that's easy and keeps your contacts within reach. There are many ways you can keep track of your network contacts, including:

- *Maintaining a Business Card File.* From any office supply store, you can pick up an expandable business card file or a three-ring binder with plastic pages designed to hold business cards. Be sure that your file is expandable so that you can add additional pages as your personal network database expands over time. An alternative method of organizing your business cards is to purchase a file box, such as one designed to hold recipes, along with alphabetical file dividers that fit within the file box. Yet another alternative for manually filing contact names is to maintain a traditional alphabetical Rolodex using inserts that you can attach business cards to.

Don't Forget

As a general rule, if you're using a manual filing system (as opposed to a computerized one), you'll want to file network contacts using their company's name, as opposed to their last name. Months down the road, you'll be able to find specific contacts faster, because you'll probably remember a person's company affiliation, not his or her name.

- *Compiling a Personal Address Book.* Address books come in all shapes and sizes. Be sure that you get one that can be expanded and neatly updated, since you'll most definitely have to edit address and phone number listings as people move or change phone numbers. If you find yourself constantly on the go, you'll probably want to purchase a smaller address book, so you can easily take it with you.

- *Using Contact Management Computer Software.* For personal computer users, there are a variety of different contact management/scheduling software packages that make maintaining a personal and professional network contact database easy. These software packages allow you to search your database by keyword (in case you forget someone's name), sort your contacts, and print out customized address books that you can carry with you. Virtually all the contact management software packages on the market also work in conjunction with all major word processors and e-mail systems, allowing you to easily address your correspondence and perform mail merge functions. In Chapter 2, which focuses on how to get yourself organized, some of the specific contact management software packages, including ACT!, Microsoft Outlook, Microsoft Schedule+, and Lotus Organized, are examined closely. If you have a personal computer, using one of these contact management software packages is an absolute must.

- *Using a Personal Digital Assistant.* In today's high-tech world, a personal digital assistant (PDA) offers the power of a personal computer in a unit that fits in the palm of your hand. Virtually all the PDAs on the market offer built-in programs to handle contact management, scheduling, and text editing/word processing. The more advanced models, such as Casio's popular Cassiopeia, actually operate using a scaled-down version of Microsoft Windows 95, and allow users to send and receive e-mail and faxes, surf the Internet, and quickly transfer files between the handheld unit and a desktop PC. A typical PDA can maintain a contact database containing hundreds or thousands of entries, and allows you to have immediate access to your contact database anywhere you need it, because these units fit in a briefcase, purse, or even a jacket pocket. With a PDA, there's no need to store and sort business cards. Once the information is entered into your PDA, it's there forever, and can be sorted, printed, or accessed with the touch of a button. No matter what type of career you're pursuing, chances are you'll find many uses for a PDA in your personal and professional life, especially if you use a daily planner, personal address book, or word processor; send and receive e-mail; and/or perform any type of mathematical calculations.

Building and maintaining your personal network contact database is only the beginning. The true benefits of networking become apparent when you begin to tap the connections, experience, talents, and knowledge of the people in your database.

How, When, and Where to Expand Your Network Database

There are countless places and ways you can meet new people and expand your personal network database. Depending on your personal situation and the industry you hope to work in, not all of these networking opportunities may be appropriate, but keep your options open and be creative.

The key to being a successful networker is getting yourself out there, in places where you'll have the opportunity to meet others. Don't get discouraged if you don't immediately encounter people who can directly help you. In addition to helping you find and land a job now, the people you meet could be useful later in your career, plus you could easily make some friends along the way.

Every time you meet someone new, you have expanded your network database. As a result, you should always be in networking mode. The trick is to keep track of the people you meet, organize these contacts, and have them at your fingertips when you need to get in touch with them.

Don't Forget

As you encounter people who are helpful, it's important to periodically stay in touch with them, and the holiday season is the best time to do that. Sending out holiday cards is an ideal way to say hello and maintain loose contact with people you've met throughout the year.

In your professional and personal life, you can expand your personal network database by meeting people in all sorts of places. Here are just a few ideas on where you can meet people with similar interests or with influence at various companies you might want to work for:

Use the Internet   Special-interest chat rooms, news groups, and forums are an ideal way to meet people from around the country (and around the world) who have similar interests as you.

Talk to People While Traveling   You never know whom you'll meet when traveling. Strike up conversations with the people you sit next to on airplanes, buses, or trains. If you're staying at a hotel, strike up conversations with people you meet when you're sitting in the lobby. When you least expect it, you might bump into someone who will offer you a job.

> *A real-life story:* Melissa is a 26-year-old graduate student at Wharton who is studying finance. While interviewing at various companies for a summer job, she was invited by one potential employer to fly from Pennsylvania to Los Angeles for an in-person interview. Sitting next to her on the airplane on her way out to Los Angeles was a vice president at a fast-growing high-tech company. During the flight, Melissa and this executive struck up a conversation, and by the time they landed, she was offered an exciting job, which she later accepted after a formal interview and meeting. The moral of this story is that even if you're en route to a job interview, you never know when a better opportunity will present itself.

Attend Meetings of Professional Organizations, Associations, and Clubs   Just about every profession has some type of national organization or association that holds regular meetings. Chances are, the organization also has regional chapters, which could provide you with a chance to meet and mingle with people currently working in the industry you're interested in. While at any library, be sure to check out *The Encyclopedia of Associations* and/or *Regional, State and Local Organizations* published by Gales Research, Inc. These directories offer detailed information about thousands of associations and organizations relating to various industries and professions.

Talk to Members of Your Health Club, Golf Club, or Country Club
If you're spending 30 minutes on a treadmill or exercise bike at a

health club, strike up conversations with the people working out next to you. Ask what type of work they do and if they've heard about any job openings in a field that interests you.

Attend Social Gatherings   Cocktail parties, family reunions, weddings, christenings, bar mitzvahs, holiday parties, and gatherings with friends are ideal places to introduce yourself to new people and promote yourself. Tell friends that you're currently looking for a job and ask them specifically if they know anyone who works for any of the companies you plan to interview with.

Don't Forget Religious Organizations   If you belong to a church, temple, or other house of worship, attend a few social functions and/or services in order to meet congregation members. Also, be sure to speak with your priest, rabbi, or religious leader, who will be able to introduce you to other members of your congregation that work in or are affiliated with the industry you want to work in.

Fall Back on Your Education   If you attended or graduated from a high school, college, or grad school, contact former professors, fellow alumni, and classmates, the career services office, and anyone else affiliated with the institution that might know someone who could help you find a job. For example, if you're interested in a marketing job, contact your former marketing professor. He or she probably keeps in touch with other former students and will know of job openings.

Contact Past Bosses   Look back upon your career and think about any of your past bosses, supervisors, or coworkers that might be able to help you. Consider people you worked for while in school, including any part-time jobs, summer jobs, or internships.

Contact Acquaintances from around Town   Think about all the people you interact with on a daily basis, who are in contact with hundreds of people from all walks of life. People like your doctor, dentist, hairstylist, manicurist, masseuse, or even the person behind the counter at your dry cleaner. All these people interact with dozens of other people each day, and probably know someone who could help you land the job you want.

Call Your Friends and Family Members Who Work in the Media
If you happen to know people who work in the media (for a newspaper, TV station, radio station, or magazine), contact them since these people are almost always very well connected. Their job often requires them to interact with and/or interview prominent people and news makers.

Do Charity Work   Getting involved with a charity is an excellent way to do some good for others, and at the same time meet people who can help you get ahead in your career. Charity events are often attended by business leaders and executives from all sorts of companies and industries; thus these events are excellent networking opportunities. (Even if you don't have money to donate to a charity, if you can donate a few hours of your time to do some volunteer work, you can still take advantage of the opportunity to network within the organization.)

Attend Trade Shows   Industry-oriented trade shows are where everyone who is anyone working in a specific industry gathers. Attending an industry-oriented trade show for the industry you want to work in might require some travel, but the benefit is that you can meet with top-level people from each of the companies involved in an industry. To find out when and where an industry trade show for your industry will be held, check out any industry-oriented publications.

Contact Past Clients and Customers   If you've had a job in the past or you're currently employed and looking for a new job, think about which of your past clients and/or customers may have job openings or know of openings in the industry you want to work in.

Attend Career and Job Fairs   Here's an opportunity to meet informally with headhunters and human resources people from all sorts of different companies. Some job fairs cater to specific careers or industries, while others have a more general focus. Keep an eye on the career section of your local newspaper for a listing of career and job fairs in your city. You can also visit the First Job Web Site (www.firstjob.com) or 1st Impressions Resume & Career Strategies' Web site (www.1st-imp.com/jobfair) for a listing of career and job fairs scheduled throughout America.

Get a Temp Job   Later in this book (Chapter 11), you'll read an interview with Lisa Elias, a branch operations manager for Kelly Services. Lisa discusses how working temp jobs (through an agency like Kelly Services), while you're actually looking for full-time employment, is an excellent way to make business contacts and demonstrate your skills to potential employers. It's very common for people hired as a temporary employees to be hired full-time after they have proved what they can offer to the company.

Read Industry Trade Magazines   Every industry has its own trade magazine or newsletter. Reading these publications will help you learn about an industry—what companies are the key players, who the top executives in the industry are, and what types of jobs are available. If you don't know the names of trade magazines that cater to the industry you hope to work in, ask someone who works in the industry, or visit a local library. For example, if you work in advertising, the magazines you should be reading on a regular basis are *Ad Week* and *Advertising Age.* People working in the music industry should read *Radio & Records, Mix Magazine, Recording,* and *Billboard.* Accountants or CPAs should read *Accounting Technology, Accounting Today,* and *The CPA Review.*

How Networking Can Be a Powerful Tool for Discovering Job Opportunities

Since over 80 percent of all jobs are never advertised, it's up to you to discover employment opportunities by talking with everyone you know. Mention that you're currently looking for a job as a (insert job title), and specifically ask people if they know of any job openings available, or if they know someone who might know of a job opening. In situations like this, you're basically looking for a needle in a haystack.

You might wind up talking with 100 people, and only two will offer some type of job lead. All you are looking for, however, is to land one suitable job that you're qualified for, and any assistance you can get along the way will make your search that much easier. It's definitely less stressful to ask 100 friends and acquaintances if they know of any job openings than it is to track down and respond to 100 suitable help-wanted ads and apply for those jobs, with no connections to the company.

A successful job search will probably require you to tap the resources of your network, plus respond to help-wanted ads or advertised job openings. By following up every lead possible, you'll land the job you want faster.

Using a Referral to Get Your Foot in the Door at a Company

Sometimes, all it takes to guarantee yourself an interview with someone at the company you want to work for is an introduction. Having a current employee at the company personally introduce you or provide a positive recommendation to someone in human resources or to a manager or executive with the company often carries a lot of weight. It doesn't matter what position the person who introduces you holds within the company, as long as the person has a good employment record.

As soon as you know what companies you'd like to work for, you should immediately begin tracking down anyone you know who works for that company or who is somehow affiliated with the company. The person you find might be a friend of a friend or a friend of a relative. Be sure to take the time to meet the person and ask him or her to make an introduction on your behalf, and you'll be able to reap the benefits of tapping that contact's resources.

What happens if you exhaust your search efforts, but can't find anyone you know who works for the company you want to work for? Well, it's time to meet someone new. Instead of sending an unsolicited resume, pick up the phone and try to introduce yourself to the person at the company you'd like to work for. For example, if you're hoping to land a job in the marketing department, one of the people you should try to meet or speak with is the company's vice president of marketing.

As soon as you determine the title of the person you should contact (your target person at the company), pick up the telephone and call the company's main phone number. Ask the receptionist or company operator for the full name and extension of the person you hope to introduce yourself to. Also, ask for that person's fax number (if you have access to a fax machine). If the company operator asks who is calling, give your name, but don't say what you're calling about unless you're specifically asked. Most company operators are instructed to forward job seekers to the human resources department instead of directly to a company executive.

Once you have the person's full name (including the correct spelling of the name, and you're sure of the person's gender), you have two options. Either you can attempt to reach this person on the phone, or you can fax the person a short letter introducing yourself. But plan out your agenda before you make contact with one of the company's busy executives. What do you want from this person? Be prepared to explain exactly what type of job you're looking for and briefly what your qualifications are. Without speaking too fast, you want to peak the person's interest in you as quickly as possible. Your goal in making contact with someone at the company, who is outside of human resources, should be to get that person to request your resume and to invite you in for an interview. Once the person requests your resume, you are no longer sending an unsolicited resume to the company.

If you choose to try reaching your target person on the phone, the best times to call are either first thing in the morning (just before business hours begin), during lunch, or after 5:00 p.m. This is when the person's secretary or assistant probably isn't screening calls, and the person you're trying to reach is more apt to answer the phone. Try to get your target person on the phone without leaving voice-mail messages. This may require you to place several calls. If you wind up speaking with a secretary, be incredibly friendly, because that secretary is the gatekeeper for the person you're trying to reach, and he or she will ultimately decide if you're going to get through to that person. Politely introduce yourself, explain that you are looking for a job in your target person's department, and note that you were really hoping to introduce yourself before sending your resume. Explain that you only need a moment of the target person's time. If the secretary explains that the person you are trying to reach isn't available, ask when a good time would be to call back, or ask if you could schedule a short telephone appointment. Be sure to say *please* and *thank you* and act genuinely grateful for the secretary's help.

Don't Forget

1. One excellent way to reach a target person is to first do some research and find a recently published article in a magazine or newspaper that featured an interview with that person. Now, when you call, you can explain that you really want to speak with the target person because you read the person's interview and you were fascinated by what the person had to say about whatever topic the article was about.

2. Another approach to take with the target person is to explain that you're interested in the person's line of work as well as the person's company, and you were hoping to get some advice about how to

break into that industry or company. This works exceptionally well if you already know something about the person you're contacting and you explain that you're a student attending a college or university and that you're about to graduate.

Should you decide to contact your target person at the company by sending a fax, write a short letter using a business-letter format. Your letter should consist of just two or three short paragraphs and should be typed or created using a word processor. Within the letter, explain the reason why you're sending it, specifically what you hope to achieve (a telephone or in-person interview), and why the person should agree to take the time out of a busy schedule to speak with or meet with you. The letter you send should be personalized to the recipient and state specifically what position you're interested in applying for.

By faxing a short introductory letter to your target person, you have a better chance of having it read and receiving a response than if you send a formal cover letter and resume that's unsolicited.

Never Become a Pest

There's a fine line between tracking down a contact and asking for help and becoming a total pest. When you leave a message for someone to call you back, be brief and keep the message simple. Make sure you include your full name and phone number. In one or two sentences, explain why you're calling. During a 2-week period, never leave multiple voice-mail messages or more than two or three messages with a secretary. If the person you're trying to reach doesn't call you back within 2 or 3 days, the person either is too busy or has no interest in helping you. In either case, move on to someone else. Persistence is important, but don't develop a reputation for being a pest when trying to reach someone within a company.

When people agree to help you, do whatever you can to accommodate their schedules, promptly provide them with whatever information they ask for, and show your gratitude. Never take advantage of people's generosity or willingness to assist you, or while acting on your behalf push them to do something they're not comfortable doing.

Remember, what comes around goes around. Down the road, the person who helped you might someday call you and ask for help. When this happens, it's your responsibility to do whatever you can to pay back the favor. Likewise, once you're happily employed, if someone approaches you looking for help landing a job, take it upon yourself to offer whatever assistance you can.

Success expert Barry Farber could easily be called a networking guru. In Chapter 11 of this book, you'll read an interview with Barry, who offers some additional advice on how to make the most out of networking in order to find and land an awesome job.

It's true that most jobs are never advertised in the help-wanted section of the newspaper or on the Internet. These jobs are advertised through word of mouth, and so to find them will require that you network. Start picking up the phone and calling all the people you know and ask them if they've heard about any job openings in your area of expertise. Talk with friends, relatives, past coworkers, previous bosses, former professors, and people you interact with on a daily basis (your hairdresser, dry cleaner, doctor, dentist, health club director, tennis instructor, etc.). You never know where a job lead will come from. Not everyone you ask is going to be able to offer you assistance. However, all you need is to land one job, so keep finding new ways to meet people and keep expanding your circle of network contacts.

One excellent way to meet new people and to find people who are working in the industry you hope to find a job in is to explore the Internet. Visit chat rooms, access news groups, and explore Web pages that pertain to your occupation. The Internet is a vast and powerful resource that should not be overlooked by any job seeker. The next chapter explores some of the ways you can use a personal computer and the Internet to assist you in finding and landing a job.

✔ Networking is the exchange of information or services among individuals, groups, or institutions.

✔ A network contact is anyone you know or have met that you can call upon to get a question answered or to ask for a professional favor.

✔ Good networking depends on having a method of organizing your contacts that's easy and highly accessible, whether it be a manual filing system, address book, contact management software, or personal digital assistant.

CHAPTER 7

Using the Personal Computer as a Powerful Job Search Tool

Do I Need to Read This Chapter?

→ How do I choose and use specialized resume creation software?

→ How do I use a personal computer to perform company and industry-related research?

→ What are some of the popular career-related Web sites, and what do they offer?

→ How do I find job opportunities on-line?

→ What is the difference between a traditional resume and an electronic resume?

A personal computer, especially one that's equipped with a modem and is set up to connect to a major on-line service (such as America Online, The Microsoft Network, or CompuServe) and the Internet's World Wide Web, can be an extremely powerful job search tool. Even if you don't actually own a personal computer, you can obtain access to one at a local college or university, a public library, an instant print shop (such as CopyMax, Alpha Graphics, or Copy Cop), or a cyber café, or by visiting someone you know who owns a computer. During your job search, you may find it helpful to rent a computer for a few weeks so that you can work from home and take full advantage of the power and advantages that a personal computer offers to job seekers.

This chapter of *Job Hunting for the Utterly Confused* makes the assumption that you are familiar with the use of a Windows-based PC computer or a Macintosh computer. If you don't happen to be one of the growing number of computer-literate people, don't despair, but don't skip this portion of the book either. Find a friend or family member who is computer-literate, and ask for help. It's an excellent idea to visit your local computer store or community college and sign up for an introduction to computers and/or an introduction to the Internet class. Becoming computer-literate is just one way you can enhance your personal skill set, which is something that makes you more attractive to potential employers.

Creating a Professional Resume Using Specialized Software

Using a personal computer equipped with specialized resume creation software (sold separately), you can design a professional-looking resume easily, and can instantly edit or customize your resume as needed. One of the biggest benefits of using this type of software is that the computer formats your resume for you. The software is also designed to help you choose the best wording and format to meet your needs. These software packages are sold at most popular computer, software, and office supply stores, such as Egghead Software, CompUSA, Computer City, Staples, and Office-Max. For the job seeker, this software can be a major time-saver and an excellent investment.

There are many ways you can create your resume:

- You can whip out a typewriter and spend countless hours pecking away at the keys trying to create a professional-looking resume. (Good luck if you take this approach!)

- You can use a personal computer equipped with a word processor. The problem with this method, however, is that you have to spend time manually adjusting margins, tabs, typestyles, and fonts in order to create a document that neatly fits on one page. Thus, you really have to be comfortable using your word processor's desktop publishing features. You're better off spending your valuable time focusing on your resume's content and not having to spend time formatting it. A standard word processor requires you to do your own formatting. Once you have your document complete, however, you can edit it or customize it quickly and easily.

- If you have some extra cash, you can hire a professional resume creation expert. This option could cost you up to several hundred dollars, plus you'll probably have to pay extra each time you want to make changes to your resume or customize it for a job you're applying for. For people who have a lot of trouble putting their thoughts and ideas down on paper, and determining for themselves what information they should include in their resume, a professional resume creation expert can provide valuable assistance. If, however, you're confident in your abilities to choose the content for your resume, there's no need to pay someone for assistance. After reading the resume-related chapter of this book (Chapter 3), you should feel confident in your abilities to create a resume on your own.

- You can write out your resume by hand and then take it to a professional typist or print shop to create the final document for you.

This method is cheaper than hiring a professional resume creation consultant, but it becomes entirely your responsibility to determine what information will be featured in your resume and what resume format you'll use.

- You can use specialized resume creation software on your personal computer, and then edit, customize, and print out professional-quality resumes as you need them. When you print out a resume that you created on your computer, be sure to use a laser printer or high-quality ink-jet printer. Print out a separate resume for each potential employer. (Don't use a photocopy machine to make copies of your resume. Either print out a new resume for each potential employer, or bring your resume to a professional print shop to have it duplicated.)

Most career counselors and resume preparation experts agree that one of the best ways to get attention when applying for virtually any job is to custom-tailor your resume for the position you're applying for.

If you visit a computer software store, you'll find several PC- and Mac-based resume creation software packages that sell for between $15 and $40. The best software packages in this category do a lot more than just print out resumes. Look for a software package that automatically formats your resume information into a variety of different layouts and that allows you to easily customize your resume for each job opportunity. This process becomes even easier when the software offers a spelling checker, "action-word" glossary, and thesaurus to help you add impact and accuracy to your resume.

Your investment in a resume creation software package will go further if the software also helps you write and format cover letters, and provides a large database of sample resumes and cover letters that you can use for reference and ideas. The best resume creation software packages also have a built-in contact manager and appointment scheduler, allowing you to keep track of everyone you contact regarding a job opportunity and to easily schedule your interview appointments.

These software packages are designed to walk you through the resume creation process. At the appropriate on-screen prompts, you select a resume format and then type in the required information about yourself, your education, your employment history, and your skills. The software will often offer ways of improving your resume by suggesting action words or phrases or by helping you to choose what type of information should be included. Whether you use one of these software packages or not, be sure to read the section of this book about creating high-impact resumes.

The biggest benefit of using resume creation software is that it takes the hassle out of the formatting and printing process. These packages are far easier to use than most word processors, and when it comes to creating resumes, they're also more powerful. Why spend hundreds of dollars hiring a resume preparation expert to create your resume, and then have to pay extra each time you need to edit your resume, when you can do it all yourself, easily, using any personal computer?

As powerful as these software packages are, they are primarily designed for formatting the look of your resume. Thus, the output they create is only as good as the informational content you input. It's still necessary for you to choose what information will ultimately be included in your resume and decide how that information will be conveyed.

Resume creation software works with a computer, but this is very different from applying for a job on-line using an electronic resume. The purpose of these resume creation software packages is to help you write and design resumes and cover letters that will be printed on 8.5 × 11 inch paper and ultimately be mailed, hand-delivered, or faxed to potential employers. Creating an electronic resume is also done using a computer, but the process and the end result are different. Later in this section, you'll learn the difference between a traditional resume and an electronic resume.

To find the resume software that best fits your needs, visit a local computer software store and read each software package's box for a list of features that each offers.

Here are some of the popular PC-based resume creation software packages you'll find available where you buy your software (Macintosh versions of several of these software titles are also available):

- Tom Jackson Presents the Perfect Resume (Davidson & Associates, $34.95)
- WinWay Resume 4.0 (WinWay Corporation, $39.95)
- Adams JobBank Fast Resume Suite (Adams Media Corp., $39.95)
- You're Hired! (DataTech Software, $19.95)
- Resume Power 95 (DataTech Software, $39.95)
- Resume Writer (Expert Software, $14.95)

Let's Take a Closer Look at *Tom Jackson Presents the Perfect Resume*

One of the best-selling resume creation software packages is *Tom Jackson Presents the Perfect Resume* (Davidson & Associates). This is a multimedia CD-ROM that operates on virtually any PC-based computer running Windows 3.1 or Windows 95. The software also works on Macintosh computers. *The Perfect Resume* is an excellent resource for all job seekers because this software package is loaded with many highly useful features and yet it is very easy to operate.

Tom Jackson is a career development expert who provides advice and instruction on a wide variety of job-search-related topics. *The Perfect Resume* takes advantage of a computer's multimedia capabilities to combine computer graphics, sound, and live-action video instruction (Figures 7.1 and 7.2).

Figure 7.1   Look for *Tom Jackson Presents the Perfect Resume* where computer software is sold. This is just one of the software packages available that can help you create a resume with ease.

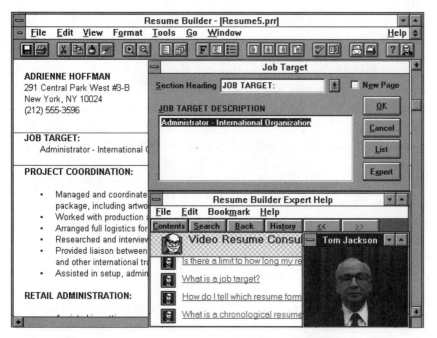

Figure 7.2   Here's a sample screen for *The Perfect Resume.*

As you'd expect from a resume creation software package, the main module of *The Perfect Resume* is the "Resume Builder." All you have to do is choose a resume format and then fill in the blanks on the screen with your personal information, education, work experience, skills, etc. The software will then automatically format your resume. To help you write a resume that will capture the attention of the potential employer, the software offers a database of over 100 sample resumes that you can use to help you generate ideas for your own resume. There's also a database of job titles, professional skills, and action words that you can incorporate into your resume and cover letters to add impact.

Many of the resume creation software packages, including this one, offer a built-in spelling checker, but you should always carefully proofread your resume and cover letters before sending them out. In fact, you should be extra careful and also ask one or two friends or family members to proofread your resume and cover letters to ensure that the documents you send out are 100 percent error-free. The slightest error in your resume or cover letter could result in your getting passed over for a job opportunity.

In addition to walking you through the resume creation process and helping you to create a professional-looking resume, *The Perfect Resume* offers a "Power Letters" module to help you write customized cover letters and follow-up letters. This module works in conjunction with the software's built-in "Job Search Manager" module, which is a contact manager designed to help you keep track of everyone you make contact with in regard to various job opportunities. Since the "Job Search Manager" works as a personal electronic address and telephone book, once you enter the names, phone numbers, and addresses of the potential employers, this information can be copied to your cover letters and follow-up letters, making it easy to send personalized correspondence.

When you start applying for multiple jobs simultaneously, you'll have to keep track of names, phone numbers, addresses, and other information about each person at each company you make contact with. Using contact management software is ideal for keeping track of this information in an organized way. For example, suppose you send out a bunch of resumes and cover letters, and a potential employer calls you back. Using contact management software, you can instantly access the notes you entered about what position you applied for, who the potential employer is, what information you actually sent, and when you sent the information.

Resume creation software, like *The Perfect Resume,* will assist you in creating the best possible resume and cover letters. When you combine the advice and instruction offered by this software package with the information offered in this book, you'll be able to create marketing tools for yourself that will get attention.

Cybersurfing for a Job

To take advantage of the career-related information offered on the Internet, you'll need to have access to a personal computer (either a desktop computer or a laptop computer) that is either PC-compatible or Macintosh-compatible. The computer should be equipped with a modem (14.4K, 28.8K, 56K, or faster), and also have a high-quality ink-jet or laser printer connected to it. You'll also need access to a local Internet service provider or to one of the major on-line services, such as America Online, The Microsoft Network, or CompuServe. These major on-line services provide access to the Internet's World Wide Web, but also feature their own on-line content, news services, and other resources that job seekers might find useful.

There are local Internet service providers in every major city. AT&T, Sprint, and MCI also offer Internet access, plus there are many other nationwide Internet service providers. All these companies offer flat-rate, unlimited access to the Internet, e-mail, and the World Wide Web for under $20 per month (although most offer cheaper price plans for people who won't be using the service too much). If you would rather use a local Internet service provider, check your telephone book or visit a local computer store and ask for a referral.

A Few National Internet Service Providers

Before you can start surfing the Web, you must sign up for access with an Internet service provider or one of the major on-line services. Each of the following companies will provide you, free of charge, with the communications software you'll need to get yourself on-line.

America Online	(800) 827-6364
AT&T World Net	(800) 967-5363
CompuServe	(800) 848-8199
Galaxy Internet Service	(888) 334-2529/(617) 433-5500
MCI	(800) 955-5210
The Microsoft Network	(800) 386-5550
MindSpring	(800) 719-4332
Sprint Internet Passport Service	(800) 887-4646

Are you feeling a bit overwhelmed by this whole job search thing? When connected to an on-line service or the Internet, you have a vast amount of job-related information at your fingertips. Whether you're looking for an entry-level position, or you have years of experience and you're looking to switch jobs or careers, the information that's available to you on-line will prove to be extremely valuable. So if you're afraid of the computer technology that's available to you, *get over it!* And if you're totally non-computer-literate, have no fear. Cybersurfing has nothing to do with the beach or getting wet.

You could easily spend countless hours in a stuffy library sifting through newspapers, magazines, annual reports from companies, industry directories, phone books, and other reference materials as you attempt to learn about career opportunities. An alternative is to hang out at home, wearing your most comfortable sweatpants and T-shirt, surfing the Internet in order to gather information that's timely and pertains specifically to your career-related interests.

Using a PC to help you discover job opportunities doesn't mean you're transforming yourself into a computer geek or nerd. To get a job that you're going to enjoy and succeed in, you must use every tool that's available to you. Here's just a sampling of the information and services available to you in cyberspace. You can:

- Gather tips and information for creating your resume
- Post your resume in electronic databases to be read by potential employers
- Perform quick and easy research on virtually any company or industry
- Learn about career fairs taking place in a city near you
- Scan electronic databases containing job listings
- Read the help-wanted sections of major daily newspapers that appear on-line
- Meet people on-line as you practice your networking skills to learn about job opportunities

No matter how you get yourself on-line, if you're looking to make great strides in your job or career search, you'll find that cyberspace is the place to be.

Scaring Up Job Opportunities Using The Monster Board

One of the best places to begin your on-line job search is The Monster Board, a service available on the Internet's World Wide Web (http://www.monster.com). In case you're not yet technologically savvy, the Internet is a worldwide network of computers. When you connect your computer to the Internet, via one of the major on-line services or a local Internet service provider, you immediately have access to the information, services, and databases from any company, government agency, university, or privately owned computer that's also connected to this tremendous network.

The Monster Board is part of a new generation of job recruitment tools that's available to you 7 days per week, 24 hours per day (Figure 7.3). This service provides job seekers, like you, with a place to look for employers and employment information, and a place where employers can present themselves to candidates with a high degree of sophistication. By accessing The Monster Board's World Wide Web site, you'll gain access to the service's:

- *Career Search Database.* A collection of job and career opportunities that's updated daily. This database can be searched by location, industry, company, job title, job area, or keyword. Best of all, you can sort through literally thousands of job opportunities (many of which are exclusively posted on The Monster Board), and the whole process takes just minutes. Every day, additional companies post their new job openings on The Monster Board, so you can expect to see at least 50,000 job opportunities in the database at any given time.

- *Employer Profiles.* The MonsterFolio offers in-depth information about hundreds of companies, as well as direct links to each company's own Internet site. The MonsterView database contains one-page overviews of thousands of companies. The information about each of the companies listed in this area is highly detailed and is designed to meet your needs as the applicant. A typical Monster-Folio contains a company's background, information about the specific job openings currently available, and the contact information you'll need to apply for a job at that company. If a company prefers to receive a resume via e-mail, details about how to submit your resume are also included. One great thing about distributing your resume via e-mail is that you'll save a few bucks, because you

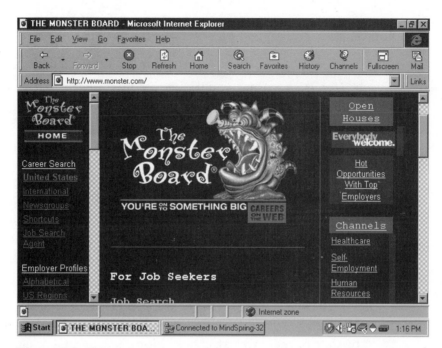

Figure 7.3   Use any Internet service provider to gain access to The Monster Board.

won't have to buy that fancy watermarked paper to print your resume on. Electronic resume distribution is both fast and cheap.

- *Resume City.* This resume database allows job seekers (that's you) to post their resume on-line, using a specific electronic format. Recruiters can easily scan this database to target candidates through keyword searches. If you have the skills and experience an employer is looking for, an employer can call you after accessing your resume on-line. This service, like everything else offered on The Monster Board (and similar services), is free of charge.

- *Resume Builder.* Use this portion of The Monster Board to help you create an electronic resume that you can post in Resume City and/or in other on-line resume databases.

- *ROAR.* This area of The Monster Board is designed specifically for college and grad school students who are about to launch their career. This portion of The Monster Board focuses on entry-level positions and job opportunities.

- *The CEO Exchange.* A forum for top-level executives.
- *Hot Tracks.* Here you'll discover tips, advice, and strategies for finding the hottest jobs. This area offers you a chance to get some advice from experts in the field.
- *Career Fair Listings.* Find out when and where career fairs will be held in your area.

So what can The Monster Board actually do for you? Well, if you're looking for a job, head for the Career Search area of The Monster Board. You need to provide three pieces of information in order to begin searching the job database. (Don't worry, the questions are easy.)

First, select the geographical location where you want to work. You can be general and select "Any," or narrow down your search by state or region. Next, choose a job discipline. Once again, you can choose "Any." However, you'll benefit more by narrowing your search and choosing one of the menu options. Finally, you can really narrow down your search, if you wish, by selecting specific companies that have job openings in your area of interest. Based on your responses to these questions, The Monster Board will search its database and provide you with a detailed listing of job opportunities that meet your needs.

Suppose you're looking for an entry-level position as an accountant at any type of company that's located in the Boston, Massachusetts, area. You can open up the phone book and start calling dozens of companies to see if job openings are available, or you can take an easier route. From The Monster Board's Career Search main menu, select the Career Search option. At the Select Job Location question, select "MA—Boston." At the Select Job Disciplines question, highlight "Finance—Accounting." For now, ignore the Select Companies option, since you want to see all the related job listings in the database. Now, click the mouse on the Search For Jobs icon, and let the computer do the work. Within a few moments, a message stating the number of job openings the computer has found that meet your criteria will be displayed. Click the mouse on the View Jobs icon to see the list of jobs that the computer has discovered. Each job listing will look something like a text-based help-wanted ad from a newspaper. Once again, use the mouse to click the box located next to the job listings you're interested in, and you'll have the opportunity to apply for those jobs on-line or obtain additional information.

On the day a search was done for this example, the computer searched the database's 14,680 current job openings for accountants and narrowed the possibilities down to 62 (all of which were entry-level accounting positions in the Boston area). This entire search process took less then 2 minutes. Image how long it would have taken you to find and then read through enough help-wanted ads in a newspaper to discover 62 potential job opportunities that might be suitable for you. Using the Internet really is a valuable, timesaving tool.

From the list of jobs that the computer compiles for you, you'll be able to examine each job posting closely, determine whom you should contact, and find out how you should make contact (telephone call, U.S. mail, fax, e-mail, etc.). If you want to learn more about any of the companies that have posted job openings on The Monster Board, the Employer Profiles area is the place to visit next.

Even if you think you know where you want to work, or in what industry, one excellent strategy is to take full advantage of the Resume Builder feature of The Monster Board. This allows you to post your own resume electronically, so that employers can find you. Is this a surefire way to get a job? Nope. But it can provide you with leads from companies that you know are hiring and are interested in you. Posting your resume in The Monster Board's resume database costs nothing, so what have you got to lose? Before posting your resume on-line, be sure to check out the section on electronic resumes later in this chapter, which describes how to create an electronic resume that works. Be aware that when you submit an electronic resume, chances are no human is going to read it. Instead, computers are going to be scanning your resume looking for keywords that the recruiter has predetermined.

The Monster Board offers an extremely easy-to-use graphics interface that makes using each feature of this service fast and fun, and because this service is part of the Internet's World Wide Web, it's readily available to anyone who's on-line. Aside from The Monster Board, there are many other job- and career-related resources available to you on the Internet, many of which offer similar services to those offered by The Monster Board.

While you're on-line surfing the Web, be sure to check out these other popular career-related Web sites. Many of these sites offer job listings that are not published in newspapers or anywhere else but in cyberspace.

- First Job: The Web Site — http://www.firstjob.com
- National Business Employment Weekly Online — http://www.nbew.com
- CareerMosaic — http://www.careermosaic.com
- JobTrack — http://www.jobtrack.com
- JobLynx — http://www.joblynx.com
- CareerNet — http://www.careers.org
- CareerWeb — http://www.cweb.com
- Kaplan Online Career Center — http://www.kaplan.com
- America's Job Bank — http://www.ajb.dni.us
- CareerPath — http://www.careerpath.com
- JobSource — http://www.jobsource.com
- Career Builder — http://www.careerbuilder.com

- 1st Impressions Career Site   http://www.1st-imp.com
- The Boston Herald's Job Find   http://www.jobfind.com

A growing number of local and regional newspapers now offer Web sites that provide an on-line version of the newspaper's career section and help-wanted ads. The *Boston Herald*'s Web site (http://www.jobfind.com), for example, offers job opportunity listings available throughout New England.

Using a Search Engine to Find Other Career-Related Web Sites and Job Opportunities

To begin searching for career-related Web sites on your own, be sure to visit an Internet search engine, such as Yahoo! (http://www.yahoo.com). A search engine is a database of World Wide Web sites (sort of like an interactive Yellow Pages) that allows you to search for Web sites and on-line information based on any keyword, phrase, or topic. At the search engine's main menu, if you type in the keyword *resume,* you'll be provided with a listing of several dozen Web sites that somehow relate to resumes. Other keywords you might want to try are *career, job, job fair,* and *employment.* See Figures 7.4 and 7.5.

Here are the Internet addresses for several powerful and popular search engines that you can use to find career-related Web sites, company Web sites, news stories, and industry-specific information. All search engines allow you to enter keywords or phrases to help you locate the information you're looking for. If one search doesn't turn up what you need, try entering slightly different search criteria.

Yahoo!   http://www.yahoo.com
Excite   http://www.excite.com
Lycos   http://www.lycos.com

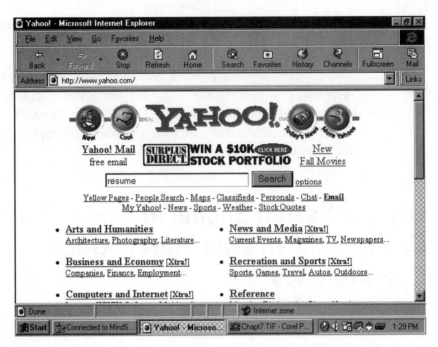

Figure 7.4   Here's the main Yahoo! screen. Enter keywords or search phrases to locate the information you're looking for.

AltaVista	http://www.altavista.com
Hotbot	http://www.hotbot.com
InfoSeek	http://www.infoseek.com
WebCrawler	http://www.webcrawler.com
DejaNews	http://www.dejanews.com

Performing Company Research On-line

Every minute of every day, new Web sites are being launched by companies throughout the world. Visiting a potential employer's Web site is an ideal way to learn more about the company. Using a search engine, try typing in the name of the company you're interested in working for, and see if that company has a Web site. For

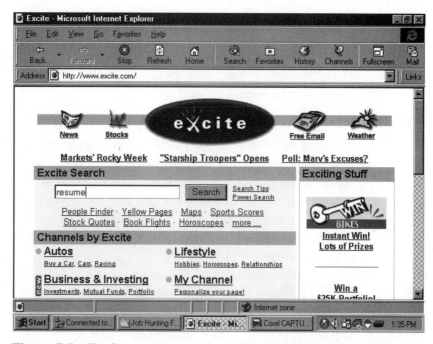

Figure 7.5   Excite works very much like Yahoo! when it comes to finding information on the Internet.

example, if you wanted to work for Lotus Development Corp., you would type in the keyword *Lotus*. From an Internet search engine, you would discover that Lotus Development has a Web site (www.lotus.com), and one of the features of this site is a listing of current job openings and information on how to apply for available jobs. If you can't find a company's Web site listed in an Internet search engine, try calling the company directly and ask whoever answers the phone if the company has a Web site, and if so, what the address for the site is. Many company Web sites feature company background information, press releases, information about the company's products and services, and other information you should know as a job applicant about to go in for an interview.

In addition to accessing Web sites operated by potential employers, you can gather information about companies by accessing industry-oriented information. Be sure to visit the Web sites for any organizations, unions, or other groups that relate to the job or career you're hoping to land.

Finally, the Internet can provide you with direct access to late-breaking news stories and published articles from newspapers and magazines (see Figure 7.6). Many of these news sites allow you to search news stories based on keywords, or allow you to create customized electronic newspapers based on the topics that are of direct interest to you. As you perform company or industry research, be sure to visit any of these Web sites to read news stories or articles about potential employers:

- My Yahoo!   http://edit.my.yahoo.com
- MSNBC   http://www.msnbc.com
- Reuters Online   http://www.reuters.com or
                    http://www.yahoo.com/headlines
- Business Wire   http://www.businesswire.com
- PR Newswire   http://www.prnewswire.com
- CNN Online   http://www.cnn.com
- Los Angeles Times Custom News Service (Associated Press)
                    http://www.latimes.com
- USA Today   http://www.usatoday.com

Electronic Library Offers a High-Tech Answer to Research

The Electronic Library (http://www3.elibrary.com) makes it possible to conduct real research over the Internet. Using this service, you can pose a question, in plain English, and launch a comprehen-

Figure 7.6 MSNBC is an electronic newspaper that you can access to read, see, and hear the latest news.

sive, simultaneous search through more than 150 full-text newspapers, hundreds of national and international magazines, a number of newswires, over 2000 books, hundreds of maps, thousands of photographs, and numerous transcripts from TV and radio talk shows and news programs.

The Electronic Library offers a 30-day free trial of its service, after which anyone can subscribe and have unlimited access to this vast information-packed database anytime for $9.95 per month or $59.95 per year. Instead of sifting through local, regional, and national newspapers and magazines looking for articles about companies you're interested in working for, the Electronic Library allows you to access thousands of media outlets and conduct complete searches in minutes.

Electronic Resumes—Beware!
Some Traditional Resumes Become
Electronic Resumes

A traditional resume is typically one printed (typed) page of information that's created to be visually appealing and easily readable by humans. Traditional resumes are usually mailed, faxed, or hand-delivered to potential employers. An electronic resume, however, is used to apply for jobs on-line. While the information offered in both types of resumes is virtually identical, the presentation of an electronic resume is different, because most electronic resumes are never actually read by a human. Instead, electronic resumes are added to databases of job applicants and then computers (operated by potential employers) scan these databases using keywords.

If you plan on sending a traditional printed resume to a medium- or large-size company, prior to submitting your resume, ask if the human resources department uses any type of automated applicant tracking system. Will your resume be scanned into a computer instead of being evaluated by a human?

Many medium- and large-size companies are now using computerized applicant tracking systems to quickly search through hundreds of resumes and narrow down their search to a handful of applicants that the human resources people will then invite in for a personal interview. Thus, if a company receives dozens or hundreds of traditional resumes in response to a help-wanted ad, the traditional paper resumes are never read. Instead, a computer that's equipped with a scanner scans the resumes into a database, sorts them electronically, and searches automatically for keywords and phrases. These scanned resumes are combined in a database with resumes that were submitted via e-mail, or downloaded from an on-line resume database. The employer's computer then breaks down all the resumes into a series of keywords and phrases. The applicants whose resumes contain the most keywords and phrases that match the list that the employer has created to describe the available job are the people who are invited in for interviews.

Tips for Submitting a Printed Resume When You Know It Will Be Scanned into a Database

When your resume gets scanned by a computer, if your resume isn't easy for the computer to read, errors can easily be made. To help avoid scanning errors, follow these 10 basic guidelines:

1. Submit your resume on white paper.
2. Be sure all printing is in black ink.
3. Use a basic font (such as Times Roman or Courier) and avoid using italics, underlines, or bold text.
4. Avoid adding graphics or lines to your resume.
5. Stick to a standard typesize (between 10- and 12-point type is ideal).
6. Use a standard resume format.
7. Incorporate "buzzwords" you think the employer is looking for. Take words or phrases directly from the help-wanted ad or job description.
8. Keep all the information on your resume straightforward and to the point. Avoid using abbreviations or industry jargon. For example, if you graduated from NYU, spell out New York University.
9. Make sure your full name is in the first line of text in your resume.
10. Avoid folding your resume or stapling it.

Changing Your Traditional Resume into an Electronic Resume

If you plan on submitting your resume to companies via e-mail, or wish to add your resume to any of the on-line resume databases that are available to applicants on Internet services, such as The Monster

Board, follow the electronic resume format guidelines provided by the employer or database operator (Figure 7.7). In describing your education, skills, work experience, interests, etc., you want to use as many keywords as possible.

In order to submit an electronic resume to The Monster Board (and most other on-line resume database services), you must take information from your traditional resume and reenter it on-line, at the appropriate prompts. Here are the prompts you will see when you create an electronic resume to be posted on The Monster Board:

Name: [Enter Text]
Address: [Enter Text]
Address: [Enter Text]
City: [Enter Text]

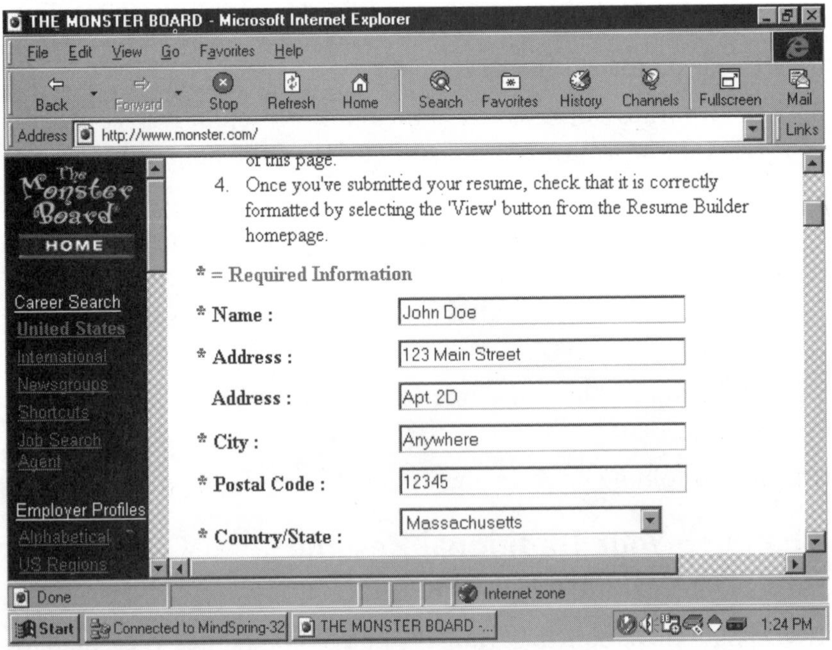

Figure 7.7 Creating an electronic resume is easy when you use the on-screen form available on The Monster Board.

Postal Code: [Enter Text]

State: [Enter Text]

Country: [Enter Text]

Phone: [Enter Text]

E-mail: [Enter Text]

Fax Number: [Enter Text]

Select Location (A list will be provided for you to choose from)

Select Discipline (A list will be provided for you to choose from)

Enter a headline for your resume. This is the first information that an employer sees about you: [Enter Text]

Cover letter, brief message, or career objective (28 lines maximum): [Enter Text]

Technical Skills (H/W, S/W Languages, etc.) (28 lines maximum): [Enter Text]

Key Nontechnical Skills (bilingual, supervisory, leadership abilities, etc.) (28 lines maximum): [Enter Text]

Current Position—From: [Enter Text] To: [Enter Text]

Job title and description of responsibilities (28 lines maximum): [Enter Text]

Previous position(s) held (company, title, skill set) (28 lines maximum): [Enter Text]

Education (degrees, licensures, certifications, designations): [Enter Text]

Areas of interest (internships, extracurricular activities, etc.): [Enter Text]

Are you willing to relocate? (Please note any specific regions): [Enter Text]

Salary Requirements: [Enter Text]

Select one of the following employment types: All, Full-Time, Part-Time/Temp/Contract

The on-line resume submission forms of most resume databases look similar. Once you enter the information, your resume will be added to a database that human resources people can access at anytime when they're looking to fill positions. Often, human resources people will access an on-line resume database if they must fill a position quickly and don't want to spend time running help-wanted ads and waiting for responses. Since posting your resume on the various on-line databases is free of charge, it's well worth your time to add your resume to at least several of them. Resume databases are a useful part of many career-related Web sites.

Before filling out the on-line resume information (which creates your electronic resume), print out the electronic submission form and spend time thinking about and formulating the best possible answers to each question asked. Try to anticipate the buzzwords that the computer will be searching for when determining your resume's compatibility with the job you're applying for. If you're submitting an electronic resume directly to a company, be sure to customize all your responses to the job. Chapter 3 will help you to write the best possible resume.

As you can see, a personal computer is a useful tool for creating your resume, writing cover letters, keeping track of contacts, scheduling interviews, performing company research, visiting career-related Web sites, tracking down news stories and industry news, and submitting electronic resumes to potential employers. If you own a personal computer, or have access to one during your job search, it's certainly one tool you should take full advantage of to make your job search process easier.

The computer and the Internet are extremely powerful and useful tools for the job seeker and should not be overlooked. If you aren't yet computer-literate, find a friend or family member who can assist you in tapping the resources available to you using today's computer technology.

Now it's time to explore that all-too-important issue of money. After all, once you land a job, you want to ensure that you'll be earning what you're worth, if not more. In the next chapter, you'll learn about salary negotiation techniques.

✔ Experts agree that a customized resume is one of the best ways to get attention, and resume creation software offers a great way to create one.

✔ The Internet allows you to search more job openings and submit your resume to more employers than was ever possible with a standard newspaper search. Find a way to get on-line and start taking advantage of this tremendous resource.

PART IV

Getting What You're Worth

CHAPTER 8

Negotiating Your Way to a Better Salary

Do I Need to Read This Chapter?

➜ How do I conduct a successful salary negotiation?

➜ When should I start talking about salary and compensation?

➜ What are the types of benefits than can make up my overall compensation package?

Once you actually receive a job offer, the next big step is the salary negotiation process. How well you are able to negotiate will most likely determine your initial salary and benefits package. Most people are very leery to participate in a salary negotiation and are willing to accept just about any offer given to them by their future employer. This isn't the approach to take.

While everyone's circumstances are different, and since how well a negotiation goes depends on the people involved, this chapter will provide you with some general guidelines for entering into a salary negotiation and offer strategies on how to emerge from that negotiation with a salary and benefits package that you're pleased with.

Conducting a Successful Salary Negotiation

The most important piece of advice you'll need when entering into a salary negotiation is to always remain calm and diplomatic, no matter what happens. Go into a negotiation with the proper mind-set. Remember, your ultimate goal is to establish a win-win situation with your potential employer. You want a job, and your potential employer is offering you a job.

Conducting a successful negotiation will require:

- Preparation
- An in-person meeting
- Communication
- Education
- Creativity
- Never being afraid to fail

Preparation

It's your responsibility to go into a negotiation totally prepared. You should know exactly what you're looking for and have a general idea (based on your research) what the employer is willing to offer. Being properly prepared will give you the ammunition you need to conduct a successful negotiation on your own behalf and will give you the added confidence that will help you to ensure you'll get what you want.

A big part of your preparation should be to anticipate your responses to any situation, before it actually happens. For example, what will you do if the employer makes an offer that's too low, or isn't willing to offer the benefits you require? Will you be willing to accept a low salary, or are you willing to play hardball and threaten to walk away and look for another job? If you actually make a "take it or leave it" threat, are you 100 percent willing to follow through on that threat? If not, don't make it.

Make a detailed checklist that includes all the topics you want to cover during a salary negotiation. This will help you to take an organized approach to your negotiation and ensure that you don't forget anything important.

Analyze what you want, but also spend some time putting together a list of what you believe the employer is looking for. Think of all the ways you can meet the employer's needs, thus giving you added value. Your strongest bargaining chip as an applicant is what you can offer to the employer based on your skills, education, experience, and accomplishments. The more the employer thinks you're worth, the higher the salary you'll be able to negotiate. In addition to pinpointing the lowest salary offer you'll consider, make a list of the top five benefits you're interested in, and put those benefits in order of importance.

Whatever happens, never immediately accept any offer. Take whatever time you feel is necessary to analyze a job offer. Once you reach an agreement, carefully review whatever employment contract you're asked to sign, and make sure that your perception of what was agreed upon is the same as the employer's. If there are any discrepancies, discuss them immediately before signing an employment contract or accepting the job.

An In-Person Meeting

Try to avoid participating in a salary negotiation over the telephone or through a series of written correspondences. Do all your negotiations in person, face-to-face with the person or people who have the power to make decisions and act on the company's behalf. Before trying to kick off a heavy-duty negotiation session, make sure you're dealing with someone at the company who has the authority to negotiate salaries.

Communication

From the moment your salary negotiation begins, you must maintain an open line of communication. In addition to being able to explain your wants, needs, and concerns, you must pay very careful attention to what the employer has to say. Listening carefully to what's said will help you determine your negotiation strategies and determine what's working and what isn't as the actual negotiation is taking place. In addition to listening, pay attention to the nonverbal communication that's taking place during the negotiation.

A good communicator will keep a positive and highly professional attitude. Don't let yourself get angry or frustrated, no matter what happens. Also, don't be afraid of silence. Not saying anything and maintaining periods of absolute silence is perfectly acceptable, and it will give you time to think about what's transpiring.

Negotiation means evaluating offers, making concessions, offering ideas, listening to what the other party has to say, and finding a happy medium where both parties are pleased with the outcome. Ideally, you want to be happy with the salary and benefits package you wind up with. You also want your employer to be happy to have you as an employee, who can make valuable contributions to the organization (at what the employer considers to be a fair price).

If the employer is trying to justify paying you less than what you're looking for, never try to defend your worth when your value as an employee is being attacked. You know your value. Don't let anyone convince you that you're worth less than you actually are. Instead, focus your efforts on promoting your merits and what you will offer to the company. Avoid trying to cover up or explain your shortfalls.

Education

Throughout your negotiation process, you must be open-minded and willing to learn about the other party's point of view. Listen carefully to your employer's objections and concerns, and based on what you learn, formulate responses that will put your employer at ease and portray you as a good investment for the company.

As a general rule, you want the employer to make the first offer in terms of a salary and benefits package. Also, as a general rule, most employers have about 20 percent flexibility when making their initial offer. So if their initial salary offer is for $30,000, they will probably consider going as high as $36,000. The job of the human resources person (or the person trying to hire you) is to get you for the least amount of money possible.

Part of your education process prior to and during the salary negotiation is to determine how badly the employer wants you and how willing the company is to deviate from its initial offer. Some companies do careful research in order to offer competitive salaries and believe that their initial offer is both generous and highly competitive. If this is the case, the company probably won't look too kindly on you incorporating heavy negotiation tactics in order to receive a higher starting salary. Whether you choose to negotiate after receiving an offer that you feel is, in fact, highly competitive is entirely up to you. Your decision should be based in part upon your research regarding how the company operates, what its hiring practices are, and what you honestly believe you're worth.

Creativity

Creativity can and often will play a pivotal role in any negotiation. Anytime you and the potential employer aren't seeing eye-to-eye on an issue, be open-minded and willing to consider alternatives. For example, if you're looking for a $35,000 per year salary, but the employer is only offering a $30,000 per year salary and is refusing to budge, be creative and make suggestions that will lead to a compromise. For example, you might ask for a better overtime plan, or request that you be evaluated for a raise in 3 months instead of 6 months. You might ask for an additional few days of paid vacation time, or ask for an improvement in the stock or investment opportunities you're being offered.

In addition to offering your own creative alternatives, invite the employer to make suggestions and offer options, and then carefully evaluate those options. Never immediately agree to a new idea brought to the table by the employer. First, consider what is being offered and think about the reasons behind the offer. What will the benefits be to you if you accept? What will the benefits be to the employer?

Never Being Afraid to Fail

Going into a salary negotiation afraid that you're going to irritate the interviewer or lose the job offer will be extremely detrimental to you. You must know what you're looking for, and if necessary, be willing to walk away from the job offer if you can't get at least the bare minimum of what you want and need in terms of salary and benefits. Human resources professionals or those who will be negotiating your compensation package will notice if you appear nervous or scared and use it to their advantage.

Get Started

Sometimes, when two parties involved in a negotiation can't agree on something, it's necessary to make one or more concessions. Since part of your preparation included determining the lowest salary you would agree to accept, you might have to make a concession and accept a lower salary than you'd like, as long as it isn't below the bare minimum that you've predetermined. If it looks like it will become necessary for you to make some type of concession(s), you can take one of three approaches, depending on your confidence level and your negotiation abilities.

1. Your first concession should be the biggest one you're willing to make. This will often be perceived as a goodwill gesture and show that you're willing to work with the employer in order to achieve a win-win scenario. After making your first concession, any remaining concessions you discuss should be of less importance to you.

2. Offer to make minor concessions and put off discussing the larger, more important issues until you've agreed upon some of the smaller issues. If you're in the process of negotiating for a $35,000 salary and the employer is offering $32,000, while at the same time, you want 5 weeks paid vacation and the employer is only offering 4 weeks paid vacation, start by negotiating the vacation time. Once you've reached a compromise on that issue, move on to bigger issues.

3. Play hardball. Instead of making any concessions, you can say, "This is what I want, and if I don't get it, I will accept a job offer from another company." If you plan on playing hardball, you must be willing to follow through on your threats or else you will have absolutely no credibility. Only use this approach if you know for sure that the employer is extremely interested in hiring you and you really are willing to walk away from this opportunity if the company won't give you what you ask for.

If you think you'll be making several concessions during the course of your negotiation, don't make them all at once. Spread them out over time, and always have something in mind that you can give up if it will cause the employer to agree to a more important issue.

Don't Start Talking Salary Requirements Too Early in the Job Search Process

During your job interview, and perhaps on the employment application as well, you will be asked at least once about the salary you're looking for. Avoid answering this question directly. Instead, respond with phrases like:

- "I expect to receive a salary that's in line with my qualifications and experience."

- "I'm interested in a job that pays well; however, I'm also interested in a job that will provide long-term career growth and a good benefits package."

- "You are in a much better position to know how much someone with my skills and experience is worth."

- "Given my other job offers, I believe something in the range of (insert dollar range, not a specific dollar amount) would be appropriate for a starting salary."

- "I will consider any reasonable offer."

You could also ask the employer one of these questions:

- "What do you currently pay employees in my position, with my qualifications?"

- "What type of salary range do you have budgeted for this type of position?"

If the employer refuses to make any sort of offer until you provide a range, start off by adding between 15 and 20 percent to your last job's salary and provide that figure to the potential employer as the salary you're hoping to receive.

The very best time to begin salary-related discussions is after you have received a firm job offer—not before. Once you know exactly what the job you're being offered entails, it's your responsibility as the applicant to do additional research and discover what the average salary is for someone with your skills and qualifications. Wage surveys are published by the U.S. Department of Labor. There are also several books available that are updated regularly that list salary ranges for various jobs. In addition to knowing what you're worth as an employee, you must know, in advance, what you're willing to work for, and that amount must be credible, based on your job and the geographical area where you'll be working.

Prior to participating in any salary negotiations, you must determine for yourself exactly how much money you'd like to earn and could earn based on your skills, education, and experience. Remember, the salary you earn will ultimately determine your lifestyle and could have a major impact on your long-term happiness. Thus, as you consider your personal salary requirements, take into account how much money you need to exist. Make sure that the figure you come up with will allow you to cover your rent or mortgage payments, car payments, living expenses, family-oriented expenses, medical expenses, entertainment expenses, travel expenses, taxes, and repayment of student loans, and allow you to put money aside for savings. Never settle for any offer that won't let you meet your basic expenses or that will lead to financial hardship in the future.

Danger!

After you have determined the lowest salary you would consider accepting, *never* reveal this figure to a potential employer, no matter what! Keep this number to yourself, and during your negotiations, always work toward a considerably higher figure.

Types of Benefits

In addition to salary, what benefits are you interested in receiving? What benefits are extremely important to you? Keep in mind, benefits offered by employers all have dollar values, so a salary offer may be lower than what you want, but the benefits package might be impressive.

A benefits package might include:

- Health/medical insurance
- Dental insurance
- Disability insurance
- Life insurance
- Overtime pay
- A pension program
- Cafeteria/meal plan
- Child care
- Savings plans
- Stocks and investment opportunities
- Bonus plans
- Paid vacations
- Paid holidays
- Tuition reimbursement
- Relocating expenses
- Free parking
- Flexible work hours

Considering a Compensation Package

Upon receiving a compensation package offer from a potential employer, you must first determine if the salary will allow you to live the lifestyle you have already established for yourself and if that offer will allow you to pay all your expenses. Is the offer higher than the bare minimum salary requirements you determined you need and want? If the starting salary offer is low, does the job have long-term rewards or career growth opportunities that you will benefit from in the not so distant future?

Not every employer will provide you with an offer in writing. Be prepared to negotiate based upon verbal offers. Upon reaching an agreement, however, insist on receiving the final agreed-upon offer in writing.

If you're applying for an entry-level position or you have little or no work experience, you won't have a lot of room for negotiation. Companies usually have predetermined compensation packages for unskilled labor and entry-level jobs, so don't risk losing a job offer by insisting on negotiating for a salary that's considerably higher than what was offered. On the same note, however, don't make the common mistake made my many job seekers and underestimate your worth.

Finally, before accepting any offer, be sure that the job offer you're about to accept is what you're looking for. Be sure to read Chapter 9, "Analyzing Job Offers," to help you determine whether or not a specific job offer is right for you.

Once you receive a job offer, it's up to you to ensure that the compensation you will be paid if you accept the offer is fair. Don't settle for a low-paying job or a compensation package that isn't comparable to what other companies in the industry offer.

It's a Wrap

✔ Do research to determine what the average salary for someone in your job, with your skills and background, and in your geographical area is paid. Keep in mind, salaries and compensation packages vary greatly by geographical region. An executive assistant working for a law firm in New York City will probably earn more than someone with a similar job in Boise, Idaho, where the cost of living is lower.

✔ Determine how much salary (and what benefits) you actually need to earn in order to survive and pay your bills.

✔ Be totally prepared, just as you would be in a job interview situation. You want to anticipate what you'll encounter during a negotiation session and be prepared to offer support for your point of view in order to ultimately receive the compensation you want and deserve.

✔ Never accept any salary offers or job offers right on the spot. Always take time to consider what's being offered and compare the offer with what you're actually looking for. The next chapter will provide you advice for analyzing job offers.

CHAPTER 9

Analyzing Job Offers

Do I Need to Read This Chapter?

➡️ How do I analyze a job offer?

➡️ How do I avoid the traps that cause many applicants to become unhappy and unfulfilled employees?

I t may seem far off into the future, but there will come a time, probably in the next few weeks, when companies that you sent resumes to will start responding by inviting you in for that all-important interview. From there, you might get invited for a second and perhaps third interview. As the job search process continues, you'll ultimately reach two of the final phases: (1) negotiating a salary and benefits package and (2) analyzing job offers that you receive and choosing the job offer you want to accept.

Even if you consider yourself to be desperate and strapped for cash, the very worst thing you can do for yourself as a job seeker is *immediately* accept the first job offer you receive. This doesn't mean you should reject the first offer you receive; it simply means you should take the time necessary to analyze the offer.

What Does It Mean to Analyze a Job Offer?

To ensure that you choose the best job for you, ask yourself if the job will provide:

- Fair financial compensation and benefits
- A work environment you can prosper in
- A chance to move your career forward
- An opportunity to work with people you will relate to and admire
- A work experience that interests you and that you'll enjoy

Ideally, you want a job that will allow you to exploit your talents and to perform work you really enjoy doing, while minimizing the things you dislike or aren't as skilled in.

It's vitally important that you have a good understanding of what you can expect from the employer in the future. The worst mistake you can make is accepting a dead-end job with an employer that won't promote you or transfer you to a position that offers more interesting work.

Before you can make a truly educated decision about which job offer to accept, you must go into the job search process knowing certain things about yourself, your abilities, and your likes and dislikes. You should also establish short-term and long-term career-related goals for yourself and have a good understanding of your needs and desires. After all, you must know what type of job you're ideally suited for and would really like, before you can analyze any job offer to determine if it's really what you're looking for.

Analyzing a job offer means finding out what the job will offer you and what you can offer to the company, and then deciding if, in your opinion, there's a perfect match. Obviously, if you receive an offer from a potential employer, that employer believes that you will be an asset and that you have something to contribute to that organization. Do you believe this is the case? If so, is the potential employer willing to pay you what you're worth? These are questions you'll want to answer for yourself, before you accept a job.

Sure, if things don't work out after you accept a job and start working, you can always quit, but that usually isn't in your best interest, plus it will require that you start your job search efforts again. By accepting a new job and going into that job knowing exactly what you're getting yourself into, you'll be in a much better position.

Analyzing a Job Offer

As you read this chapter, look back at Chapter 1 and review the answers you provided to the questions posed to you. No matter what type of job you're hoping to receive, once you receive a job offer from a potential employer, there are a number of things you want to evaluate before accepting that position:

- The company's background
- The job description
- Your work schedule
- Who your coworkers and boss will be
- The work environment and corporate culture
- The compensation package
- Work-related travel
- Your ability to fulfill the job requirements
- Future opportunities

The Company's Background

Prior to your first job interview with the potential employer, part of your research should have included finding out as much as you possibly could about the company. This includes:

- Reviewing the company's annual report (if it's a public company)
- Reading newspaper and magazine articles about the company
- Talking with current employees
- Reviewing press releases and other information from the company
- Developing a good understanding of what the company is all about
- Determining what the company's reputation is among its customers and what type of market share it holds within its industry

If you cut corners prior to your job interview and didn't research the company as thoroughly as you should have, now is the time to do so. Accessing the Internet to research a potential employer is an excellent strategy. You can also read back issues of industry-oriented magazines or newsletters. Try to discover what the company's strengths and weaknesses are. Is the company growing? If so, how long has this growing phase been taking place? Is the company in an industry that's overly competitive or saturated? Is the company facing difficult times? Is downsizing in the company's future?

Is the company following a well-established and well-thought-out business plan? In the next 5 to 10 years, what changes will the company undergo in order to stay on the cutting edge? How will these changes affect you as an employee? The more you know about the company itself, the more educated decision you'll be able to make when it comes time to actually accepting or rejecting a job offer.

Job Description

Knowing about the company you may soon be working for is important, but you also must acquire a true understanding of the exact position you're being hired to fill. Thus, one of the first things you should ask for (if you haven't already done so by this phase in the job search process) is a detailed job description—in writing. What are the responsibilities of someone in your position? Who will you be answering to? How does the division you may be working for fit in with the rest of the company? In a typical day, week, or month, what will you be spending your time doing? How is your success measured? What skills will you be required to use? Will you be encouraged to think for yourself while on the job, or simply follow directions and predetermined procedures?

In addition to obtaining a written job description, ask the potential employer if you can be introduced to one or more people currently employed by the company who hold the same or a similar position as the one you're being offered. Prior to accepting a job offer, take some time to talk to these potential coworkers to learn as much as you can about the position and what it actually entails.

One of the common reasons why new employees don't like their jobs is because of miscommunication between themselves and their employer prior to being hired. It is your job as the applicant to ensure that the job you are about to accept is exactly how it was described to you. To help ensure that you're accepting the job you expect, ask the employer to verbally describe the position to you in detail and compare the verbal description with the written job description you request. Obviously, these two job descriptions should be identical.

If an employer is reluctant to provide you with adequate information and thoroughly describe the position you're being hired to fill, you should seriously consider the possible reasons why this information is being withheld. If you believe you're being misled in anyway, either decline the position or speak with several current employees to ensure that you have a good understanding of what will be expected of you if you accept the job offer.

Don't Forget

Leave nothing to chance. As you discuss a job offer with your potential employer, have the employer review with you the job description, in detail, and define each and every term used within the description. For example, if the job description says "light typing and filing," what does this mean? If you accept the job, will you be typing and/or filing 1 hour per day, 5 hours per day, or 4 out of 5 days per workweek? How you define a job-related term or requirement might be very different from how it's defined by a potential employer, so it's critical that you and the employer are working with the same vocabulary and understanding of what your job will entail. Ask the employer lots of questions about the position. Good communication will ensure that there are no misunderstandings later, after you actually accept the job.

Your Work Schedule

What hours will you be expected to work? Are you expected to work a 9 a.m. to 5 p.m. day? How long will you have for lunch? Will you be given any breaks throughout the day? What happens if you're late for work? Can you make up the time that evening? Is the employer flexible with your work schedule as long as you get your work done on time and meet deadlines? What happens if you need to leave work early or take an extended lunch due to personal or family emergencies (how tolerant will the employer be)? How often, if ever, will you be required to work late or on weekends? (This is particularly important if the employer doesn't pay over-time.)

Who Your Coworkers and Boss Will Be

If you accept the job offer, who will you be answering to? What is the hierarchy of positions, and where does your job title fit into that hierarchy? Is your personality similar to your supervisor's? Do you have anything in common, outside of work, with your potential supervisor(s) and coworkers? Prior to accepting a job, try to get introduced to your supervisor(s) and as many coworkers as possible, and see if you can meet for lunch or coffee in order to get to know them. Sharing common interests or a similar personality with those you work with is definitely one of the factors that makes a job enjoyable. After all, you'll be spending a considerable amount of time working with these people. If, over time, you can develop friendships with fellow employees, you'll find your job will be less stressful and more fulfilling over the long term.

The Work Environment and Corporate Culture

How structured is the environment you'll be working in? Will you have your own office or cubicle, or will you have a desk located in a common office area? Do employees have freedom to express their own "personalities" by decorating their own workspace? What management style will your supervisor or boss be using? What is the dress code of the company, and how strict is that dress code? Are employees encouraged to express their ideas and suggestions and incorporate their own creativity into their work? What type of office equipment, technology, and resources will you have available to you in order to complete your work?

The Compensation Package (Salary and Benefits)

Are you being offered a fair and competitive salary and overall compensation package based on what you're worth to the company and what people with similar job titles are being paid at other companies in the same industry and/or geographical area? Chapter 8 explained the importance of getting paid a fair salary and how you should consider what benefits you're being offered based on your need for those benefits and what monetary value they have. For a high percentage of full-time workers, their job is a repetitive and unending cycle of working hard during the week to earn a salary, which offers just enough money to pay the bills. An ideal job allows you to improve upon your lifestyle while at the same time allowing you to pay off debt and/or put money away as savings. Thus, as you analyze a job offer, you must ensure that you'll be compensated enough financially to pay your bills and at least maintain your current lifestyle. If you wind up working full-time and have to tap into your savings on a regular basis in order to make ends meet, you will wind up in serious financial trouble in no time. Likewise, you must ensure that the job you accept allows you to plan ahead for your retirement.

Work-Related Travel

Some jobs require travel or the use of your personal automobile for business-related purposes. If travel is required, determine in advance how preapproved and unexpected travel expenses are paid for. Are you expected to lay out the money, submit receipts, and later get reimbursed? If so, how long does it take to get reimbursed? Do you get paid for mileage put on your vehicle? If you have to travel by plane and/or stay at a hotel, who makes the travel arrangements and how are they paid for? What expenses are covered while you're on a business trip? Is there a limit to how much you can spend on meals, etc.? Will you be given a company credit card?

Your Ability to Fulfill the Job Requirements

Once you know what the job entails, based on your conversations with the employer, current employees, and the job description you have acquired, you must determine if you have the knowledge, skills, and experience that will allow you to be successful if you accept the position. Will the job allow you to exploit your abilities and knowledge, challenge you, and keep you interested in your work on an ongoing basis? If you accept the job, will you be getting in too deep over your head? Will you require additional training? If so, how much training will you need, and will you be compensated for your time while training? Does the work interest you? Even if you have the skills necessary to fulfill the job requirements, is this work you enjoy doing? Accepting a job you know you're good at, but you hate, simply because it allows you to earn a paycheck isn't a long-term formula for success. In fact, your chances of getting burned out or bored with your job after a few months are much higher if you don't love what you're doing. Having a passion for your work is one of the key ingredients for lifelong success. In an ideal job, you want to wake up in the morning excited to go to work, and leave work every evening excited about returning the following day.

Future Opportunities

Throughout this book, you have been warned to avoid falling into the most common trap facing job seekers—whatever you do, don't accept a dead-end job that offers no way to move forward in your career. Ask about opportunities for advancement within the company. How will you, as an employee, be evaluated? How often will this evaluation take place? What are the steps required for an employee to receive a promotion? What career path can someone who accepts the position being offered to you expect to follow? What is the time line for following this career path? How long will it be until you'll be eligible for a promotion, assuming you're a good worker? What type of training or tuition reimbursement is offered? What type of on-the-job training or outside schooling will be necessary in order to be eligible for a promotion?

If there are no advancement opportunities available once you accept the job, are you willing to spend the remainder of your career (or your time working for that employer) performing the same job function day after day, year after year? When you become bored or dissatisfied with your job, will you be willing to start your job search all over again to find a new position, or will you be too lazy and wind up spending your professional life totally bored, frustrated, and miserable? As an employee, you always want something to work for (i.e., a promotion or a raise). This will help to keep you excited and motivated about your work, give you something to work toward, and provide you with an ongoing sense of accomplishment. If you're not constantly being challenged and working toward a goal that allows for career growth, then you're working in a dead-end job.

Even if you don't have aspirations to become a top-level executive and you're not interested in working your way up that corporate ladder, find an employer that will allow you to transfer between divisions and use your experience and skills in a variety of jobs.

As you can see, there are many things you'll want to know about a potential employer and the specific job you're being offered, before you actually accept it. Once you have all the information needed to make an educated decision about whether or not to accept a position, you must take the necessary amount of time to consider your options.

With all the information you have gathered about the employer and job offer in hand, look back at Chapter 1. Start comparing the answers you provided in the "Get Started" section with the information you have acquired about the job that's being offered to you.

If you had trouble determining your likes and dislikes, pinpointing your work-related skills, and answering the questions posed in the "Get Started" section of Chapter 1, consider consulting with a career counselor. A professional career counselor can assist you in your career planning, help you to pinpoint suitable job opportunities, and offer you standard aptitude tests to assist you in determining your skills, interests, and best employment opportunities. Virtually all high schools, colleges, universities, and other educational institutions have career counselors available to students and alumni, free of charge. You can also find a career counselor by looking in the telephone book, checking the Internet, asking people you know for a recommendation, or visiting a career fair in your city.

The people who are the happiest in their careers are the ones who absolutely love what they're doing. While on the job, they're doing what they're good at and what they enjoy, plus they're constantly being challenged and improving upon themselves. If you can honestly say that the job you're about to accept offers these and other benefits, then chances are you've found a job you'll prosper in. Never settle for a job due to desperation. If you need income during your job search, consider accepting a temp position so you can earn money and take some extra time to pursue permanent career opportunities.

Accept a Job You'll Be Happy In

In this section, we'll go through the list of questions posed in Chapter 1 and see how they apply to analyzing your job offer(s). Now is the time you want to compare some of the answers you provided when you first started reading this book with the information you have uncovered about your potential employer(s) and the job(s) you're being offered.

Question 2 asked, "What would you most like to change about your life?" Now that you have a job offer and you have a good understanding of what that job entails, ask yourself, if you were to accept the job offer, would you be taking a positive step toward changing your life for the better? For example, if you answered this question by writing, "I hate working such long hours in my current job," does this potential job give you the opportunity to have a more flexible work schedule or work fewer hours, yet make the same or more money? If you answered this question, "I would like to make more friends and have people I can enjoy my free time with," then will this job give you the opportunity to meet new people with common interests that you might become friendly with outside of the work environment? When you accept a new job, you're going to experience a major change in your life. You want this change to be for the better, and for it to somehow improve upon something about your life you are not currently happy with.

In Question 3, you were asked to outline five things you could do to bring about positive changes in your life. Does accepting the job you're being offered in any way relate positively to one of those five things you listed in your answer?

Questions 4 and 5 asked you to evaluate your current lifestyle and to think about what you'd want your lifestyle to be like in the future Based on your answers to these questions, will the job you're being offered allow you to maintain and perhaps even improve upon your lifestyle in the immediate future, and ultimately achieve the lifestyle you want for yourself in the long term? Based on your answer to Question 6, do you see any relationship between what you believe you could start doing today to improve upon your lifestyle and the lifestyle that the potential job will allow you to achieve?

Money can't buy happiness, but it can certainly buy you a place to live, a car, clothing, and everything else you need to exist in the world (with the exception of love and personal relationships). In Question 7, you described your current financial status. How will the job you're being offered allow you to improve your financial status? Will you be able to pay off debts, put money into a savings account, pay all your regular bills and expenses? Will you have money available in case of an emergency or to go on a vacation? Based on your answer to Question 8, how can accepting a job offer allow you to fulfill any of the five things you believe you can do to improve your financial status in the next 1 to 5 years?

In Question 9, you listed what you consider to be the very best things about your life. Perhaps you listed your relationship with your spouse or children. Maybe you listed that you have a best friend whom you can rely on for anything and everything. Whatever you listed, how will these things be affected if you accept the job you're being offered? Will you have more time or less time to spend with your spouse and kids? Will you be able to spend 2 weeks per year visiting Disney World instead of 1 week? Think carefully about whether the job will make the best things in your life better or if it will have a negative impact on these things that are clearly important to you.

All people have something in their lives that they dislike or would like to improve upon. Being able to achieve success in virtually any aspect of your life means being able to recognize opportunities and take full advantage of them. Based on your answer to Question 10, what opportunities would the job offer you're considering provide that would allow you to change or improve upon the worst things in your life? Be creative when considering the answer to this question. Think about opportunities that might not be totally obvious.

For example, if you believe that one of the worst things in your life is that you aren't exposed to enough natural sunlight (because the job you've been working at for the past 10 years requires you to work in an office with no windows), then perhaps the job you're considering will allow you to work in a building with large windows or skylights. Everyone will answer these questions differently, and what you want out of life and your new job might be totally different from what someone else might want, so think about your own needs and desires.

As an adult, you should have a pretty good idea about what you're good and bad qualities are as a person, what you most like about yourself, and what you think other people like and dislike about you. In Questions 11, 12, 13, and 14, you were asked to write down specifics about your personal qualities. Take a look at the answers you provided and see how they will benefit you or hamper you in the job you're being offered. Consider both the positives and negatives. Based on your answer to Questions 13 and 14, will the job you're considering allow you to change the negative qualities about yourself that you listed and to grow as a person?

Everyone sometimes feels inadequate. That's normal. There are highly trained doctors, who are the best in the world at what they do, who think to themselves everyday how much they could benefit by learning new medical procedures and by expanding their field of expertise. In Questions 15, 16, and 17, you were asked to outline some of the skills you believe you need to improve upon in order to perform your job better. Will the job you're considering provide you with on-the-job training or the opportunity to attend evening classes in order to acquire the additional knowledge you need? Will you be given a chance to practice the skills you feel you could improve upon? Will the job allow you to expand your overall skill set and make you a more valuable asset to the company? In the job interview, you sold yourself to the employer based on what you could offer to the company. Now that you are being offered a job, it's important to consider what knowledge and experience the employer can and will offer to you.

Many of the most successful people in the world have managed to combine their job with what they love to do (i.e., a hobby or special skill that they enjoy doing). Now that you have written down (as the answer to Question 18) some of the ways you enjoy spending your free time, is there any way that your own hobbies or special interests can be incorporated into your professional life. For example, if you love playing computer and video games and you have training as an artist, perhaps you can get a job creating storyboards or backgrounds for video and computer games and work for a game developer. If you enjoy downhill skiing and you have an accounting background, maybe you can find a job working for a ski equipment manufacturer, sporting goods store, or ski resort. Maybe you went to school to become a marketing or public relations specialist, and your hobby involves using tools and building things in your basement. One job you might enjoy would be working in the marketing or PR department of a hardware store chain or tool manufacturer.

Once again, finding ways to combine your interests with your occupation may require a bit of creativity, but the benefits will be tremendous when you're working in a job that you love and that really interests you.

People should have goals that relate to their career, their personal life, and their family. No matter what your goals are or how ambitious you are as a person, the job you ultimately accept should allow you take a step (or multiple steps) forward toward achieving your goals. As you consider a job offer, think carefully about the goals you wrote down as an answer to Question 19, and determine how the job you are considering will help you achieve any or all of the goals you listed. If the job opportunities won't help you achieve any of your goals, that job isn't for you.

Even if you've never held a job in your life, chances are you have accomplishments that you're extremely proud of. It is hoped that you listed those accomplishments as your answer to Question 20; if not, spend a few minutes thinking about what you've accomplished in your life—at work, at home, etc.—and figure out why you consider what you listed to be important to you. Think back to what skills and knowledge you used to achieve those accomplishments. Now, consider if you'll be able to duplicate or expand upon those accomplishments in the job you're being offered. Will this potential job allow you to achieve things that you'll be proud of?

The skills you have developed over your lifetime, from on-the-job training and as part of your education, all contribute to who you are as a person. No two people have the same combination of skills, and it's your special combination of skills and talents that makes you who you are, which is why you have been offered a job from a potential employer. In Question 21, you were asked to outline some of your skills and special abilities. The key to finding a job you're going to enjoy and prosper in is matching yourself up with a position that will allow you to focus on and spend your time doing the types of work-related tasks you're good at (maximizing your skills and special talents). At the same time, you want a job that will allow you to avoid those tasks that can be allocated to someone else who is better qualified to handle them.

Throughout your lifetime, you should always be on a quest to improve your skill set and talents. This can be done by reading, obtaining training, learning from others, and taking on new types of work-related challenges. The more skills you have and the better you are at them, the more valuable you become as an employee and the faster you'll be able to earn promotions and achieve your ultimate goals. Learning a new skill can be as easy as reading a magazine article, self-help book, or how-to manual and then putting your new-found knowledge into effect. As for the skills and special talents you already have acquired, always keep trying to perfect those skills by practicing and by finding new and innovative ways to use those skills both at work and in your personal life.

If you're having difficulty narrowing down and pinpointing some of your skills (don't worry, everyone has them), think back to when you were in school. Which subjects really interested you and which did you excel in? Was there a correlation between the courses or subjects you liked and how well you did in them? Think about what skills you used in order to earn good grades in those subjects you enjoyed and did well in. Did they require writing term papers, performing research, memorizing facts and figures, doing mathematical or scientific calculations, using your imagination and tapping your creativity, reading, problem solving, working in groups, preparing oral presentations, meeting deadlines, or working with computers and/or technology? If you performed any of these skills and were good at them while in school, these are skills you have already acquired. Looking at your answer to Question 22, think about the skills you used in school to earn the best grades and consider how you could incorporate those skills or talents into the job you're considering.

Some of the most successful businesspeople and entrepreneurs in the world have managed to combine their talents, special skills, and hobbies and create a career for themselves. In Question 23, you wrote down some of your hobbies, interests, and work-related activities that you enjoy. As you evaluate any job offer, try to determine if there is any way you could incorporate any of these interests into your work. For example, if you really enjoy surfing the Internet for fun at home and you know your way around cyberspace as well as you know your hometown, strongly consider finding a job that will require you to use the Internet as a work-related tool. If you consider yourself to be an avid reader, perhaps a job that requires you to read information that you're interested in would be suitable for you. One of the weakest skills of many people is their ability to write and communicate using the written word. If you happen to enjoy writing and have a talent for it, you should consider finding a job that will allow you to do a considerable amount of writing and that might allow you to take advantage of your creativity. Even in the business world there are plenty of jobs that require strong writing skills and creativity.

Just as people have different strengths and combinations of special skills and talents, people also have different weaknesses. Some people are good at writing and enjoy it, but are awful when it comes to dealing with numbers. Question 24 asked you to carefully consider what you think your personal weaknesses are. While it's not necessary for you to stress your perceived weaknesses to a potential employer, it is absolutely vital that you know in your heart what you're capable of doing and what you're not. This will allow you to find ways of using your strengths to compensate for your weaknesses and ultimately land a job that allows you to focus on your strengths. Chances are that whatever job you wind up accepting will require that you do some tasks that you don't enjoy or simply aren't good at. These tasks will probably take you longer to accomplish and require you to spend more energy trying to focus on getting them done. Part of growing as a person means facing challenges head-on, with a positive attitude. When you're forced into a work-related situation that feels like you're in over your head, you can take the easy way out and quit, or you can put forth whatever energy it takes to learn how to accomplish your objectives. Yes, this will take hard work, a positive attitude, and motivation—but by not being afraid to fail, facing those challenges (and your perceived

weaknesses), and finding ways to face them head-on, you will ultimately overcome them. By doing this, you will expand your skill set,
grow as a person, and become adept at tasks that you once thought
were impossible for you to accomplish.

With the proper instruction, an excellent attitude, a drive to succeed, hands-on training, and practice, you will discover that there is
very little you can't achieve, no matter what you perceive your
weaknesses to be. The important thing right now, as you're looking
for a job that you'll be successful in, is to know what you're good at,
understand what your limitations are, and determine what skills you
believe you can handle but will need to work extra hard to accomplish. By knowing and understanding yourself, you'll be in a far better position to analyze a potential employment situation and
determine if it's right for you.

Just as there are a countless number of occupations and types of
jobs that you could potentially qualify to fill, there are an equal number of work environments. The work environment, atmosphere, or
corporate culture of a company will determine a lot about what it's
actually like working there. Before you can properly analyze the
work environment at a company you have received a job offer from,
you must consider what type of environment you work the best in.
You were asked to consider this when answering Question 25. Make
sure, when you answered this, that you took into account your own
personality, your strengths and weaknesses, your likes and dislikes,
and all the various work experiences you had in the past. Even the
smallest work-environment-related issue can have a tremendous
impact on your happiness and productivity on the job. For example,
if you're a nonsmoker, you probably don't want to be working everyday in a small, enclosed room with a bunch of smokers. Even if
they're not allowed to light up at their desks, the smell of smoke will
still be on their clothing and in their hair. If you're working in close
proximity to these people, the smell of their smoke will eventually be
extremely noticeable. Likewise, it's a proven fact that humans prosper in sunlight, and keeping people out of natural light can nega-

tively impact them emotionally over a period of time. Thus, when investigating the work environment at the job you're being offered, inquire about the lighting situation where you'll actually be spending your time. Are there windows in the room? Can the windows be opened? Are their shades on the windows? Will you be able to breathe fresh air throughout the day? Is proper climate control (heating and air conditioning) provided? If there are no windows, what type of lighting is provided? The geographical location of the employer can also make an impact on whether or not you enjoy a job and prosper in it. Outside of your office, will you see cornfields or busy city streets? Will you hear birds chirping or sirens blaring? When you look out the window, do you see trees and grass, or skyscrapers, pollution, and billboards.

As you evaluate your job offers, think about where you worked in the past and what you liked and disliked about that work environment, and consider the following when analyzing what the work environment will be like if you accept the job you're being offered:

- The office decor
- Lighting
- Air ventilation
- Accessibility to rest rooms and parking
- The proximity from where you'll be working to your nearest coworker(s)
- Who your coworkers will be
- What type of direct supervision you'll receive while on the job
- What type of management style you'll be forced to accept
- Who your direct supervisor and/or boss will be
- What the dress code at the office is
- What office equipment, technology, and resources you will have at your disposal
- Anything else that will have even the smallest impact on your ability to work at your highest level of productivity and potential

If you've held a job in the past, chances are you can tick off a list of things that you absolutely hated about that job. In Question 26, you should have outlined some of the things you used to complain about in regard to your previous employment situation. Did you hate your boss? Was your work space too small? Were you required to work too hard for too little pay and receive no reward(s) from the employer for that extra effort? Were your coworkers obnoxious? Were you forced to wear an ugly uniform or abide by a strict dress code? Perhaps you spent your workdays doing mundane tasks that were unchallenging and boring. As you consider the job you've now been offered, consider all the things you hated about your previous employment experience and make sure that none of these things will be repeated if you were to accept this new position. Learn from your experience and avoid repeating past negative experiences.

For Question 21, you were asked to think about and list all the skills and abilities you have as a person. Now, as you responded to Question 27, you should have narrowed down your list to those skills that relate directly to your job. What makes you a highly attractive employee and the perfect person to fill the position you're being offered? Do the skills required for the job you're considering mesh nicely with the work-related skills you consider yourself to be extremely good at? Obviously, since you were offered the job in the first place, the potential employer thinks you have what it takes to be successful in the job you've been offered. However, you're the person who will be doing the job, so it's important that you too believe that your qualifications are in sync with the job's requirements. This is a judgment call you'll have to make for yourself based on your knowledge of what the job entails and your knowledge of who you are and what your skills are.

Question 28 is extremely straightforward. Before you started your job search, you were asked to write down the qualities you would be looking for in that new job. Now that you have a job offer, match up your list of responses to what the job actually offers. Is there a match? Likewise, Questions 29, 30, and 31 also requested that you consider and write down what you'd be looking for in terms of coworkers in your new job. Once again, consider what you wrote down as the answers to these questions and compare those responses to the people who would be your coworkers if you were to accept the job that you've been offered. Are these people that you can work well with and that share common interests and personality traits with you? If, in Question 31, you pinpointed types of people you simply don't work well with, for whatever reason, will you be able to avoid those people in your new job?

In Chapter 6, you learned about the importance of networking. Question 32 encouraged you to list all the network contacts you have that might be able to help you analyze the job you've been offered. Prior to accepting any job offer, contact people you know who work for your potential employer or within the industry you'll be working in, and learn as much as you can about the potential job from those people. Try to determine what their perception of the employer is, whether or not the company has a good reputation, and whatever else you can discover. In this case, even listening to the gossip about the employer might prove beneficial, so contact everyone you can think of that might be able to offer you some information, and then listen carefully to what you're told.

In a perfect world, people wouldn't have to apply for jobs. They'd simply be hired to do whatever it was that they really wanted to do for a living and were good at. The people who are the happiest and most successful on the job are those who manage to come as close as possible to actually working in their dream job. That's why you were asked to describe that dream job in Question 33. Now that you've actually been offered a job, is there anything about that job that resembles your dream job? If not, is there anything you can do as a potential employee to bring about a greater similarity? Keep in mind, the closer the match is between your dream job description and your actual job description, the more apt you are to really love your work and be successful at it. Check out the answer you provided for Question 37 as well. Is the help-wanted ad and job description you wrote for your dream job anything like the help-wanted ad and job description you responded to for the job you are being offered?

Out of all the jobs you've had in the past, which ones were the closest to what you would consider to be your dream job? What was it about those jobs that made them enjoyable? What similarities are there between your past jobs that you've liked and the one you're now considering? Compare your response to Question 34 with what you perceive your new job will offer if you accept it. Once again, you're looking for similarities so you can find a job that is the closest thing to what you would consider your ultimate dream job.

In Chapter 8, work-related benefits are discussed. In Question 35, you were asked to outline what types of benefits you need and want. Since you listed the three most important benefits to you, be sure that the job you're being offered will provide those benefits (or something similar). Benefits are an important part of your overall compensation package, and it's critical that you believe that your job offers you fair compensation for the work you're providing. If a job you're being offered doesn't offer a benefit you really need, such as health insurance or child care, is the financial compensation (salary) that's being offered enough so that you can pay all your regular bills plus pay for that insurance or child care out of pocket?

Along with benefits, how do you like to be rewarded? As you considered this when answering Question 36, did you think about how important overtime pay, extra vacation pay, coffee breaks, promotions, and pay raises are to you? Finally, does the job you're considering offer rewards for working hard? Are the rewards that will be offered in line with what you want? If the employer doesn't pay overtime, will you be rewarded in other ways for working long hours?

People have to make career-related decisions for themselves in order to ultimately be happy. You can't let a parent, spouse, friend, or anyone else force you into a career, even if you're good at the tasks required to be successful in that career, because it is you that ultimately has to be happy in the job you choose. To help you make educated career-related decisions, it's sometimes helpful to follow in the footsteps of someone you really admire. By choosing a mentor and trying to become as knowledgeable about that person as you can, you will have access to someone with experience, someone who can offer you advice based on personal experience and help you make smart career choices.

In Question 38, you should have written down at least one person, living or dead, that you admire. What is (was) it about that person that makes you admire him or her? What could you learn from that person? Even if the person is no longer living, simply by studying the person's career and the business and professional decisions the person made, you can learn and make more educated decisions about your own life. Following in the footsteps of a mentor doesn't mean copying everything the mentor does. You are your own person and need to make the decisions and career choices that best fit your needs, personality, and lifestyle. You can, however, obtain valuable guidance and advice from a mentor.

Throughout your lifetime, you are constantly developing your personal reputation—how other people perceive you based on your actions or implied actions. As long as you're still alive, you can always fix a poor reputation by changing your ways, treating people more kindly, and demonstrating a genuine concern for others. Once you pass away, however, you're stuck with whatever reputation you developed while you were living. In Question 39, you were asked to think about how you want people to remember you once you're gone. Based on your answer, what can you start doing right now— this very minute—to ensure that your reputation becomes exactly what you want it to be. Both on the job and in your personal life, you must always be striving to maintain a good reputation by treating others fairly and honorably. Doing this not only will allow you to maintain a good reputation but also will improve the overall quality of your life, because you will continue to earn the honor and respect of those around you (family members, friends, coworkers, employers, etc.). As you contemplate accepting the job you're being offered, think about how you'll treat others and what positive impact you'll be able to make. Does this employment opportunity allow you to be the person you deep-down really want to be?

Finally, as we reach the end of the questionnaire from Chapter 1, you're asked in Question 40 to define what personal and professional success means to you. As you answered this question, did you take into account your short-term and long-term goals? Did you contemplate exactly what you hope to get out of life? Now, as you consider accepting the job you've been offered, the most important question to ask yourself is whether or not accepting the job will help you take a step closer to achieving what you perceive as success in your personal or professional life. If accepting the job does not allow you to grow as a person and move closer to achieving your goals, you could be walking into a dead-end job, so proceed with extreme caution! If the job you are being offered won't help you, either directly or indirectly, to achieve your dreams and goals, it's probably not worth accepting.

Dealing with Multiple Job Offers— Choosing the Best One

The trick to choosing the best job for you when you're lucky and skilled enough to receive multiple offers is to compare each job offer with the questions posed to you in this chapter and in Chapter 1. Once you've done this for each job offer, compare the job offers with each other. Based on your wants, needs, likes, and dislikes, it should become pretty obvious which job is the best for you. Obviously, salary and compensation is a major issue; however, pay careful attention to your future growth potential in regard to each employment opportunity. By accepting a job that pays slightly less today, will you be able to work your way up to a much higher paying job in a few months? Is the potential for promotions and pay raises greater at one employer than another? Are the benefits more generous at one employer even if the salary being offered is lower? Are you willing to be paid a bit less in order to work in an environment you know is much better suited to your likes and needs? Would you prefer to work with one group of people at one job instead of the people who would be your coworkers at another job? In which job will you be the most challenged, and most importantly, where will you be the happiest?

Never jump into making any type of career decision. Take the time you need to analyze each job offer carefully. Weigh the positives and negatives about each job and compare them with what you're looking for. Determine what compromises you're willing to make and which employer will offer the best compensation and most growth potential.

If you're currently employed and you'll soon have to tender your resignation prior to starting your new job, be sure to read the following chapter, "Quitting without Burning Bridges." It will help to you maintain positive professional relationships with your current coworkers and bosses, while at the same time, allow you to move forward in your career.

✔ Communication is the key to understanding a job offer. If you enter into a job knowing what to expect and what's expected of you, you'll be better positioned to achieve success.

✔ Finding a job is very important, but finding the right job that you'll be happy and prosper in could mean the difference between loving your work and being miserable during every moment you're on the job.

✔ Your destiny lies in your hands. Make educated and well-thought-out decisions, taking into consideration your short-term and long-term needs and desires.

CHAPTER 10

Quitting Without Burning Bridges

Do I Need to Read This Chapter?

➡ How do I quit my job without burning any bridges?

➡ How do I maintain my professional reputation as I change jobs?

F inding a new job can become extra challenging if you're currently employed with a full-time job and you want to keep your job search efforts a secret from your current employer until you actually land a new job and you're ready to quit your current one. Most career counselors agree that it's always better to remain employed while looking for a new job. If you're employed and have a paycheck coming in, you'll be less desperate and won't feel forced to accept the first job offer that comes along. You'll be more comfortable to take your time, analyze each job offer, and find a job that's really the right one for you.

The most important thing to keep in mind is that you should never quit a job on a whim or without carefully thinking through all your alternatives. When you quit a job, you should have a plan (and, one hopes, another job) in place. Even if you have a fight with your boss or you believe that you're being treated unfairly and want to tell off your employer and quit on the spot, this is absolutely the worst strategy you can adopt for leaving a job.

Think Before You Quit Abruptly

There are countless reasons why someone leaves one job to pursue a career with another company, but to maintain a good reputation within an industry, it's important to act professionally when you actually quit a job. Getting into a fight with your boss, shouting, "I quit!" and then stomping out of the building forever is never the best way to handle things. Even if you think your boss is an incompetent jerk, in the heat of anger never let your negative feelings cause you to act unprofessionally. If you get into a major disagreement with your employer, never make a decision to quit impulsively. Spend a few days thinking about your decision, and if you decide it's time to move on, start looking for a new job before actually tendering your resignation with your current employer.

Once you've actually landed that new job, be prepared to give your current employer the traditional 2 weeks' notice. Some people give notice and then use their accumulated vacation or sick days to avoid showing up for work. This is not appropriate behavior. Even if your new employer wants you to start work immediately, he or she will almost always understand that as a matter of loyalty and professional courtesy, it is necessary for you to stay with your current employer for those 2 weeks after giving your notice.

During those last 2 weeks on the job, no matter what your reason is for leaving, offer to do whatever you can to maintain a positive relationship with your coworkers and boss. One way to do this is by offering to train your replacement, or at least write down how you perform certain tasks so that your replacement won't be totally lost when taking over your old job. Make your exit from the company as smooth as possible.

No matter how much you hate your current employer, purposely causing problems, stealing from the employer, or sabotaging business deals are all actions that are unethical, totally inappropriate, and often illegal. After you give notice that you plan on leaving your job, some companies will request your immediate departure, and will promptly cut off your computer access and escort you out of the building, especially if you're leaving on a negative note. Prior to quitting, try to ascertain how your employer handles employees that quit, and if possible, try to talk with a former employee who quit under similar circumstances to yours. Knowing what to expect in terms of the reaction from the employer is always helpful.

As you actually leave the company for the last time, take with you only your own personal belongings and nothing that is considered the company's property. Make a point to return, directly to your boss, your office keys and any company-owned equipment that was in your possession. If possible, for your protection, obtain a written memo stating that everything was returned promptly and in working order. Remember, any equipment, such as a laptop computer, that was purchased by the employer for your use remains the property of the employer, and attempting to keep that equipment is considered stealing.

If you're planning on taking a copy of your personal client list, for example, make sure you have legal rights to take this information. All companies have different restrictions that its employees are legally bound to through noncompete agreements and employee contracts. Prior to making a copy of your client list or trying to take customer accounts with you to your new job, it may be useful to consult an employment attorney and learn your rights to avoid getting into legal problems with the employer.

Down the road, you might need to use your current employer as a reference. Simply walking off the job and leaving the company in a bind is not the best way to maintain positive relationships. Lisa Elias, branch operations manager for the Framingham office of Kelly Services, says, "It's very important to never burn bridges. The results of your actions will follow you throughout your career, especially if you stay within one city and keep working in a specific industry. You'll find that most people within an industry know each other, and your reputation will follow you from job to job." Likewise, you may very well wind up working with your boss or your coworkers again down the road, so maintaining a professional and positive relationship is always beneficial.

A Basic Strategy for Quitting a Job

Before you take that giant leap forward and quit, make sure that this is really what you want to do. Ask yourself why you're quitting. If you're having problems with a coworker or boss, can you work things out and stay on the job? Instead of quitting, can you arrange for a transfer within the company? What will you do if the employer considers you a valuable asset to the company and is willing to offer you incentives for staying on the job?

Once you quit, will you have another job lined up, or will you be unemployed? Make sure that you have money set aside in savings so that you'll be able to support yourself and pay all your bills, without a regular salary, for a few weeks or months until you land a new job. Be prepared for a worst-case scenario, and plan on being unemployed for several months. Prior to quitting, if you haven't already landed a new job, have a detailed plan in place for kicking off your job search.

When you're actually ready to quit your current job, spend some time thinking about how you'll quit, what you'll say, and how you're going to maintain a professional relationship with the employer. Arrange a private meeting with your boss or with the appropriate person within the company, and offer your resignation in person, following it up in writing with a friendly and professional letter. Never get into a shouting match or argument. Whether you're leaving your full-time job or a temporary employment position, never simply walk off the job, and always try to give your current employer proper notice. Many employees develop friendships with their coworkers and bosses, so if this is the case for you, you might want to take the extra time to explain why you're planning to pursue another job, and do what's necessary to maintain the friendships you've developed.

Quitting a job can be both a scary and exciting thing, because it involves major changes in your life. The prospect of starting a new job that looks like it'll be exciting is a wonderful feeling, especially if you're leaving a job that you hated.

In the next chapter, you'll read interviews with a handful of experts who offer career and job-search strategies that you'll definitely find useful. Through these interviews, you'll obtain yet another perspective regarding the whole job search process.

✔ Never act unprofessionally when tendering your resignation.

✔ It's always advisable to offer your employer at least 2 weeks' notice prior to your departure from the company.

✔ As you actually plan your exit from a company, be sure to read your employment contract carefully to ensure that you won't create any legal problems. Many companies require employees to sign noncompete agreements, so if your new job involves working for a competitor, make sure you're not violating the agreement you signed when you first started the job you're now leaving.

✔ Make sure you have legal ownership of any documents, client lists, information, office equipment, or other items that you plan on taking with you. If necessary, consult with an employment lawyer who can provide legal guidance when moving from one job to another.

✔ No matter what the circumstances are behind your quitting your existing job, avoid burning bridges or allowing a confrontational situation to develop.

PART V

Advice from
the Experts

CHAPTER 11

◆◆

Face-to-Face with Some "Get a Job" Experts

◆◆

Do I Need to Read This Chapter?

➡ An interview with "success expert" Barry Farber, the host of a nationally syndicated radio show, author, lecturer, and creator of the *Diamond in the Rough* audiocassette series from Nightingale Conant.

➡ An interview with Sue Nowacki and Steve Burt, who operate a resume writing and career strategies business, called 1st Impressions. Together, Sue and Steve have over 25 years of experience in professional resume writing and career strategy development.

➡ An interview with Pam Meyers, the president of HRI, Inc., a company that provides human resources services to small and medium-size companies in a wide variety of industries.

➡ An interview with Lisa Elias, the branch operations manager for the Kelly Services office in Framingham, Massachusetts, one of the country's largest temp agencies.

◆◆◆

N ow that you have a good idea what the whole job search process is about, this section will help you to put all the pieces together. You're about to read a series of interviews with experts who have extensive experience helping people like you to launch their careers or land awesome jobs.

Each of these interviews has been added to *Job Hunting for the Utterly Confused* to give you additional guidance as you embark on your own job search. All the individuals interviewed for this section are highly qualified and extremely knowledgeable. They are, however, providing their own opinions and strategies for helping you land a job. Take all of this advice to heart, but follow the advice that you believe applies to your personal situation or that you feel will help to give you that all-important edge as an applicant.

Meet "Success Expert" Barry Farber

What exactly is a success expert, you ask? Well, as a businessperson and salesperson, Barry Farber has achieved a huge amount of success; yet his career path has led him toward becoming a success expert, with the goal of helping others, from all walks of life, to achieve their own personal and business success. Over the years, Barry has interviewed some of the world's most successful business leaders about what makes them successful. He has spent years studying what these people have in common, and what qualities and personal traits are required for everyday people to achieve similar success.

Barry has gathered vast amounts of knowledge about what motivates people, and he broadcasts this wisdom each week on his nationally syndicated radio show. He also travels around the country giving in-person seminars and lectures on personal achievement strategies, plus he's the author of the best-selling book *Diamond in the Rough* and creator of the audiocassette success training program *Diamond in the Rough,* from Nightingale Conant.

In this section, Barry shares advice for job seekers on how to land an awesome job that will lead you to joining the ranks of the millions of successful people in the world. Anyone who listens to Barry's *Diamond in the Rough* 6-hour audiocassette program discovers that the most successful people in the world aren't always the top-level business executives. How you ultimately define your own personal or business success can be totally different from how the CEO of a Fortune 500 company defines personal and business success. Being successful means achieving the personal and business-related goals and dreams you set for yourself, not spending years trying to match someone else's success or fulfill someone else's dreams.

The first step toward success in the business world is to land yourself a job that will provide you with a vehicle for moving up the corporate ladder through hard work and determination. The last thing you want is a dead-end job that will lead to frustration and depression. Thus, before becoming successful in your career, you first must become a successful job seeker. By following some of Barry's advice that's outlined in this chapter, you'll be well on your way.

Get Started

Through his extensive research and hundreds of interviews with high achievers, Barry has compiled a list of 10 common traits that most successful people share. Obviously, one person probably won't have all these traits, but as you delve into your career, you should strive to adopt as many of these success-oriented strategies into your daily life as possible.

1. Successful people maintain a positive mental attitude, even during times of extreme adversity. Bad stuff might happen, but you have to deal with it and move on.

2. Always learn from your failures, setbacks, and the adversity you face. After experiencing a setback, immediately try to ascertain what you could do differently the next time you're in a similar situation.

Continued

3. Attack fear and use it as a motivator that pushes you into action. Never be afraid of failure.

4. Maintain a massive amount of enthusiasm about everything you set out to do. This includes developing confidence in your self and learning how to foster that confidence in ways that are highly beneficial.

5. Put forth an extreme amount of effort in whatever it is that you do. Understand that nothing involving great accomplishment comes without great effort, and that nothing is offered on a silver platter.

6. High achievers never stop investing in their minds. Read everything you possibly can about your chosen career and industry, plus read about topics of interest to you in order to stay on the cutting edge. Successful people never stop trying to learn more, and they do whatever they can to obtain new knowledge. Remember, no matter what career path you choose to follow, knowledge is power!

7. Constantly setting long-term and short-term goals is an absolute must for achieving any type of success. By defining success for yourself, you can devise a personal plan for achieving it.

8. Tap the knowledge and follow the guidance of your personal mentors. Being able to learn from mentors and people you respect is an important ingredient for achieving success.

9. People who become successful don't take on a "stab-em-in-the-back" attitude toward their coworkers, superiors, customers, clients, or business associates. Always deal with people honestly and develop a reputation that conveys your personal integrity.

10. Most successful people go out of their way to serve others. The age-old saying, "What goes around, comes around," applies. If you help others to achieve their goals and dreams, they are more apt to return the favor.

Barry explains:

The key to landing a good job in today's business world is being able to set yourself apart from the slush pile of other applicants. You have to be different and always maintain a positive attitude.

Get Started

Unfortunately, receiving rejection is part of the whole job search process. According to Barry:

Rejection is a way of life. I spent 20 years of my life in sales, and as a salesmen, to be successful, you have to learn how to love rejection and use it to make you smarter.

Over the years, Barry has developed three steps for dealing with rejection:

1. Try to figure out what you did that caused you to receive rejection, and do it differently the next time.

2. Obtain as much detailed feedback as you can from the person who rejected you. Discover what you did wrong and what the reason was behind the rejection. Is there a deficiency that you can overcome?

3. Let rejection motivate you. Rejection is just one person's opinion. If you don't receive a job offer after participating in an interview, chances are you're being rejected by a single person who didn't believe you met the criteria for the job. When someone rejects you who doesn't know you, you can never take that rejection personally. A human resources person typically will read your resume and then spend maybe an hour talking with you. From this limited exposure to you, the interviewer knows very little about who you are and what you stand for. Learn what you can from the experience and move on. If you're totally convinced that you're suitable for a job that you were rejected for, reapply. There is nothing wrong with being persistent and driven to land a specific job that you really want and are qualified for.

Barry notes:

Once you know your goals, you have faith in what you're doing, and you know exactly what it is that you're going after, any rejection you receive will bounce off of you. Any top achiever has overcome massive rejection and setbacks, but they have learned to overcome rejection, never to take it personally, and to use it as a motivator to get themselves to work harder in the future. People who are successful have built a foundation for their success upon their many failures.

To land the job you're looking for, Barry suggests that you begin by taking a good long look at yourself and choosing a small handful of companies that you'd really like to work for. He advises:

Don't just mail out dozens of resumes to companies you know have openings for someone with your qualifications. Once you've selected between three and five companies that you'd really be excited to work for, go to the library or surf the Internet and learn everything you possible can about those companies. Talk to people who work for the companies you're interested in, and if possible, talk to the company's clients or customers to learn even more. Do whatever it takes to learn about the company. Obtaining just a general overview of a company isn't enough to set you apart from other applicants. You have to develop a true understanding of the company's business philosophy, discover its strengths and weaknesses, and know how the company fits within its industry. You absolutely have to go a step beyond what other applicants are doing in terms of performing research.

One strategy for developing contacts within a company or industry, and for gaining knowledge, is to find mentors who are already successful. Barry suggests:

Approach top-level executives within the companies you're interested in working for, and ask them for some career guidance and advice. To reach some people it will take persistence, but eventually you'll reach that person. When I needed to reach someone once, after nine weeks of leaving voice mail messages and talking with their assistant, I finally left a message saying, "Every night before I go to sleep, I speak to God. Why can't I talk to you?" I received a call back from that person within 15 minutes after leaving that message. Sometimes, all it takes is a bit of creativity and lots of persistence. You should never be intimidated to call someone in order to learn from them. You'd be surprised how many top-level businesspeople are happy to share their experience and advice with someone trying to break into their industry. Even if you never get to speak with the top-level person you set out to contact, chances are that person will provide you with a personal referral to someone within their organization who can help you. A personal referral from a top-level person who works for the company you hope to get a job with will carry a lot of weight.

As you try to reach an executive you'd like to adopt as a mentor, it's important to be persistent, but always to be professional and never become a nuisance. Barry adds:

The best times to call someone who you're having trouble reaching are early in the morning, during lunch, or after business hours, when the person is more apt to answer the phone.

Barry explains:

Before any applicant will receive a job offer, they must participate in the biggest selling effort of their life, because they have to sell themselves to the employer. Part of your sales pitch should be to demonstrate all of the detailed research you have done about the company. You want to show a strong understanding about what the company offers, what its strengths and weaknesses are, and what you can contribute to the organization.

Sometimes, it's necessary for applicants to go out on a limb in order to win over an interviewer. In making this point, Barry shares this strategy:

One fool-proof method I have discovered for landing virtually any job that you're qualified for is to tell the interviewer that you're willing to work for the company, free of charge, for 30 days. Tell the interviewer, "During a 30-day trial period, I will show you the work ethic, excitement, enthusiasm, and the value that I will give to the job on an ongoing basis, and I will prove my value to the company. If after the 30 days, I haven't proven myself, you can let me go and not pay me a cent. When, however, I do prove my value and capabilities, I expect to be paid for the 30 days and be kept on board with a full-time job." Applicants that take this approach will stand out, because they demonstrate that they're willing to work hard and put themselves on the line for something they feel strongly about.

Following this advice, says Barry, certainly takes a sense of confidence in yourself and plenty of motivation, but the extra effort you put forth will pay for itself many times over:

Always show people who have helped you gratitude by sending hand-written thank-you notes, and never stop networking. As an applicant, you should always be looking for people who can make an introduction for you to a company and help you get your foot in the door. You never know what job opportunities you'll discover simply by talking with people.

Job seekers should consider finding a job to be their biggest short-term goal. According to Barry:

Less than 3 percent of the world's population actually take the time to write their goals down, and that's a mistake. Taking an organized approach to landing a job means developing goals, setting deadlines for yourself, and writing down your goals and achievements. As you begin your job search, on a piece of paper, write down your ten top goals that you want to achieve during the next 12 months. These goals can include anything that relates to your career, family, personal life, etc. Once you have developed your list of ten goals, choose the one goal that will have the biggest benefit to you once it's achieved, and write it down again on a separate sheet of paper. This time, however, write down your top goal in the form for a question. If your top goal is to increase your income by $50,000 per year, on the second sheet of paper, for the heading, write down, "What can I do during the next 12 months to increase my income by $50,000 per year?" Next, write down 20 different action-steps, which are things you can start doing immediately, to help you achieve your goal. The action-steps can be big or small, but you must write them down so you can begin to develop a plan for achieving your goal. Finally, take one of those 20 steps and choose one that you can act on immediately. Nothing is more important than taking action.

By taking action, not only will you feel closer to your goal, but you will also keep getting closer to achieving it. Humans need things to keep them focused and on track, because in our daily lives, there are many things that will offer distractions and detours. Writing down your goals and developing steps for achieving those goals is a proactive and easy-to-follow technique for achieving them. This technique can easily be applied to finding a job.

Since your top goal is to find and land a job, write it down on the top of a piece of paper. Next, rewrite the goal as a question—"What can I do to find and land a job?" Finally, start making a detailed list of the actions you'll need to take in order to find and land a job, and at the same time, set deadlines for yourself to accomplish each item on your list. During your job search, keep this goal sheet with you at all times, and refer to it several times each day, starting when you wake up in the morning. The last thing you should do at night before going to sleep is to review your goal list, check off action steps you have accomplished that day, and choose which action steps you plan on tackling the next day. By referring to your goal list, you will keep your goals fresh in your mind and keep yourself motivated. You'll also be able to identify detours and setbacks in your life and avoid them.

Barry goes on to say:

I believe that by elevating someone else's success, you elevate your own success. When you call up someone and explain that you're looking for a job in their industry and that you're interested in learning from people who have achieved success, you are feeding a person's ego by asking them for their assistance, because you consider them to be a good mentor. Not only will you enhance your own knowledge by learning from mentors, you'll also develop powerful connections and contacts that you can benefit from in the future. As you do research, cut out articles from newspapers, magazines, newsletters, and trade journals that interview or profile people you'd be interested in learning from, and make a point to contact those people. When you contact them by phone, fax, mail, or email, tell them you read about them in an article and you're very interested in what they had to say. Take the time to do the little things necessary to set yourself apart from other applicants. Often, it's the little things that generate the biggest and best results.

In addition to hard work, Barry suggests that applicants learn as much as possible about what a company's expectations are for its employees:

> Try to talk with as many people as you can who currently work for the company. Discover what the company looks for in a model employee and strive to meet and then surpass those expectations. Through your research, develop an understanding of the big picture. Don't just focus on your area of expertise, or on the department you hope to work in. Never be afraid to contribute to a company in ways that are outside of your job description. Supervisors and managers always take note of people who hustle. Those are the people who earn the promotions and get the most responsibility.

However, when stepping outside of your area of responsibility, be sure that you don't step on other people's toes. Many businesses have very political environments, and there can be a fine line between helping people out and making them feel threatened by your actions. Work with others, not against them.

You can learn much more about what it takes to be successful by experiencing Barry's *Diamond in the Rough* audiocassette success training course, which is available from Nightingale Conant, by calling (800) 323-5552.

Resume Preparation Advice from Some Real Pros

Being able to write an awesome resume takes skill as a writer, creativity, plus a good knowledge of the job market. After all, you're providing a document designed to sell yourself to a potential employer, so that document must capture the attention of the reader; highlight your achievements, skills, and experience; and profile you as the ideal candidate for the job opening you're applying for. Chapter 3 of this book will guide you through the resume preparation process and help you create your own resume that will get you results. Many job seekers, however, choose to hire a professional resume writer to assist them in creating their resume.

Sue Nowacki and Steve Burt are both professional resume writers. Between the two of them, they have over 25 years of experience in the professional resume writing and career strategies business. Both Sue and Steve are members of the Professional Association of Resume Writers and the National Association of Resume Writers. Sue is the publisher of an international newsletter for career professionals called "Smart Presentations," which provides a bridge of communications between professional resume writers and those in hiring positions and career counseling. Steve is a Certified Professional Resume Writer and is a registered resume service vendor/consultant for the State of Florida Department of Vocational Rehabilitation.

Together, Sue and Steve launched a resume preparation company, called 1st Impressions, Resumes & Career Strategies, in February 1996. Currently they offer their writing services to job seekers across the country and around the world. Sue and Steve became business partners after establishing Espan's Career Management Forum on CompuServe. Sue explains:

> Our role in the forum was to guide forum activities and offer career support and strategies to the members who visited there. We answered questions on issues of resume preparation and career strategies, including how to handle tough interviews, career gaps, changing career direction, targeting companies of interest, references, resignations, and a variety of other career-related issues. We provided written material for the forum's library, and we held live conferences on issues of career management and resume preparation.
>
> Each of us has written resumes for people in nearly every field imaginable, at every level. Our clients come from the United States as well as several other countries. We are also very familiar with curricula vitae and preparation of documents for foreign markets. We launched 1st Impressions, Resumes & Career Strategies on the Net on February 2, 1996. While working on the CompuServe forum, we

realized that our philosophies regarding resume writing and approaches to a career search, as well as our sense of professional ethics and our desire to provide premium client services, meshed neatly. We discussed providing resume writing services on the Internet as an opportunity to offer services to a wider market and decided that this would be something we would enjoy doing together. Steve had operated his private resume service for 13 years, and I had operated my private resume service for nearly 11 years before we decided to team our skills and backgrounds and make this a partnership.

In addition to providing resume writing services to job seekers, the duo continues to operate a highly informative Web site designed for job seekers. Sue notes:

We've worked hard to make the 1st Impressions, Resumes & Career Strategies web site [http://www.1st-imp.com] a great resource site for job hunters. Our site is updated daily, so that the information is always current and fresh, giving our visitors something of interest during every visit. Our site offers hundreds of direct links to the best career-related information and web sites on the Internet. We provide articles, free of charge, on various aspects of the career search process, including resume preparation, interviewing, networking, targeting companies, and more. We provide information on current career news, colleges, internships, career fair schedules, and disability resources. We provide a career counselor page, which answers job hunters' most frequently asked questions. There's also an interactive message board where visitors can post their career questions and receive professional guidance.

Obviously, some people choose to create their own resume, while others don't mind spending some money to hire a professional in hopes that it will give them the upper hand when their resume is added to a huge pile on a potential employer's desk. Sue explains that virtually every job seeker can benefit from hiring a resume preparation expert:

With careful attention to the selection of a resume writer, anyone, at any level in their career, can benefit from the writing and expertise that a professional resume writer offers. Just as a good CPA knows tax law, a good resume writer knows resumes, employment issues, and career strategies that will give clients a distinct advantage in their job search process.

The professional resume writer is especially equipped to help individuals deal with issues such as:

- Complicated backgrounds
- Problem areas
- Career changes
- Lengthy absences from the work force
- Concern over lack of qualifications or education
- Sketchy work histories

Additionally, Sue believes that people who have trouble organizing and presenting information in written form, who may have poor writing skills, or who don't have access to state-of-the-art computers and laser printers will also greatly benefit from the professional services of a resume writer.

Sure, by putting in the necessary effort, people can create their own resumes. Likewise, Sue says:

People can also prepare their own tax returns, serve as their own attorneys, or fix their own cars. The reason for using any professional service is to take advantage of a professional's specialized knowledge and experience. Job hunters may not have the time, interest, or opportunity to study resumes, research current hiring practices, and learn about effective career strategies. They may not have access to hiring managers or human resource professionals to guide them at the same depth as a professional resume writer who is dedicated to the field. It's the job of the professional resume writer to remain current in today's hiring practices and employment laws and to fully understand the whole process of the job search. We can provide our clients with an advantage over those who choose to write their own resumes. Investing in a professional resume writer's services can be an investment toward your future. It can mean the difference between being invited to an interview or simply adding one more resume to the slush pile.

Most people will write only a handful of resumes during their entire career. A professional resume writer will write hundreds of resumes each year, with thousands written over the course of their careers. Thus, from this specialized experience, professional resume writers tend to know what works and what doesn't.

Like many resume writing companies, 1st Impressions offers a wide range of services to job seekers, including:

- Detailed resume critiquing
- Professional resume construction (writing, design, and presentation) for entry-level, technical, and top-level positions
- Targeted resumes to specific positions
- Delivery of a binary resume file to the client (MS Word document, or converted to client's word processing software program)
- Resumes converted to ASCII format for Internet use
- Scannable resumes
- Resumes converted to HTML format for posting on a web page
- Posting of the resume to a private page on our web site
- Posting of resume to various Usenet Newsgroups
- Professional cover letters (broadcast, modifiable, and targeted to specific positions)
- Resume and cover letter submission services (via mail and fax)
- Resignation letters
- Reference letters and lists
- Letterhead creation
- Professional printing

So, how much does hiring a professional resume writer cost? Sue answers:

The cost can depend on geographic area, level of difficulty of the resume, additional services used, number of prints provided, etc., but typically, resume services charge anywhere from $25–$350. Higher cost doesn't necessarily define a better service, but very low-priced services do seem to fall under the "you get what you pay for" category. We charge $125 for a package of services, and we are up front about all our fees prior to beginning work. Be wary of any service that does not discuss fees at the onset.

Sue adds:

We work on a one-to-one basis with our clients. Through detailed interviewing and ongoing communication exchanges, we develop a solid working relationship with each client. We not only take the time to learn what our clients' background and current goals are, but we make ourselves available to answer all of their career-related questions. We provide career strategy guidance to help them overcome problem areas and ultimately reach their career goals. Because of the professional relationship we develop with our clients, we're also often rewarded with the "rest of the story," as clients contact us to let us know about the jobs they've secured.

As in any service business, we have competitors who are good at what they do and competitors who aren't. The good ones offer quality products at fair prices with reasonable turnaround times, and they back what they offer, never making empty or unfulfilled promises. We believe strongly in providing top-quality services. We back our promises, services, and products fully. Not only are we aware that we compete with the good, top-quality resume services, we also know we're competing with poor-quality resume services, those whose poor reputations have created a negative impression in the minds of consumers. Good resume services rely on direct referrals from previous clients, and these referrals will only come from happy clients. Our services are also distinguished from many of our competitors' by the number of years we've been in business and because our team approach allows us a broader knowledge base from which to draw.

When it comes to deciding whether or not to hire the services of a professional resume writer, make sure that you're not basing your decision on any of the most common misconceptions that many seekers have about these services.

According to Sue:

The biggest misconception is that a professionally written resume will get them a job. It won't. What it will do is give them an advantage over their competition in securing an interview. Securing an interview is the resume's sole purpose. Another misconception is that professional resume writers have ESP powers or a crystal ball that allows them to write a resume without input from the client. Many people who hire good resume writers are surprised by the amount of information they are required to supply, but a good resume can only be achieved through the information the client supplies the writer. The more communication that takes place between client and resume writer, the better the resulting resume.

Elsewhere in *Job Hunting for the Utterly Confused,* information on resume preparation software packages is provided. These software packages work on a PC- or Mac-based computer and are designed to help job seekers develop and print professional-quality resumes. While the purpose of resume preparation software and a professional resume writer is the same, the benefits of using each are different. Thus, some people will benefit more from using resume software, while others will find it more useful to hire a human to help them prepare their resume.

Sue points out:

Resume software programs are a good way to organize your thoughts and information, but lack flexibility. They operate on a "fill in the blanks" format that fails to take advantage of a client's unique skills, talents, achievements, abilities, and concerns. They tend to produce generic-looking documents. A generic resume isn't going to move your document to the top of the slush pile. A professional resume writer goes beyond simply organizing dates, places, and titles. He or she takes advantage of the individual's unique circumstances. A good resume writer recognizes what the client has to offer and presents this information in a way that a potential employer will find valuable.

Through interaction with the client to maximize their strong points and minimize their negative points, the resulting resume will be far superior to the generic document that resume software produces.

Once you decide to hire a professional resume writer, you will quickly discover you have many choices about whom to hire. Sue explains there are specific questions you can ask to help you choose the best possible resume writer or resume preparation firm:

A resume writer should be very willing to answer any relevant question a potential client asks. Since the client should be working closely with the writer during the writing process, open communication and a good working relationship is vital. If the resume writer seems offended or put off by questions, or refuses to answer openly, find another writer.

Quick Tips

Questions to ask a resume writer before hiring him or her:

- How does your service work?

- What are your credentials? How long have you been writing resumes? Do you remain current in today's hiring practices? How?

- How do you obtain a client's information? Do you have your clients fill out a form from which you create a resume? Do you involve your clients in the process of creating the resume? To what extent do I get to participate in the resume creation process?

- Do you provide a one-on-one consultation or interview with your clients? How long is an average initial consultation or client interview?

- Do you target resumes to specific situations, or do you create one resume for all situations?

- Do you use a "fill in the blanks" computer program?

- What do your resumes look like? Do you use a specific format? If not, how do you customize resumes to individual situations?

Continued

- Do you use laser printing? What type of stationery do you recommend?

- Do you know how to create a scannable resume? Do you know about "keywords"? Can you create a resume I can post on the Internet? If I ask to have a computer diskette containing my resume file, will this be made available to me? How long do you keep resumes on file?

- What is your turnaround time?

- What other services do you offer? Do you create cover letters, resignation letters, reference lists, etc.? Do you do resume submissions on request?

- Do you provide career strategy help? Can you help someone who is interested in changing career goals? How do you handle gaps in employment, "problem" resumes, clients in the so-called hard-to-hire group, or clients who are uncertain of career direction? Do you provide information on interviewing strategies, networking, locating potential companies, or target positions?

- In your opinion, who is the resume being written for?

- What is your price schedule? What do I receive for my investment? Will I know what the charges are up front? Will there be any hidden charges?

- If I'm dissatisfied with your work, what happens?

Whenever someone hires a person to perform a service, it's always an excellent idea to ask for samples of the person's work, or request referrals in order to ensure you're hiring a professional who will offer you the best possible service. In the resume writing business, you'll find that some firms will be happy to provide you with sample resumes they have prepared for other clients, while others will answer all your questions, but hesitate to provide you with actual samples of their work.

Sue explains:

In our private local practices, it's quite normal for us to show many samples of our resumes to potential clients who visit our offices.

However, we don't do this with our Internet service because in order to show a resume example to an Internet client, we'd have to send them an actual file or printed copy rather than examples that would remain in our office. Not only would this be an easy way for our competitors to acquire samples of our work, nothing would prevent potential clients from modifying these samples for their own use. Our concern isn't that the client would then choose not to use our services but, rather, that they might do themselves a disservice by trying to modify someone else's resume into one for themselves that doesn't have their particular background or focus in mind. It would be the same as someone looking at another person's tax return and using it to help them prepare their own return. The resulting tax return (and resume) could be worse than if the tax return (or resume) had been done from scratch, without a sample. Even though we don't provide samples, we gladly answer any questions clients may have. In addition, we make our biographies available on our Web site, so that potential clients can read about our level of experience. Our approach and philosophy should also be quite evident to anyone who takes the time to review all the sections of our Web site. Potential clients can also "test the waters" by having us perform a critique on their existing resume before hiring us to perform the full rewrite. This allows a client to see how we work as well as gain valuable information from our recommendations and guidance on how to improve their resume on their own, if they choose to go that route. Then, if they decide they'd like us to write their resume, we apply the critique fee as a credit towards the writing fee.

Hiring the wrong person to create your resume can cause you to waste valuable time and money. Sue offers these suggestions on things to watch out for when evaluating a resume writer you're thinking of hiring. She explains that if you don't choose your resume writer carefully, you can end up with someone who doesn't:

- Value you as a client or take the time to get to know you and your unique circumstances
- Answer questions
- Deliver what he or she promises
- Understand what the resume's true purpose is

- Create a resume presentation that is effective, achievement-focused, or targeted to the intended reader

- Understand current employment laws or practices

- Deliver the level of quality for which you paid

Quick Tips

Benefits of hiring a professional resume writer:

1. The advantage of a professional resume writer's expertise in writing, presentation, and career strategies allows you to make the most of what you have to offer to a potential employer, and express this in written form—in a way a potential employer will find valuable.

2. You'll have an ongoing professional partnership and someone to guide you through the process of resume preparation and the job search. You can utilize this throughout your career search process.

3. Additional services, such as professional printing, creation of targeted or broadcast cover letters, creation of a resignation letter that will keep contacts instead of burning bridges, submission services to take away some of the time demands of job searching, HTML resume creation, and Internet posting.

4. Time factor. A good resume writer can have a resume finished in a day.

5. Access to state-of-the-art computer and printing equipment, which an individual may not have.

Hiring a resume preparation firm or a professional resume writer is different from hiring a career counselor, although some of the services offered overlap. Sue notes:

Career counselors assist people in making career decisions. They may help clients determine educational routes to take in order to achieve certain desired goals. Or, they may assess client abilities, skills, and natural interests to the various career fields or educational options available. They may help clients overcome bad past situations, such as dealing with the emotional effects of being fired, downsized, verbal abuse, or sexual harassment at work. Counselors use detailed interviews, written tests, examinations, and evaluation tools in order to help their clients narrow the field of choices and determine areas of strength. Some career counselors will offer assistance in resume preparation, but most are more experienced in helping their clients map out goals and determine options.

Some resume writers offer career guidance, too. Those that do will use an interview and communications process that takes the time to get to know the individual client's unique background and experiences, both positive and negative. They determine areas of strength, learn what the client's short and long term goals are, cover areas of concern, and assist the client in mapping strategies to meet their short and long term goals. However, most clients seeking professional resume help are in need of securing immediate employment as quickly as possible. The professional resume writer can provide these individuals with the tools necessary to achieve that immediate goal as well as discussion and counseling about long term plans of action for achieving future goals.

Clients who come in with serious concerns, such as having been recently fired, are taught ways to approach this with a potential employer, and, through the process of creating the resume, often achieve a renewed sense of value and worth from their past achievements and professional experiences. Having a resume created can be an uplifting experience, an opportunity to recognize and take credit for all they've achieved.

A good resume writer has to be an interested and compassionate interviewer, perceptive enough to recognize achievements and accomplishments that even the client may not fully appreciate. He or she must then take this information and present it in written format that will give the client a distinct advantage in securing the next step to their immediate goal, the interview. A professional resume writer who offers career guidance will also assist the client in interviewing skills and strategies, as well as methods and avenues available to enhance and broaden his or her career search.

People who choose to create their own resume should allow plenty of time to choose the content of their resume, select a proper format, and determine the best wording. Leave plenty of time to create multiple drafts before achieving a final, professional-looking document that can be sent to potential employers. When you hire the services of a professional resume writer, however, you can often expect prompt service and a speedy turnaround.

As for 1st Impression's services, Sue tells what they do:

We provide the first working copy or review draft of the resume within 24 hours after receiving a completed order. The time frame for completing a resume is greatly influenced by the client. Since we work closely with our clients, we're depending on their input and information. Most resumes are completed within two days, while others may take as long as a week. We're not certain how fast turnaround time is for other resume services, but we assume that the good ones have turnaround times similar to ours.

Short Cuts

In order for a professional resume writer to provide you, the job seeker, with the best possible service, it's your responsibility to provide the best possible information. As soon as you actually hire a resume writer or resume preparation firm, you should be prepared to provide the following information:

- Your full name, address, phone number(s), fax number(s), e-mail address, and all related contact information
- A detailed explanation of the types of jobs or companies you will be targeting with your resume
- A listing of current and previous employment: name of employer, location, job titles, dates of service, and responsibilities held within each position (relevant to the position now being targeted)
- Educational history: name of institution, educational achievement, date of completion

> • Special skills applicable to the targeted position: for example, computer skills
>
> • Professional associations of which the candidate is a member or active participant or with which the candidate is affiliated

It'll be your job to provide the most accurate and detailed information possible, so that the resume writer you hire can transform that information into a targeted and well-written resume. How you actually provide this information to the person you hire to create your resume will vary. According to Sue:

> Be leery of resume writers who work strictly from a form without any communication exchange between the two of you. Your input is vital to this process. At 1st Impressions, we use a combination method to acquire the information we need from our clients. We provide those without an existing resume a form that will give us the basic information we need to get started.

In addition to basic questions regarding positions held, educational background, and specific technical skills, be prepared to answer questions like:

• What types of positions or companies will you be targeting with your resume?

• What characteristics, both personally and professionally, do you possess that allow you to do this work well?

• What aspects of your work do you enjoy the most?

• What made you decide to pursue this type of work in the first place?

• Do you have any special concerns or questions regarding this career search?

These questions give the resume writer an initial framework to work from. Sue adds:

We've found e-mail to be the most efficient method for us as well as the most convenient method for our clients. This method gives clients the opportunity to respond to our inquiries at their convenience, the time to formulate good responses, and the benefit of fast responses from us. During this exchange, we discuss their goals, their concerns, their strengths, what a potential employer will be looking for in a candidate for the targeted position, what their options are, how to handle a change in career path or goals, how to handle gaps in employment, etc. Our goal is not only to help our clients achieve interviews, but achieve interviews for jobs in which they will find the most satisfaction.

In addition to choosing what information you plan to include in your resume, if you are planning to create your own resume, you must select an appropriate format. Various resume formats are discussed in Chapter 3 of this book. A professional resume writer, however, can help you select the best format to showcase your skills, knowledge, and experience. Sue explains:

Because our resumes are achievement-based, we choose a format and presentation most likely to gain the positive interest of a potential employer. We are skilled in making the most of a client's true strength and potential, while minimizing negative aspects. Yet, we always give our clients the final say in their presentation. When necessary, we help clients minimize negative aspects of their employment history, both in the resume and in the interview strategies we offer.

Quick Tips

After your basic resume is created, it will be necessary to customize the document to specifically target the job you're applying for. The best way to customize a resume is to consider:

- The position for which the resume is being applied

- The intended reader (the person holding the key to the interview)

- The interests of the client (the type of work the client wants to do). For example, if you focus on skills the client really doesn't want to do and the client is hired because of those skills, the client will be unhappy in this position. By listing information focused on a targeted position, company, and reader, the resulting resume will be stronger and more effective. In other words, don't list any information that isn't directly relevant to the position.

- Include all background information: job history, experiences, accomplishments, and educational achievements that directly relate to this targeted position and company.

When choosing a resume writer or resume preparation firm, make sure that the person who will be creating your resume knows how to create electronic resumes, which can be submitted via e-mail or posted on the Internet's World Wide Web.

Sue explains:

In addition to the word-processed file that can be sent by e-mail as an attached binary file, there are two resume file formats that are used for electronic exchange—HTML coded and ASCII coded file formats. An HTML coded resume is a resume created using Hyper-Text Markup Language. It is uploaded to the Internet as a Web page and looks much like the standard printed version of your resume with typical formatting features like bold print, italics, tabs, and underlining.

An HTML formatted resume can be used for:

- Submission to Web sites that accept HTML formatted resumes for posting.

- Your own Web page.

- E-mailing to prospective employers. Netscape and Microsoft Mail utilities both allow you to mail your actual Web page. Other mail programs such as Pegasus Mail and Eudora Mail will create a "hot link" in your e-mail message where the reader can click on your Web address and go directly to your Web page.

Sue adds:

An ASCII resume is a text-only version of your resume. It bears no resemblance at all to the standard paper version of your resume since it is stripped of all boldface, italics, tabs, and underlining.

An ASCII formatted resume can be used for:

- Posting to Web sites with resume databases where employers search for prospective employees.
- E-mailing to prospective employers if you don't know what word processing software they're using (ASCII text can be read by all word processors). Posting to Usenet Newsgroups. There are around 250 news groups devoted to job postings and resume postings. Many of these news groups are very active for both employers and job seekers. For example, the misc.jobs.offered news group posts over 30,000 job openings per week. Misc.jobs.resumes posts over 1,000 resumes per week.

Whether you choose to create your own resume or use a resume writer, Sue believes the five elements a resume must have in order to capture the attention of the reader are:

1. Professional appearance.
2. It must be logically organized, well written, presented in a manner that allows quick reference to the information, and easy to read.
3. The resume should focus on the targeted position.
4. Everything in your resume should be totally accurate. (Be honest.)
5. Your resume should include lots of quantitative information and achievement statements.

Finally, no matter how your resume is created, Sue offers this additional advice to job seekers:

Don't go for gimmicks, they don't work. Brightly colored paper (fluorescent, for example) or overly unique presentational styles don't work. They may get you noticed, but not necessarily in the way you hope. You want your resume to impart a positive and professional impression about you. Just as you want to be taken seriously in your job search, you want a resume that presents you as a professional individual with a lot to offer. Your resume is your personal representative. In most cases it's your initial introduction to a prospective employer. You want this document to make a great first impression.

To learn more about 1st Impressions, here's how to contact them:

First Impressions, Resumes & Career Strategies
6225 NW 71st Street
Gainesville, FL 32653
Fax: (352) 371-0673 or (904) 794-5803
E-mail: suenowac@aug.com
Web site: http://www.1st-imp.com

Job Search Advice from the Point of View of a Person in Human Resources

During your job search, you will encounter human resources people who represent the companies where you are applying for a job. HR people represent the employer. Their job is to evaluate potential employees as they search for people who meet their predetermined criteria. In this interview, Pam Meyers shares her years of experience as an HR professional. From her point of view, she offers advice on how to conduct yourself as the job applicant.

Currently, Pam Meyers is the president of HRI, Inc., an independent company that provides HR-related services to small and medium-size companies that don't have human resources people on their own staffs. HRI, Inc., was founded in 1993; however, Pam has worked for years doing HR work for large corporations. Pam's primary job is to provide recruiting assistance to her client companies:

On behalf of our clients, we place their "help wanted" ads, perform college recruiting, conduct telephone and in-person interviews, and we do reference checking.

When Pam is looking to fill job openings at any of her client companies, most of the time she runs help-wanted ads requesting that potential applicants send in their resume and cover letter prior to calling to schedule an actual interview. She notes:

> Most of the time, I specifically request applicants send both a cover letter and a resume. The reason for this is to see how well an individual can communicate on paper and to see how well potential applicants can follow directions. Even if an ad specifically requests that applicants mail in a resume and cover letter, we'll still get plenty of applicants who don't follow directions and fax us just their resume. When someone can't follow simple directions, to me, that says a lot about the candidate. I usually read all of the applicants' cover letters and then scan their resumes. I pay careful attention to how clearly and concisely a cover letter is written. I also take notice if a resume is too wordy or contains information that should not be included. The best types of resumes I have seen are those that use bullets to highlight specific points and major accomplishments. I personally hate it when a resume lists a previous job and then includes several paragraphs of text describing what they have done.

Pam says that she often sees two-page cover letters come in that go into great detail about the last 10 or 20 years of the applicant's life. Since Pam specifically looks for cover letters that are concise and to the point, overly wordy cover letters do not get the most attention. She advises:

> A cover letter should not re-state all of the information that's listed in your resume. I believe that it's important for the stationery that is used for the resume and the cover letter to match perfectly. I particularly like neutral-colored paper; however, when I'm looking to fill a job that's in a highly creative field, such as advertising, I tend to look for creativity within the resume and cover letter package. For jobs in corporate America, it's more important to maintain a neutral and

highly professional format for a cover letter and resume. Personally, I don't think an applicant that uses colored inks to enhance a resume actually benefits from this.

When Pam invites an applicant in for an interview, she observes the person carefully:

I look at how the applicant is dressed and how they walk up to the reception area. I look to see if they present themselves in a professional manner. One of the biggest mistakes I have seen applicants make when they show up for an interview is to be chewing gum. Another common mistake is to show up to an interview dressed very casually for a very professional level job. Once you actually land a job and start working there on a day-to-day basis, there may be some leeway in the dress code, however, when you're showing up for an interview and you want to make a good first impression, dress in formal business attire. I advise against wearing too much jewelry. This applies to both men and women. If wearing a certain piece of jewelry is extremely important to you, then by all means wear it. Otherwise, you might consider not wearing too much jewelry to the interview.

Remember, dressing in formal business attire does not mean wearing a $300 suit or outfit. You just want to look clean-cut and professional.

Once your interview with an HR professional gets under way, Pam strongly advises against using canned answers to questions posed to you:

When it comes to obvious questions, of course you're going to have pre-planned answers. For less common questions, try to provide answers that are honest, positive, and that demonstrate that you're putting some thought into how you're responding. There's a difference between being prepared to answer interview questions and regurgitating stock answers to questions.

In order to discover more about an applicant during an interview, Pam tries to ask questions that will help her learn about the person's values and morals:

I often ask applicants how they measure their standards of success in their job, and why the applicant has chosen their line of work. Other questions that tend to reveal a lot about a person are "Describe your system for controlling errors in your work" and "Have you ever missed a deadline and what were the circumstances when you did?" When an interviewer asks questions that involve ethical issues, I recommend that applicants answer those questions based on what they would actually do or what they believe, not by providing a response they believe the interviewer would want to hear. Sometimes an employer is looking to discover what your ethical standards are and whether or not you're willing to stand up for what you believe in.

When Pam interviews candidates for sales positions, she often asks, "Sometimes we have to bend the truth a little when dealing with a particularly difficult customer. Can you give me some type of example of when you've had to do this?" Another question she asks is, "How far do you think salespeople in your field will go to make a sale, and how far have you gone?" She comments:

These questions really show where the applicant is coming from. I strongly recommend that applicants answer these types of questions honestly. Employers are looking to see if you're going to lie or tell the truth, and how you answer says a lot about you.

There are several types of personal questions that an interviewer is not allowed to ask. Many HR people and interviewers with a lot of experience have their own ways of gathering personal information without actually asking illegal questions. Pam states:

Never volunteer personal information! I have done many interviews during which the applicant just starts talking, and they provide all sorts of personal information that's really none of my business. Among HR people, there's an ongoing joke that you don't have to ask an applicant those illegal personal questions because if you just sit back and let them babble, they'll provide the answers without being asked the questions. If an interviewer comes right out and asks one of those illegal questions, such as if you're married, you can respond by saying that you don't believe that your marital status has any relevance to the position you're applying for. Don't be intimidated into answering questions you're not comfortable with. If a company insists on asking illegal questions, you should seriously think twice about accepting a job working for that company.

Many job applicants get nervous during an interview, and they become even more nervous when they think that the interviewer is actually seeing signs of their nervousness. Pam suggests that instead of coming out and saying that you're nervous, you should muddle through the interview:

> The applicant may think they're coming across as being very nervous, but most of the time, this nervousness is only in the applicant's head, and it's not obvious to onlookers, so you shouldn't bring attention to it. Most people who start off nervous become relaxed after the first few minutes.

When an HR person is interviewing numerous people for a job opening, there are many mistakes that applicants make that almost immediately remove them from contention for the job. Pam remarks:

> I look at someone's attitude. Once in a while, an applicant will have the attitude that I'm wasting their time, and that's simply not acceptable. Sometimes an applicant will adopt the attitude that the job they're applying for isn't good enough for them, and that's a total turn-off. Too many people have a really bad attitude about their work. This will hurt your chances of landing a job, and it will also hurt you in the long run. People with bad attitudes get passed over for promotions and tend to have trouble developing good relationships with bosses and coworkers.
>
> I like interviewing people that have clear objectives and who ask good questions. As an interviewer, one question I really like to be asked is about the employer's management style and the corporate culture. Obviously, we all work for money, but it's not appropriate to ask about salary or benefits during the early stages of the interview.

Just about anyone offering career advice will tell you that it's necessary to go into an interview having done research about the company. When applicants have multiple interviews with various companies in a short period of time, they tend to cut corners and skip doing that all-important research. This results in the applicants trying to B.S. their way through the interview. Pam observes:

> Applicants who aren't prepared tend to fumble a lot and provide answers that aren't well defined or well thought out. They also ask stupid questions about the company that would be obvious if they did some basic research. I can't stress enough the importance of doing research and going into an interview totally prepared.

Demonstrating your credibility as an applicant is also important throughout the entire interview process. Pam adds:

> If you're applying for a job at your current employer's competition, never give out classified information relating to your current employer, because that's not ethical.

As you and the interviewer delve into your employment history, if there's negative information in your past, the good news is that these days employers are more interested in what you've done instead of where you have been. Pam offers this advice:

> To take focus away from negative information in your resume, don't use a chronological format. During the interview, you must be totally honest about your employment history, but you don't want to come right out and say that you were fired. Be prepared to put a positive spin on your negative employment information. Offer a very brief explanation of any negative information, and say what you learned from the experience. Keep in mind that most employers are going to check with your previous employers and references to verify the information you provide. If something you say somewhat contradicts what a previous employer or reference says, your chances of getting hired become very slim. It's more common for an applicant to be denied employment because the employer discovers that the applicant lied about being fired, not because they were actually fired.

Pam stresses that being fired is very different from being downsized or terminated from a job due to circumstances beyond your control:

If a previous employer goes out of business or closes a division, that's something the job seeker had no control over, so it will never be held against them. What can hurt an applicant's chance, however, is if they have been unemployed for a long period of time after they were laid off. The longer someone waits to go back into the job market, the harder it will be to land a new job, especially in a technology-related field.

I personally believe that it's better to begin looking for a job while you're still employed, as opposed to quitting and then starting a new job search. If you're currently employed and looking for a new job, that shows that you're looking to improve yourself and your career. The best piece of advice someone once gave to me is that the best time to look for a job is when you don't need a new job. This allows you to carefully analyze offers and not be forced to accept a job out of desperation. It's always beneficial to have the luxury of being able to take your time and explore job opportunities and to wait for the best job to come along.

In between jobs, Pam believes that doing temp work can be extremely beneficial:

Working in a temp position between permanent jobs will help you to expand your skills and keep money coming in. If it takes you a while to find a new permanent position, doing temp work is an excellent way to explain gaps in your employment history. An alternative is to spend your free time in between jobs attending classes or obtaining training to expand your skills and knowledge. Verbal and written communication skills are critical for virtually every job, so if you're weak in these areas, you should definitely spend some time perfecting these skills.

Acting in a professional manner and having a clear objective in mind about what you want to do are critical for landing a job. Pam explains:

It doesn't matter if you want to be a cashier in a department store or the CEO of a Fortune 500 company. For your career to go anywhere, you must know, in advance, in what direction you want it to go. One final comment I'd like to make is in reference to the advice that many applicants are given about coming out and asking the interviewer for the job they're applying for during their interview. This is certainly a good idea, but wait until the later part of the interview. If you ask for a job too soon, the employer is going to wonder how you know you want the job, because you don't know too much about it yet. If, at the end of the interview, you know you really want the job, then come out and ask for it with totally sincerity. Finally, never talk down to the person interviewing you, or go out of your way to flatter the interviewer. This strategy is almost always transparent and will usually backfire.

After the interview, as an HR professional, Pam expects to receive a thank-you note from the applicant. In fact, some of her clients will make their final decision about hiring someone based on whether or not the applicant sends a thank-you note within 24 hours after the interview. Pam says:

> From my point of view, I don't care if the thank-you note is handwritten or typed. My advice is to keep the note professional and short. Thank the person for taking the time to interview you, specify the date of the interview and what job you applied for, and conclude by saying that you look forward to hearing from them. It's definitely appropriate to make reference to something positive that happened during the interview in order to jog the interviewer's memory about who you are. From an HR person's perspective, if I interview thirty or forty people for a job opening, it gets pretty difficult to keep everyone straight in my mind. The people who I seriously consider hiring are the ones who set themselves apart from the crowd.

Waiting is part of the job search process. After participating in an interview, you should be patient and not start calling the employer on a daily basis in order to ask if a decision has been made yet. As Pam notes:

> If you don't hear from an employer within a week or two, then it's appropriate to make one follow-up phone call. I have seen many people not get hired because they became a pest and started calling the employer everyday after their interview.

She adds:

When you submit your resume, make sure that your phone number is displayed clearly at the top of the page so the employer can contact you easily. If you don't already have an answering machine, go out and purchase one. Nothing is more frustrating, from my point of view, than having to track down an applicant one of my clients wants to hire. Get yourself an answering machine or hire an answering service. Either one of these alternatives is inexpensive but highly worthwhile.

Pam Meyers can be reached by calling (800) 440-6706, or by visiting HRI's Web site at http://www.hriinc.com.

Job Seekers Can Benefit from Doing Temp Work

Opportunities that most job seekers overlook are those available through temp agencies. Companies of all sizes, in virtually every industry, periodically require temp workers to replace full-time workers absent from the workplace due to long-term medical problems, maternity leave, extended vacations, or sabbaticals. Companies also hire temp workers seasonally or to accommodate sudden growth in their business. When a company needs temp workers fast, they turn to temp agencies, like Kelly Services, that are located throughout the country (check your Yellow Pages for a listing of temp agencies in your area).

Quick Tips

For job seekers, there are many benefits to accepting a temp position in between permanent, full-time positions while you're participating in the job search process. These benefits include:

- You'll have a paycheck coming in while you're searching for a new job.

- You can expand your networking database and meet new people.

Continued

- Many temp employees eventually get hired as permanent employees, once they prove themselves on the job.
- You can learn and perfect new skills and obtain free training.
- You'll receive free resume preparation and career counseling services.
- If you're not sure what type of career you want to pursue or what industry you want to work in, accepting temp positions at various companies allows you to experience firsthand the corporate culture at many types of companies, without making long-term commitments.
- Your work schedule can be as flexible and long-lasting as you want it to be. You can often be placed in a temp position within 24 hours and work around your job search schedule.

To help you decide if you should pursue temporary employment opportunities and work with a temp agency while you're looking for a permanent position, Lisa Elias, branch operations manager for Kelly Services in Framingham, Massachusetts, offers some insightful advice in this interview. Prior to working for Kelly Services, Lisa worked in the career services office at a college.

Kelly Services is a staffing services company that has offices across America and throughout the world. In addition to being able to place candidates in local-area jobs, the company maintains a central database and can place workers in jobs in virtually any city they're interested in working in. Lisa explains:

Kelly Services specializes in temporary staffing; however, we also do some permanent position placement. Many recent college grads find it a lot easier to begin their professional life by working temp jobs through an agency. This allows them to get their foot in the door at companies they might want to work for permanently and prove their abilities. Working a temp job can often lead to a full-time, permanent position within a company. We often place people in jobs that they're interested in, or we can use our expertise and place people in jobs they're qualified for and that we believe they'll do well in.

Some of the services a company like Kelly Services offers are free job training to qualified applicants and free resume preparation and career consultation. Our client companies pay for the services we offer to our temp workers. We can help someone develop computer skills or other skills that are highly marketable. Our job is to match applicants with jobs that they're best suited for. If someone comes in and wants to work for a financial services company, we have clients all over the country and we can often place that candidate in a temporary job he or she is interested in.

Often, once a candidate for temp work steps through the door at a Kelly Services office, that person can be placed in a job within 24 hours.

Many people don't realize that temp agencies offer much more than just short-term job opportunities. According to Lisa, Kelly Services, as well as most other temp agencies, have long-term temp positions that can last for weeks, months, or up to a year. Likewise, with so many different types of work opportunities available, based on an applicant's qualifications and experience, a person can earn highly competitive salaries. Most temp agencies help to place people in middle-management jobs as well as entry-level positions.

Lisa remarks:

For people who don't know what exactly they want to do, and they've never worked in any type of office environment, we can place those candidates in a variety of different short-term temporary assignments. This will give them exposure to what it's like working for large, medium, and small-size companies with different corporate cultures.

People come to us with all sorts of different work requirements, and we do our best to accommodate people's needs. We can help people who already have full-time, permanent jobs find extra work in the evenings and on weekends to help supplement their income. Other people come to us for short-term assignments in order to keep busy and earn extra income while they're looking for a permanent job. For a temp service to really help an applicant, it's important that the applicant be totally honest with us about what exactly it is that they're looking for.

Lisa often encounters job seekers who have a company in mind that they'd really like to work for. However, that company doesn't have any permanent job openings available. According to Lisa, this is where a temp agency can be very helpful:

> A temp agency, like Kelly Services, can often help that person get their foot in the door by placing them in a temporary position at that company. While you're at the company, you can learn about the work environment, network, prove your abilities and sell yourself as the ideal employee for a permanent position when one becomes available.

If you choose to work for a temp agency and accept short-term work assignments, it is critical that you treat that assignment as seriously as you would treat a permanent employment position. Lisa stresses the importance of always maintaining a highly professional attitude:

> It's a very small world and whether you're working in a temporary or permanent position, when you're on the job, you're always building up your reputation. Maintaining a good reputation is important for anyone who is on any type of career path. If a temporary work assignment doesn't work out, never just walk out the door. Immediately call the agency that placed you in the job, and stay on the job at least for the remainder of the day, unless you're told by the agency to do otherwise. Never do anything to sabotage the company you're working for prior to leaving. Remember, as a temp worker, you are an employee of the temp agency you're working with, so if you want to be placed in other jobs in the future, don't do anything unprofessional when you're on the job at any work assignment. If you're working in a temp job and a permanent position you applied for comes through, it's common courtesy to give the temp agency ample notice before leaving.

To learn more about Kelly Services, from anywhere in the United States call toll-free (888) 465-3559.

Well, there you have it—advice from a few experts on a variety of job-related topics. As you come to the end of this book, you now have the basic knowledge necessary to put your job search efforts into full swing. Knowing what steps to take in order to land an awesome job is only the beginning. Now it's all up to you. You must dedicate the time and energy necessary in order to discover job opportunities, submit resumes, perform company research, schedule and participate in interviews, negotiate salaries, and analyze job offers. While you can hire a resume writer or a career counselor to assist you in this process, much of the work and all of the responsibility lies on your shoulders. Whether or not you land a job you'll love is entirely up to you! Keep this in mind as you read the final chapter of this book and then begin your job search efforts.

CHAPTER 12

Conclusion: Where Should You Go from Here?

By reading this book in its entirety, you now have the basic knowledge and steps to follow for finding and then landing an awesome job for yourself. Unfortunately, there are no guaranteed answers or tricks to finding a job. It's going to take hard work, confidence, and persistence. Throughout your job search efforts, it's important to maintain a positive attitude. This can become difficult, especially if you receive rejection. Keep in mind, rejection is a normal part of the job search process—learn from it and move on. Don't let yourself fall into a state of depression or become overly anxious about any one job opportunity that comes your way. If one job falls through, find five more opportunities to pursue.

As you kick off your job search efforts, take a deadline-oriented and well-organized approach to everything you do. Not only will this save you time and help you avoid confusion, but it will also position you as a highly organized person, which is something that most employers will appreciate. Don't be afraid to ask a friend or relative for assistance as you embark on your job search. Have your friend or relative proofread all your outgoing correspondence (your resume, cover letters, thank-you notes, etc.), and have them perform mock job interviews with you so that you can practice answering questions that will be posed to you during interviews.

At each step in the job search process, try to predict what you can expect, and in your mind, visualize a positive outcome. Think about what it will take to make that positive outcome actually happen, and then do everything within your power to make what you visualized in your mind a reality.

Enter into your job search knowing what you want out of life, and specifically, what you want out of your job. Never settle and accept a job due to desperation. Find a job doing something you have a passion for, and find an employment opportunity that will keep you challenged and excited about what you're doing on an ongoing basis. Throughout your career, you should always be working toward an ultimate goal or dream, and the job you accept should be a stepping-stone that takes you at least one step closer to making your goal or dream a reality.

All people (including you), no matter what their age, sex, height, weight, skin color, race, intelligence, or religion, have the ability to achieve whatever it is they set out to do, simply by focusing their efforts and working hard. If someone tells you "you're not qualified" or "you're not smart enough" to fill a certain position, don't listen, especially if you know in your heart that you're capable of doing whatever the job entails. Sure, obtaining additional training might be required, or you might have to obtain some additional work experience first, but don't let anyone stop you from living up to your ultimate potential. When you have a will to accomplish something great, you'll eventually find a way to do it.

Only you know what you're capable of achieving, and the higher you set your own standards, the more success you'll achieve as long as you maintain your focus, keep working hard, and act ethically in any situation. Always be on a quest to expand your knowledge and skill set. Learn everything you can from others, by reading, by taking classes, and by challenging yourself to constantly achieve even greater levels of success.

Let the information provided in this book be a starting point for you to launch what will ultimately be your own highly successful career. Follow the advice within this book that pertains to you, and then develop a career path and plan for yourself that will allow you to achieve whatever it is that will help you obtain success (no matter how you define this term).

What happens in your future depends on you, not luck. Don't sit around waiting for a better job opportunity to come along. Take a proactive role in your life and seek out the job opportunities you want to pursue. Be creative in your efforts and never stop networking.

Job Hunting for the Utterly Confused was written to provide you with the basic knowledge and skills you'll need to find and land a job. Don't be afraid to consult other sources of knowledge, such as a career counselor or professional resume writer, or to seek the advice of a parent, coworker, classmate, or friend. However, never allow others to make career-related decisions for you or force you to follow a career path you're not interested in. Sometimes it might become necessary to take a risk when it comes to forwarding your career. Prior to taking that risk, think about the positive and negative consequences. If you're married and have young children, can you afford to accept a job at a start-up company that could go under at any time. How important is job security based on your current financial status? Risk taking can lead to great rewards, but be extremely careful when risking the well-being of a spouse and siblings, especially if you are the primary source of income for your family. Obviously, any job you ultimately accept will have an impact on your immediate family, so consider their needs as well as your own, prior to accepting any job offer.

Finally, never stop looking for new opportunities that might materialize when you least expect them to. Even when you're on the job, knowing how to recognize an opportunity, and then take advantage of it, is a skill that will generate great rewards for you throughout your career. When opportunity knocks, be on hand to answer the door!

Now, you're done reading this book, so get to work! Start calling up all your contacts and friends. Visit the career guidance office at your college or university. Start reading the help-wanted ads of your city's newspaper. Read publications like *National Business Employment Weekly*. Surf the Internet and visit career-related Web sites, and do everything within your power to track down the most exciting and rewarding career opportunities available to you.

Index